Gift of Tears

This thoroughly revised and updated second edition of *Gift of Tears* includes new research and examples of recent events to help illustrate the effects of loss. Containing a strong practical element, the book guides the reader through the process of contemplating and eventually confronting their own relationship to loss.

Written by experienced counsellors and psychotherapists, the book contains candid and readable discussions of central issues, including:

- How to understand and work with anger and guilt.
- Attachment patterns and loss.
- Historical changes in attitudes to death and bereavement.
- Death as particular form of loss.

Gift of Tears is intended for anyone who finds they have to cope, in the course of their daily lives, with the grief of others. It will prove invaluable to counsellors, therapists, mental health professionals and all those helping the bereaved.

Susan Lendrum and **Gabrielle Syme** work as psychotherapists, counsellors, supervisors, trainers and consultants to psychotherapy and counselling courses. They have lectured widely and run workshops on loss and related topics.

'In this book, Susan Lendrum and Gabrielle Syme have faced all the difficulties inherent in dealing with grief, in oneself and in others, and overcome them superbly. These pages are immensely readable, useful and enjoyable (it's always a joy to meet good writing!), and I, for one, am grateful to have had the chance to read them. For this book has two functions; it teaches counsellors, but it also teaches the individual reader to face the reality of his/her own feelings about death and loss. And it is something we all have to do. I can't commend it too highly.'

Claire Rayner, President of the National
Association for Bereavement Services

Gift of Tears

A practical approach to loss and
bereavement in counselling and
psychotherapy

Second Edition

Susan Lendrum and Gabrielle Syme

Brunner-Routledge
Taylor & Francis Group

HOVE AND NEW YORK

First edition published 1992
by Routledge
11 New Fetter Lane, London EC4P 4EE
29 West 35th Street, New York NY 10001

Reprinted 1992, 1993, 1994, 1995, 1997, 1999 (twice) and 2000
by Routledge

Reprinted 2001 and 2002
by Brunner-Routledge
27 Church Road, Hove, East Sussex BN3 2FA
29 West 35th Street, New York NY 10001

Second edition first published 2004
by Brunner-Routledge
27 Church Road, Hove, East Sussex BN3 2FA

Simultaneously published in the USA and Canada
by Brunner-Routledge
29 West 35th Street, New York, NY 10001

Brunner-Routledge is an imprint of the Taylor & Francis Group

Copyright © 2004 Susan Lendrum and Gabrielle Syme

Typeset in Times by RefineCatch Limited, Bungay, Suffolk
Printed and bound in Great Britain by Biddles Ltd, King's Lynn
Paperback cover design by Caroline Archer

This publication has been produced with paper manufactured to
strict environmental standards and with pulp derived from
sustainable forests.

British Library Cataloguing in Publication Data
A catalogue record for this book is available from the British Library

Library of Congress Cataloging in Publication Data
Lendrum, Susan, 1942–
   Gift of tears : a practical approach to loss and bereavement in counselling
and psychotherapy / Susan Lendrum and Gabrielle Syme.—[Rev. and
updated ed.].
      p.   cm.
   Includes bibliographical references and indexes.
   ISBN 1-58391-932-5 (hbk)—ISBN 1-58391-933-3 (pbk)
   1. Loss (Psychology)   2. Bereavement—Psychological aspects.   I. Syme,
Gabrielle, 1943–   II. Title.
BF575.D35L46   2004
155.9′3—dc22   2003026167

ISBN 1-58391-932-5 hbk
ISBN 1-58391-933-3 pbk

This book is dedicated to Robert and the children and grandchildren

Before the beginning of years
There came to the making of man
Time with a gift of tears,
Grief with a glass that ran.
A.C. Swinburne, *Atalanta in Calydon*

Contents

Exercises

Tables

Introduction to first edition

Many of those who work with people in a helping capacity or just as fellow humans come across loss in the course of these human interactions. For instance, we might notice tears in a friend's eyes as we chat over coffee about last night's television programme. In a more formal context, as a teacher for example, we might be puzzled by the behaviour of a child whose parents are divorcing; or as a social worker, be troubled by an elderly person's difficulties when faced with residential care; or as a doctor, feel anger when a patient talks of his redundancy notice; or as a nurse, feel anxious when talking to relatives of a dying patient; or as a father, feel helpless when a daughter cannot be reconciled to the loss of a pet; or we may be just confused when a neighbour cannot seem to get over her youngest leaving home. Of course, we may also have been, indeed we may also still be, or may soon be, that awkward child, that lonely old person, that redundant worker, that bereaved relative, that abandoned parent. There is a sense in which all of us have suffered and share in the suffering of every kind of loss.

When the two of us sat down to write this book we remembered how we had met, one of us a physiologist and the other a linguist, and had talked to one another of the very different losses we had each experienced. We remembered how frightened and alone we had each felt with our separate griefs and how often we had hidden our tears from other people. By the time we met we had each been enabled, through the presence of another person, to work through our separate griefs and to lay down some of the burdens we had been carrying. We had also worked, in different contexts, with many who had suffered loss. We decided to set up courses together to train those who were working with the grieving. We were aware of the fear of grief in society and yet we also knew, with Swinburne, that grief is an integral part of the time-span of human life and that tears are the natural response.

In thinking about the elements that had helped reduce our own fears, we realised what we valued in particular. At an emotional level, we remembered the invaluable presence of another in our grief work, and at a cognitive level, the knowledge we had received from training. Knowledge gained from studies of adult and child bereavement and from studies on the effectiveness of different helping responses; knowledge about depression and about the responses to loss of people from other cultures and ideas from both the humanistic and the more psychodynamic tradition have all thrown light for us on how to BE with a person who has suffered a loss.

In this book we attempt to share what we have learned, emotionally and cognitively, from these different sources. By condensing what has been a necessarily long and drawn-out process we may well make it all seem simpler than it is. The mistakes we have made with clients, trainees, colleagues and friends were no doubt as important as our other sources of learning. But we hope that, even in the simplified form of this book, our experience can be of some use to the man or woman faced by another's grief and wondering: 'What on earth do I say now?', 'How can I handle these tears?', 'Why do I feel scared?', 'Why am I angry?'.

Anyone working with someone who is grieving will experience strong feelings themselves. Indeed, we hope this book will evoke feelings in you, as well as thoughts and ideas. As we discovered for ourselves, such strong feelings can sometimes be overwhelming unless they are spoken in the presence of someone who will accept – and not judge. For this reason we would strongly encourage you to use this book not on your own, but with others, in a group as part of a training programme, or in counselling supervision, or with a trusted colleague or friend.

Strong feelings are part of the natural response to loss, and tears their human expression. We know the value of tears in releasing and expressing feelings, and we know that counsellors need to learn to feel comfortable with tears. This ease with tears is acquired in part through an understanding and acceptance of our own and others' tears and associated feelings; in part through learning how to respond to feelings in others; and in part through the use of professional help in working with those who have suffered loss. Our relative ease with tears has been made possible through the many men and women who have taught us and shared their lives with us.

Counsellors and the counselled can be male or female. We have therefore sometimes used 'he' and at other times 'she'. If the counsellor is female, we have usually made the counselled male. In all such cases, the 'he' can be read as 'she' and vice versa. However, there are some cases where it is important for counsellor and counselled to be of the same sex; an example is the story of Vilna. When referring to children in general, rather than to a particular child, we have used 'she' throughout.

We have deliberately avoided the word 'client' in the early chapters, as we are aware that many people who use counselling skills, when listening to someone's sorrow and grief, would not necessarily see themselves as offering counselling to a client. However, later in the book, particularly from Chapter 10 on, where we use exercises and vignettes to illustrate the points we are making, we have for clarity used the words 'client' and 'counsellor'. Some other words used commonly in our language take on different and perhaps deeper meanings in this book, for instance 'feelingless-ness' and 'way-of-being'. Their meanings should emerge from their contexts.

All the characters and stories recounted in this book are fictitious and truthful at the same time. They have been drawn from our experience (in life and as practising counsellors), but transformed and combined so as to detach them entirely from any possible resemblance to people we know. If you think you have met one of our characters then you will have discovered that life is no less painful than fiction and that human loss is universal.

Introduction to second edition

Twelve years have passed since we wrote this book and the world has changed in many ways. It seems that loss and bereavement have become a more acceptable subject for discussion in society; there are 'sitcoms' around the theme of loss, the national bereavement organisation Cruse has expanded hugely and there are many more local bereavement support groups. 'Counselling' is now an almost automatic response to any traumatic event involving loss of life in the West. While there may still be many misconceptions about what 'counselling' actually is, there is generally more acceptance of its value in helping people to feel and to think more constructively about themselves and others. The increasing recognition and professionalisation of counselling may also be reflected in a more 'therapeutic' slant to this new edition.

There has been a burgeoning of counselling courses, with such a variety of both content and standard that we saw the 'Training in loss counselling skills' chapter as too narrow and no longer relevant to such a wide field. We have summed up the essential principles of loss counselling training in the chapter on supervision. We have also updated and expanded the appendices.

Since our first edition, interesting and important research has emerged on the 'dual process' nature of grieving and on the 'continuing bonds' that normal grievers usually maintain with those they have lost. Both these findings have confirmed hunches we have shared, drawn from our experience. Strengthened by the research findings, we have now been able to use these phenomena more clearly and constructively in the text and have brought in Worden's 'tasks of mourning' from his book *Grief Counselling and Grief Therapy* (1991).

Research into the different ways in which men and women communicate has also enhanced our understanding of the difficulties that couples often experience in trying to share grief or to move through grief together.

We are also each 12 years older with a total of 24 years' more experience! This experience confirms the power and influence of unrecognised loss in people's lives and the importance of helping people to try to face their losses without rancour so that they, in turn, can help to understand the experience of loss both in themselves and in their children. This is particularly important at a time when a third of all marriages end in divorce – a complicated loss if ever there was one!

The importance of consultancy, often equated with 'supervision', has become more clearly recognised and we are increasingly convinced of the value of quality supervisory consultancy.

We returned to the hoary old dilemma about whether or not to offer worded examples of possible counselling interventions. One side of the argument insists that suggesting any wording for the counsellor constitutes a danger of undermining her authority and autonomy. It can be perceived as prescriptive and authoritarian. The other argument suggests that beginner counsellors may be so overwhelmed with anxiety that having some reasonably accepting and thoughtful examples can be helpful. On balance we have decided that offering some words, however inadequate to the intense situation, can at the very least get someone started in thinking what to say. And if they are stimulated – even by irritation with our words – to find words of their own, then so much the better!

The aim of the book was, and remains, that of stimulating others to work things out for themselves, knowing they are not completely alone or abandoned in the business of trying to help others with that most universal human experience: loving and losing loved ones.

Acknowledgements

We wish to acknowledge the many clients, students, supervisees and others whose losses have touched our lives and from whom we have learned so much. Our children in particular have taught us, often with great patience, how to respond more usefully to the losses in their lives.

We are grateful to CarolAnn Allan, who has worked in the background bringing the appendices up to date and correcting our word-processing errors.

Part I

Loss and nurture

Chapter 1

Early attachments and loss

Natural or necessary losses

To be born, a baby must leave the womb; to grow up and leave its mother, a baby needs to be weaned. The child entering school and learning about the world needs to leave its parents, and adolescents have the task of leaving their own family in order to set up their own separate lives. These 'leavings' constitute much of the loss that human beings in our culture experience as part of the natural process of growing up and eventually of death.

In thinking of these stages only as development or 'growing up', it is easy to forget the place of loss in growth and change. These losses, which happen to the majority of us, usually evoke strong feelings. As babies, such feelings find powerful and direct expression. Think of the baby sleeping who awakens and lies quietly for a bit, but suddenly starts to cry lustily, as if it cannot bear to be alone any more. The cry is usually very compelling to the mother and appears to demand a response and a re-establishment of human connection. The younger the baby is, the shorter the time it can bear on its own. Weaning a baby is not just a nutritional process but also an emotional process in which the infant gradually manages longer periods on its own; with maturity comes the capacity to be alone. People who study babies propose that this is because babies gradually develop the knowledge that their parent will return and that the loss or absence is survivable meanwhile. In other words, as we mature we discover inner resources and knowledge. Without increasing periods alone and the consequent experience of loss, we would not mature. These losses are termed 'necessary losses' (Viorst, 1989). Each one of these necessary losses resulting from separation needs to be recognised and comforted. Given enough comfort, each loss successfully managed is a step towards independence and growing self-awareness. We do not necessarily remember these losses but we are shaped by them, for they are internalised and form part of our unconscious memory. In other words, they are not forgotten but become part of our inner emotional world. The unconscious memory of them begins to build a sense of inner strength. We have learnt that loss is survivable, and as we begin to face loss more consciously we can discover inner resources.

Mothers 'know' about and draw on these internalised resources in their handling of their babies and children, responding intuitively with the comfort they need.

To focus on your own 'intuitive' knowledge of loss, consider the example in Exercise 1.1 of a child lost and separated from his mother in a crowded shopping centre.

Exercise 1.1 Lost child

It is 4 p.m. on a wintry afternoon. Tom (2) and his mother, Mary, are in the shopping centre. Mary is tired and keen to get home. She thinks Tom is still in tow. Tom, however, has been distracted by some moving toy he's just spotted. After a minute or two he turns to tell her and realises she's not there. As that moment, he emits a piercing and penetrating scream which seems to blot out all other sounds.

You can use your imagination to continue the story, knowing how Tom would feel.

If you were able to get inside Tom's skin you will have noticed some strong feelings. These probably included shock, disbelief, terror, fear and anger. Your ability to recall these feelings draws on your memory and your understanding that others feel similar things in similar situations, i.e. your empathic capacity.

You also know that Tom's mother's experience of the same event will be different. This is told in Exercise 1.2 (p. 5).

In thinking about Mary's feelings you will have recognised fear, anger, frustration and relief. You can respond to the story because you know intuitively how people are likely to feel in a frightening situation of loss or separation. Tom's frightened, angry cry was his way of trying to get his mother back. Mary's anger fuelled her drive to get through the crowd. Anger is one of the very strong feelings that arises when we fear a separation, and is a regulator to try to ensure that the attachment bond remains intact. Even when she found Tom, it took time for her fear and anger to subside.

Exercise 1.2 Mother's response

As Mary suddenly realises that Tom's not there, her heart misses a beat. She hears the piercing scream and tries to rush towards him, but the centre is crowded and her way is barred. Despite her tiredness she finds sudden energy to get through the crowd and reaches Tom within a few seconds. She shouts and rages at him for a minute. As she gradually calms down, she realises he is frightened too. Fighting back her tears, she puts her arms round him, cuddles him, calms him down and sets off home. When they get home they tell the family through their tears about their frightening afternoon.

Use your imagination to list the various feelings Mary experienced.

Fortunately the loss was brief and her fear manageable, so she was able quickly to comfort him in the way he needed. The relief of getting home and telling the rest of the family allowed the tears to flow. The 'gift' of their tears gave the family a sense of their interconnectedness and a recognition of the importance of Tom.

The powerful feelings of shock, fear, terror, anger and frustration evoked in Tom and Mary through even this very brief separation are not surprising. Research into the power of human attachment, and especially the bonding of young children to their attachment figures or carers, most frequently their mothers, confirms that such unforeseen separations are very frightening for good reasons.

Some studies of attachment behaviour

Sigmund Freud, who recognised the enormous influence of childhood experiences on adult emotional life, wrote about the strength of early attachments. He recognised this most basic of all human drives towards forming and sustaining attachments to others, yet seemed to understand it, initially at least, as simply a feeding relationship; primarily as cupboard love. Of course for the newborn baby the balance between life and death hangs upon the success of this relationship and the attendant ability to deal with hunger, pain and illness. But is this all there is to the mother and baby relationship?

John Bowlby, a psychoanalyst interested in childhood development, thought not. He was interested in more recent studies by biologists such as Konrad Lorenz and Nicolaas Tinbergen, who observed patterns of behaviour in birds and other animals. They noticed that many species of bird forged strong and specific attachment bonds. Lorenz's goslings 'locked' on to the first moving object in sight (usually the mother goose, but occasionally Lorenz himself!); many of Tinbergen's birds, having 'locked' on to a bird of the opposite sex, had remained mates throughout life (Bowlby, 1969).

The newborn baby does not, of course, 'lock' on to the first moving object and will be relatively undiscriminating about the person who attends to its needs in the early months. At this stage the baby is thought to be unaware of itself as a separate person. By about six months, however, a very marked preference for one person develops. It is as though the baby, having recognised its separateness and aloneness, 'decides' to counter this terrible aloneness by falling in love with the very person recognised as 'other' and yet who is also familiar. Anyone judged 'unfamiliar' is likely to be firmly rejected at this stage. As women suckle babies and, in our culture, generally also tend to their physical needs and interact with them in the process, mothers are usually, but not necessarily, the chosen attachment figures. It appears that the need for human connection is fundamental. 'The love of others comes into being simultaneously with the recognition of their existence', wrote Ian Suttie in 1935. As soon as we can distinguish 'you' and 'me' we seem almost to fall in love, perhaps to try to assuage the terror and isolation of that very separateness.

Experiments by Harry Harlow (1961), using a range of wire model 'monkey-mothers', showed that baby rhesus monkeys would thrive best and form attachments only to wire substitutes that were covered in cloth and gave 'contact comfort' – in other words, that were 'cuddly'. In other experiments where the infant monkeys were alarmed or in a strange setting, only those with cloth models were comforted sufficiently to start to explore. It looks, therefore, as though monkeys are 'programmed' to stay close to a cuddly mother, thus finding protection from predators that might harm them. Only with this security are they able to explore, play and mature. This attachment behaviour is found in the young of most species of mammals and birds. Its likely function is self-preservation, in that an immature animal seeks close proximity to an adult, which in turn will protect it from danger.

Baby humans seem also to be 'programmed' to stay close to their mothers to find protection from danger. Babies who did not have a mother or mother-figure to stay close to and who were hospitalised from birth were studied by

René Spitz in America in the early 1940s. He found that babies whose hunger, pain and illness needs had been methodically attended to, but who had 'only 1/8th of a nurse', were severely retarded developmentally, both mentally and physically (Spitz, 1945). It would seem that a reliable early attachment is of vital importance to healthy development, and the cost of breaking that bond, as in institutional care with a low carer to baby ratio, or with 'wire mothers', may be very high.

Quality of attachment

In the 1970s, attachment behaviour was observed in more detail by a team led by Mary Ainsworth, one of Bowlby's co-workers (Ainsworth *et al.*, 1978). For a year she observed infant–mother dyads in their home, seeing them for four hours every three weeks. At the end of this year's observation she conducted a standardised 'strange situation' procedure. In this the reactions of these infants now aged between 12 and 18 months, when left alone for three minutes in a standardised strange situation and then reunited with their mothers, were observed. She found three distinct patterns of response. The majority of babies were upset during the separation episode and explored little. On their mother's return they would respond strongly, seeking close bodily contact, and insist on interacting with her. A second group of babies showed no distress during separation and on reunion avoided contact and interaction with their mother. The smallest group of all were anxious, even before separation, and were enormously upset during the separation, but on reunion, although they wanted close contact, they resisted interaction. Ainsworth described the first group of children as 'securely attached' (B attachment category) and observed that the mothers of these children were sensitive and positively responsive to them. The other two groups were said to be 'anxiously attached' and either 'avoidant' (A attachment category) or 'ambivalent' (C attachment category). The avoidant children had mothers who were interfering as well as rejecting and with an aversion to physical contact. These mothers were frequently angry but showed little facial expression. The ambivalent children's mothers were not rejecting, seemed to enjoy physical contact but were singularly insensitive. Ainsworth and her team concluded that attachment behaviour and response to separation are markedly affected by the mother's personality.

When Ainsworth's work was followed up by Mary Main and her colleagues (1986, cited in Main, 1994), it was found that a small group of babies did not fit the three categories identified by her, but showed a mixture of A and C. They were insecure but showed disorganised attachment behaviour and were disoriented in the presence of their parents during the strange situation procedure. At about the same time it was found that some maltreated infants also showed this disorganisation. These maltreated infants had either psychiatrically disturbed or cruel and frightening parents. This gave a fourth attachment category known as disorganised/disoriented (D). When observed with their parents in the strange situation procedure they often freeze all movement and have a trance-like expression. Another example of disoriented behaviour is clinging while crying hard but at the same time leaning away with their gaze averted.

It is important to stress that these categories are not diagnostic. An insecure attachment is not pathological but indicates that there is a developmental risk of maladaptive and problem behaviour. The patterns are of interest because they help us to understand the response of people to subsequent losses. What is observable is that those with more secure attachments have a noticeable vitality in their relationships. More recent research observing infants with their mothers has given us greater understanding of these patterns.

Attunement and psychoneurobiology

Daniel Stern (1985) picked up Bowlby's notion of the working model of the mother in the infant's mind and contributed further to our understanding of the interpersonal world of the infant. His studies observing mother–infant behavioural interaction and the intense sharing of an inner feeling state led him to recognise a phenomenon he called 'affect attunement'. He is referring to the way in which one person, by synchronising their interactions to another, recognises, validates and shares feelings and communicates without necessarily using words. The 'affect attunement' of the ordinarily intuitive mother means that she tunes into, and resonates with, the baby's feelings in its resting state. Then, as these feelings increase and decrease in intensity, she modulates her affective stimulation so that the baby remains in a comfortable, positive state. The mother's capacity to do this with her infant is especially important because the interaction contributes to the development of the infant's capacity to feel (Schore, 2001) and therefore gives the baby a subjective sense of self.

About the same time as Stern's studies of behaviour were recognising the importance of the development of feelings in the infant, some neuroscientists, psychobiologists and developmental biologists were exploring the development of the infant brain and mind. They discovered that different parts of the brain are particularly sensitive to external stimuli at different times. These timings are critical, and if the external stimuli are absent then the growth and maturation of the brain are inhibited. The development of the occipital cortex depends on the proto-conversations between the primary caregiver (mother) and the baby, which are the visible and communicating signs of the 'attunement' described by Stern. Proto-conversations are the way in which interpersonal awareness and emotions are mediated between mother and infant via movements of the arms and head, eye-to-eye orientations, vocalisations and hand gestures (Trevarthen, 1993). This 'reciprocal facial signalling', described from different theoretical perspectives by Stern and Trevarthen, enables the internal feeling state of the baby to be expressed, and relies on the mother being psychobiologically attuned to the internal state of the infant rather than its overt behaviour. As Trevarthen (1990) notes, 'the intrinsic regulators of human brain growth in a child are specifically adapted to be coupled, by emotional communication, to the regulators of adult brains'. Or, put another way, brain–brain interaction in a positive affective relationship is essential for brain growth and emotional development. For the first three years of a child's life the right brain dominates, during which the development and growth of the brain depend on these 'vital emotional communications' between the mother and the infant (Schore, 2001). This not only confirms Stern's earlier studies on the importance of communication, but demonstrates its intrinsic role in brain development. The communication between internal emotional states constitutes an integral part of attachment behaviour.

Eisenberg (1995, cited in Schore, 2001) stated that attachment transactions also mediate 'the social construction of the human brain'. Attachment is not just an overt behaviour, but attachment experiences influence the development of the orbitofrontal cortex, which is the socio-emotional part of the brain. This area of the brain is connected with the autonomic nervous system, which is responsible for the bodily feelings associated with emotional states. For example, fear is felt as increased heartbeat and a desire to urinate, both mediated by the autonomic nervous system. It is also connected with the limbic system, which is involved in 'affective responses to events and in the mnemonic processing and storage of these responses' (Carmichael and Price, 1995; cited in Schore, 2001) and in the ability to process facial expression without any conscious awareness (Critchley et al., 2000; cited in Schore, 2001). From these functions it can be seen how critical the full development of this system is for the regulation of emotion, for the development of empathy and for the capacity to adopt different emotional states when interacting with other people. In general, when the communication system between infant and caregiver is well developed, the infant will grow up with the inner capacity to regulate emotion and to adopt different emotional states when interacting with other people. In other words, the baby will be developing the inner resources to connect with others, to think and to work its way through the processes of grief as a securely attached individual.

Secure attachment

Short separation

Let us return now to Mary and her son Tom (Exercises 1.1 and 1.2), and let us assume that Mary and Tom had been able to form a secure attachment. As Tom had developed within this basically secure relationship there had always been someone there for him to turn to in threatening situations. As he had begun to crawl and then walk his movement was always 'away', moving towards independence and discovery of the world. All this was possible within the secure knowledge of Mary's presence, with the occasional backward glance for reassurance. Gradually the 'secure base' that Mary offered out there began to be assimilated and to develop within Tom so that she did not always have to be in sight. He could tolerate her absence and could reconnect to her when she returned. When he did lose her in the shopping centre he emitted a scream so powerful, and full of 'hope-of-retrieving-her', that Mary was quickly with him and the period of loss brief. She was able to comfort him, he felt secure again and the loss was managed.

This early secure attachment of Tom's provides inner resources that will help him to manage later in stressful and even threatening situations. However, if the attachment is anxious then it is more difficult to explore and to cope with separation. Thus the capacity of infants to manage a threatening and stressful situation, such as the loss of an attachment figure, will depend on the quality of the early attachments. Additional factors that affect this capacity are the duration of the loss, the frequency of losses with little recovery time, the maturity of the child and the presence, warmth and caring capacity of other familiar figures.

Longer separation

To illustrate the effect of a longer separation on a securely attached child, let us return to Tom and his mother in Exercise 1.3 (p. 11). In this instance the separation could be described as traumatic or circumstantial rather than natural.

The further feelings you may have thought about may be frustration and panic; you may even have wondered about hopelessness and despair. In this story Tom's angry cry did not bring his mother back, so he started rushing frantically around as though he were searching for her. He still thought he would find her and felt hopeful. Yet his mother's longer absence this time had raised his fear and panic to such an extent that he had almost given up hope and begun to feel the despair of disconnection. This made it more difficult for her to soothe and reassure him. Tom's experience of loss is summarised in Table 1.1 (p. 12).

Tom's response to the longer separation is typical of the responses found by James and Joyce Robertson when they made some very poignant films in the 1950s documenting the reactions of children separated from their parents on admission to hospital or a residential nursery. The majority of the children over the age of six months were found to respond to the separation in predictable ways. Initially they would protest loudly, search frantically and cry, showing acute distress. To an onlooker it was clear that the children were moving heaven and earth to retrieve their lost mothers. This phase was followed by despair, in which they became inactive and withdrawn, though they

Exercise 1.3 Child in hospital

Unfortunately, a few months later Tom fell off the slide and bumped his head so badly that he was dazed for some minutes. When he was violently sick some time later, Mary decided to take him to casualty. They kept him in hospital for observation. She was able to stay with him. When Tom nodded off, she took the chance to go and telephone her husband to tell him where they were. There was a long queue for the telephone, and Mary had to wait for about 20 minutes to complete her call.

Meanwhile Tom had woken up and, realising that his mother was missing, he screamed. When she did not reappear, he started rushing frantically all over the ward. Nobody could comfort or calm him. The nurses were beginning to feel frantic. He suddenly went quiet. However, the peace was short-lived and Tom soon repeated his frantic searching, to be followed again by a quiet and withdrawn period.

When Mary returned, his withdrawal shocked her. He initially 'ignored her' and she had to coax him into letting her cuddle him.

Use your imagination to identify the different feelings that Tom experienced.

might well repeat the word 'Mummy' monotonously with the odd tear appearing. Children would frequently return to protesting and then back into despair more than once before the third stage was reached.

In this third stage the children became detached, apparently not noticing when an individual nurse came and went. The longer the stay in hospital or nursery, the worse the situation became. Although children would try to form an attachment to a nurse, for instance, she would then leave to go off duty. The more often these transient mother figures were lost, the more detached these children became, eventually ceasing to show any feelings or any care for anyone, as in the pictures that emerged from the Romanian orphanages shortly after the fall of Ceauşescu. There were no more tears and the child's

Table 1.1 Summary of a child's experience of a sudden longer loss

Child's feeling	Child's inner thoughts	Child's behaviour
Mother goes away		
Shock and anger	Can't believe she's gone.	Scream to recover mother.
Angry longing	I want her – she can't really be gone.	Rushing around searching; crying.
Despair and hopelessness	She must have gone.	Withdrawal.
Emptiness	I'm alone.	Silence. (Short-term denial of needs and feelings.)
Mother returns		
Scared	Dare I believe what I see?	Watching and waiting. Lets self be hugged but does not respond.
Fear wanes	I'll risk believing.	Begins to respond.
Relief	I can believe. I'm not alone.	Reattached.

need for comfort and recognition was denied. These original observations have eventually had profound effects on hospital policy in the UK, so that it is now common for hospitals to enable parents to stay with their ill children, just as Mary stayed with Tom.

Insecure attachment

Later research, in work by Bowlby and others, has shown that the quality of a child's early attachment will influence both the persistence with which she tries to form new attachments and the quality and persistence of her withdrawal. Where the early attachments are reasonably secure the child will be upset by frequent separations and may make a lot of fuss about each departure, but she will persist for longer in trying to make attachments and will not become withdrawn. Overall she will be less damaged by each departure.

Where the early attachments are insecure and more anxious, the child's response is quite different, as is illustrated in the story of Sally.

Sally's mother was diagnosed with a brain tumour when she was two weeks old. This was operated on almost immediately but the surgeons were not able to excise all of the tumour. Over the next year Sally's mother spent a lot of time in hospital, so Sally was looked after by a lot of people while her father tried to continue to work. When Sally was 2½ years old her mother was well enough for her parents to go away on holiday without her. She stayed with her grandparents, whom she knew well. To her parents' surprise, she made no fuss at all when they left, ignoring them completely and playing with her toys. Nor was she any trouble to her grandparents while they were away. Indeed, she seemed even 'easier' than usual. When her parents returned she refused to go and meet them, preferring to play with the children next door. From then on she seemed very detached, preferring her own company.

This little girl has already had many painful departures in her life and she seems to have tried to manage this by cutting off her feelings altogether. On the surface she appears quite quiet and settled and much less trouble to carers than the securely attached child. But underneath she may be denying the very feelings and experiences that, however uncomfortable they were at the time, are part of the natural grieving process.

These differences were also apparent when Sally's parents returned. Even for the securely attached child, it would have been difficult. She would probably have ignored her mother initially and have needed considerable coaxing to relate to her again. For the insecurely attached child such as Sally, it may be impossible for her to risk a relationship again and she remains detached, cut off from her parents and denying her true feelings. This could be understood as a logical conclusion to the disconnections she has experienced, and is her attempt to protect herself from being hurt again.

In Tom's case he was deprived of Mary for so long that he was overwhelmed with despair and at first needed to deny his relationship. Fortunately, he was attached securely enough to Mary to have the capacity to bear the anxiety of separation and the angry feelings he experienced towards her. It took Mary time to comfort him and to remember that his angry feelings were entirely appropriate to his situation. In spite of the more severe difficulties associated with this loss, Tom was nonetheless able to reattach and 'manage' the loss. For others, like Sally, the experience of loss is not managed by reattachment but by continued denial of feelings and withdrawal from relationships.

Where the early attachments are very anxious and insecure, the number of losses too frequent, the duration too long or the capacity of the attachment figures to offer comfort and support very low, then the direct expression of feelings and needs becomes increasingly difficult and instead the true feelings are denied. This denial of the existence of feelings is a way of separating and thus 'protecting' ourselves from feelings too frightening or too painful. In this way we can come to convince ourselves that we are unaffected by the loss, and in turn convince others of this make-believe. When this happens grief may seem to disappear, but signs of locked-in feelings such as coldness and disconnection signal that grief has 'gone underground' or become blocked. A relationship of trust is required to free this block so that the denied feelings of childhood can find expression. A skilled and experienced helper will be able to facilitate the expression of these locked-in feelings.

The basic attitudes that facilitate the expression of feelings will be looked at in Chapter 3 and the specific skills in Chapter 10.

Summary

- Loss and separation form an intrinsic part of human emotional development. Such losses are therefore known as 'necessary losses'.
- Readers know from their own life experience the emotional responses of both a parent and a child when they are suddenly separated.
- Attunement and attachment behaviour are central to the growth and maturation of the 'socio-emotional' brain.
- The survival of young animals depends on attachment behaviour.
- Studies on attachment behaviour in young children show that attachment can be secure or anxious, and within the latter category can be ambivalent, avoidant or disorganised/disoriented.
- The response of a securely attached child to a short natural separation and a longer unexpected separation can be predicted.
- The response of an anxiously and insecurely attached child to a short natural separation or a longer unexpected separation can also be predicted and differs from that of a securely attached child in two major ways. These are that the child will remain detached and become cut off from her true feelings, and she will protect herself from excessively painful feelings by denying their existence.

Chapter 2

Adult attachment patterns

In Chapter 1 the four attachment categories of children were described. They are significant because they help in understanding the emotional reactions of children to separation and loss. This is elaborated in considering children's reactions to loss and grief in Chapters 8 and 13. It is also significant for us that these attachment patterns carry on into adult life. Evidence for this has come from the work of Mary Main and her co-workers. They developed a story-telling technique to assess the 'attachment status' of children of 10–12 years old (George and Solomon, 1996; cited in Hesse, 1999) and a structured interview, the Adult Attachment Interview (AAI) (George *et al.*, 1985), which could be used to assess the attachment status in adults.

The children were given pictures to complete or asked to talk about their families, and again some clear patterns emerged. The secure children demonstrated what Holmes (1993) has called 'autobiographical competence', i.e. they were able to give a coherent account of their lives even when events were painful: for instance, 'When my Dad died, Mummy was very upset and we all went to live with Gran'. The avoidant children, however, had great difficulty in giving any sort of account and in remembering events from childhood, and the ambivalent children gave muddled, incoherent accounts.

The adults were given an hour-long interview which was devised to 'surprise the unconscious' with questions about such topics as childhood, parents, feelings of rejection, major losses, giving ample opportunity for contradiction and inconsistency between statements. The interviews were then scored for a number of components, but in particular for the adults' ability to present a coherent picture of their attachment figures and attachment-related events in their lives, and to be able to describe and evaluate these experiences whether they were good or bad. From these differences in narrative competence a classification was made. Four categories were found in adults: 'secure/autonomous', 'dismissing', 'preoccupied' and 'unresolved/ disorganised'. These categories had close parallels to the infant standardised strange situation groupings of 'secure', 'avoidant', 'ambivalent' and 'disorganised'. In Table 2.1 (p. 16) we attempt to illustrate this comparison using an adaptation of Hesse's table.

Table 2.1 Adult attachment interview classifications and corresponding patterns of infant strange situation behaviour

Adult state of mind with respect to attachment	Infant strange situation behaviour
Secure/autonomous Coherent, collaborative discourse. Valuing of attachment, but seems objective regarding any particular event or relationship. Description and evaluation of attachment-related experiences are consistent, whether experiences are favourable or unfavourable.	**Secure** Explores room and toys with interest in pre-separation episodes. Shows signs of missing parent during separation, often crying by the second separation. Obvious preference for parent over stranger. Greets parent actively, usually initiating physical contact. Usually some contact maintained by second reunion, but then settles and returns to play.
Dismissing Not coherent. Dismissing of attachment-related experiences and relationships. Normalising with generalised representations of history unsupported or actively contradicted by episodes recounted. Transcripts tend to be excessively brief.	**Avoidant** Fails to cry on separation from parent. Actively avoids and ignores parent on reunion. Little or no proximity or contact-seeking, no distress and no anger. Response to parent appears unemotional. Focuses on toys or environment throughout procedures.
Preoccupied Not coherent. Preoccupied with or by past attachment relationships or experiences, speaker appears angry, passive or fearful. Sentences often long, grammatically entangled, or filled with vague usages. Transcripts often excessively long.	**Ambivalent** May be wary or distressed even before separation, with little exploration. Preoccupied with parent throughout procedure; may appear angry or passive. Fails to settle and take comfort in parent on reunion, and usually continues to focus on parent and cry. Fails to return to exploration after reunion.
Unresolved/disorganised During discussion of loss or abuse, individual shows striking lapse in the monitoring of reasoning or discourse. For example, individual may briefly indicate a belief that a dead person is still alive in the physical sense, or that this person was killed by a childhood thought. Individual may lapse into prolonged silence or eulogistic speech. The speaker will ordinarily otherwise fit the other three categories.	**Disorganised/disoriented** The infant displays disorganised and/or disoriented behaviours in the parent's presence, suggesting a temporary collapse of behavioural strategy. For example, the infant may freeze with a trance-like expression, hands in air; may rise at parent's entrance, then fall prone and huddled on the floor; or may cling while crying hard and leaning away with gaze averted. Infant will ordinarily otherwise fit the other three categories.

Source: Adapted from Hesse (1999), p. 399.

Apart from this correspondence between the adult and infant categories, it was found that parents who were secure had secure children, dismissing parents had avoidant infants, preoccupied parents had ambivalent babies and unresolved/disorganised adults had disorganised infants. Further confirmation of the validity of these observations is that when first-time parents were assessed for their attachment category prior to the birth of their baby, the researchers could predict the baby's strange situation category in about 75 per cent of cases (Fonagy *et al.*, 1991; cited in Hesse, 1999).

Surveys have now been done on the distribution of these attachment categories in the general population. Secure attachment is found in about 70 per cent of the mother–infant dyads, so this is physiologically and numerically the norm (Holmes, 2001).

These studies seem to have implications. First, attachment patterns in childhood are transmitted from the parent to the child. Second, these early childhood ways of responding to people continue into adult life. Both these implications suggest that early relationship patterns become 'internalised' in the mind, leading to an 'internal working model' of relationships that seems to function as a template for personal interaction in adult life. This applies to relationships with other adults but, more importantly, if we become parents these inner models guide how we interact with our own children. This internal working model also affects how closeness, loneliness, separation and loss are handled.

Early separations and losses

In Chapter 1 we described the childhood attachment patterns and the pattern of emotional and behavioural responses to shorter and longer separations. It would appear that these early experiences become inner working models which are carried into adulthood, so that the responses to separation and loss can be predicted depending on the type of attachment relationships that have existed in childhood.

At the end of the spectrum where children have been securely attached, in both later childhood and adult life they will be able to trust others to understand, validate and comfort the strong feelings associated with separations and other kinds of loss, and will be able to tolerate these for themselves. At the other end, where children have in one way or another been insecurely attached, as adults they will be unable to trust others to validate their feelings and may react in a variety of ways. Some may deny the strong feelings, detach from the experience and appear untouched or even deadened. Others may seem to be stuck in one part of the pattern and express only one feeling in an exceptionally concentrated way, which can seem bizarre to observers. Indeed, this can be so extreme and intense that some people refer to these grief responses as 'abnormal', 'atypical', 'unnatural', 'morbid' or even 'pathological'. We have found it more useful to think of all these human responses to loss as lying along a spectrum of responses ranging from less to more complicated forms of a common fundamental pattern. Extreme behaviour patterns in adults may indicate a particularly complicated form of response to loss. In Chapter 5 we will look at how the impact of attachment difficulties, or poorly managed or excessively frequent childhood separations and losses, affect a person's inner working model and thus the management of grief.

Of course most people's responses will be somewhere between the two ends of the spectrum, with wide variation in terms of the kind of response, the intensity and duration of denial, the ability to trust themselves to make sense of their experiences and not to be overwhelmed by these feelings, and the ability to trust others to validate and comfort them.

A knowledge of this spectrum of human responses and its relationship to attachment history is very useful in working with the grieving. It enables helpers to understand more about individual difference and to focus appropriately. It can also enable them to assess early whether a person might need a particular approach, which might include a longer-term helping relationship focusing on early separations and losses.

Summary

- Studies of children's autobiographical competence throw up categories that correlate with patterns of secure and insecure attachment.
- These categories, in turn, correlate with categories of adult narrative competence.
- In practice there is a strong correlation between the categories of adults as parents and their own children.
- Childhood relationship patterns continue into adult life.
- Early relationship patterns appear to become 'internalised' into 'inner working models' which function as templates for relationships in adult life.
- Difficulties and insecurities in early relationship patterns usually lead to more complicated responses to loss and separation for both children and adults.

Chapter 3

The nurturing environment

Aspects of the counselling approach

In the first chapter we pointed out how Tom's mother felt fearful and angry when she lost him, but was quickly able to accept her feelings. She could then nurture Tom by comforting and consoling him when she reached him. We also considered the role that feelings play in responses to loss, and their function in ensuring care and comfort in young humans and, indeed, in young mammals. The response to loss, of course, becomes more complex and differentiated as we grow and develop, but some very basic reactions remain with us all our lives and are part of our essential humanness. Accepting these reactions is part of our ability to comfort and console others. Mary had an accepting attitude to her own feelings. She trusted, accepted and listened to them, perhaps intuitively, and thus was sensitive to Tom's needs. Her ability to do this depended to a large extent on her own experience of secure attachments. As she was nurtured, so was she able to nurture. Her sense of emotional connectedness was strong.

Peter Hobson's (2002) studies of autistic and non-autistic babies demonstrate that normal babies are predisposed to take part in intense emotional interactions from within hours of birth. They form a 'vital and energetic interpersonal linkage' between themselves and their caregivers. It is through this emotional connectedness that a baby discovers that 'a person is the kind of thing with which one can feel and share things, and the kind of thing with which one can communicate'.

This description of intense emotional communication from a baby links with both affect and the psychobiological attunement between mother and baby outlined in Chapter 1. According to Hobson (2002), such an emotional connectedness is also the prerequisite for a baby to acquire the capacity to think. Hobson (2002) observes that 'we cannot watch someone else's feelings and fail to react with feelings in ourselves. We have a basic human response to expressions of feelings in others – a response that is more basic than thought.' This is poignantly expressed by William Blake's poem 'On Anothers Sorrow' (Blake, 1992).

Can I see anothers woe
And not be in sorrow too.
Can I see anothers grief,
And not seek for kind relief?

Can I see a falling tear,
And not feel my sorrows share,
Can a father see his child,
Weep, nor be with sorrow fill'd.

William Blake, *Songs of Innocence and Experience*

As adults we are aware that we have the capacity both to think and to feel, as well as the capacity to think about feelings. This is dependent on the development of the socio-emotional part of the brain, which we described in Chapter 1. Being able to think about our own feelings and being able to imagine the feelings of others is the cognitive basis for empathy. Of course empathic exchanges happen all the time without awareness of this cognitive base, but sometimes the empathic contact is weakened and the connection becomes fragile. For instance, feelings can sometimes be experienced so intensely that it becomes difficult to think about them. Indeed, some feelings can be so painful that we manage to avoid experiencing them altogether by unconsciously removing (repressing) them from our conscious awareness. But this system is not foolproof and when, like Blake, we are touched by the sorrow of others, we will find strategies to remove ourselves from the pain by cutting off or limiting our empathy to these others. Thus, when 'seeing another's woe', some people will be able to 'be in sorrow too' and stay in emotional connectedness with the other person, while others will have difficulty with this and will find ways of protecting themselves from the sorrow by disengaging from the other's experience.

When new mothers are not closely emotionally connected with those around them, they may experience their babies' cries of pain as though it were their own pain. This may be so intense that the emotional connectedness with their baby is threatened, they may feel attacked by the babies' increasingly desperate cries and their empathy begins to falter. The subsequent guilt and disconnection may manifest as 'post-natal depression'. There are, of course, many other contributing factors to post-natal depression, such as loss of an earlier way of life, but this inner disconnection may be one of the most painful elements. Counselling can enable women to move towards a more empathic and forgiving way of seeing themselves, and thus of recognising their own pain. They are then more able to separate themselves psychologically from their babies, and respond to them as separate human beings with whom they are able to connect emotionally.

Counselling training aims to develop a person's capacity to stay with another's sorrow and remain in emotional connectedness with the other. In general, a counsellor is wanting to find a way of helping people to trust, accept and listen to themselves and their feelings. Counselling is characterised by a set of attitudes, towards both self and others, that aims to foster trust and self-acceptance. These attitudes are often there when people are trying to help and comfort one another through their emotional connectedness. Sometimes when they are not around we encounter unhelpful and even painful responses. Exercise 3.1 offers you the opportunity to use your own experience of life to find the range of attitudes and capacities you met when you needed help and comfort.

Exercise 3.1 Helpful and unhelpful responses

Go back into the past, near or distant, and think of a time in your life that was difficult for you. Try to remember the event itself, think about that time, ponder on what was happening then and see if you can recall how other people responded to you. You will remember things that were said as well as attitudes that you sensed. Try to categorise these into responses that were helpful or unhelpful.

HELPFUL RESPONSES   **UNHELPFUL RESPONSES**

A major aim of this book is to help you use your own experience as an integral part of learning about loss counselling. It is useful in this context to think about the event that you chose in Exercise 3.1 and consider the ways in which loss was a part of the event, or indeed the core of the event.

You may find yourself feeling quite angry now as you remember these unhelpful responses. Generally the unhelpful responses are linked with the listener being non-accepting, having judgemental attitudes, being a poor listener or finding it difficult to remain in emotional connectedness with the other because of the pain that is touched in them by the story of the other.

This often leads to statements such as:

You'll get over it	Cheer up
Don't cry! Crying only upsets you	Give us a smile
Least said, soonest mended	It was meant to happen
Every cloud has a silver lining	There's light at the end
It'll all come out in the wash	of the tunnel

and, in the case of loss and bereavement, statements such as:

Don't be morbid	You're better off without him/her
Never speak ill of the dead	It's time *you* got back to normal
	[six weeks later!]
Of course you'll find someone else	It's God's will
There are more pebbles on the beach	It was meant

All these remarks can make the person who is hurt feel devalued, angry and misunderstood. Although the listener may be trying consciously to respond to the person in distress, with the best of intentions, their unconscious fear of pain may lead them to disconnect emotionally and fill the silence with some protective platitude. They may also reflect society's difficulty in accepting death and the strong feelings that we have about pain and dying.

Helpful responses, on the other hand, usually include a recognition of feelings and an understanding that the feelings being experienced may be frightening for that person, and that those who are frightened or lost may behave in odd ways. They will usually recognise that what is happening is unique for that individual. The person in trouble who receives helpful responses has the experience of receiving undivided attention, and does not feel they are a burden to the listener. These helpful responses lead to the person in difficulty feeling accepted and understood so that the experience of hurt and pain is truly recognised. This capacity to accept and not judge is the first of three basic attitudes which characterise the 'way-of-being' of a counsellor. A counsellor in training not only will learn about appropriate responses, but will also be encouraged to adopt and foster the basic attitudes underlying any responses. This first attitude is usually called 'acceptance'.

A second attitude is demonstrated when listeners are able to sense, very accurately, what is being felt by the other and yet not be overwhelmed by those feelings. This is what counsellors call empathic understanding or 'empathy', i.e. the capacity to feel with others and to enter the world of their feelings as if it were one's own without the distancing effects of either fear or pity. Fear makes it difficult for us really to hear the true experience of the other, and pity can become a barrier that puts down the other person. This is succinctly worded by Dea Trier Mørch (1982) when she says: 'You don't help another person with pity. You don't have to suffer too. You have to be what you are.'

The origins of empathic relating are in our earliest relationships. The capacity for empathy may be enhanced or diminished by subsequent relationships and experiences. Counsellor selectors are looking for this basic empathic capacity when they select counsellors for training. This capacity can be enhanced through training and supervision.

A third attitude, called 'congruence', or sometimes genuineness, is less easily understood. We are in a state of congruence when we can be real and genuine and not make ourselves out to be what we are not. Our inner feelings are clear to us and are reflected in our behaviour. Congruent counsellors accept themselves as they are and convey this sense of self-acceptance to the other. This enables a more trusting and safer relationship to develop.

These attitudes are, of course, not exclusive to counsellors, but are those fostered in counselling and psychotherapy training of all kinds. Truax and Carkhuff's (1967) seminal research on therapeutic relationships demonstrated that when these attitudes are present in the helping relationship then growth, change and healing take place. These findings have been replicated in various Western countries. A summary of this way-of-being is given in Table 3.1.

Table 3.1 Basic attitudes of counselling

Counselling is most effective when the counsellor can:
1   offer complete and unconditional acceptance;
2   feel and communicate empathic understanding;
3   Be congruent or genuine.

One of the difficulties in writing about acceptance, empathy and congruence in a book is that they are not as easy to demonstrate as they might sound. There are times when they are particularly difficult to experience and demonstrate towards another person. Knowledge of ourselves enables us to recognise when our feelings are not congruent. If an incongruent feeling develops and persists so that it intrudes on the ability to listen, then it is worth reflecting on this and deciding where this feeling is coming from. A counsellor's response to loss in her own life may be sparked by the experiences or feelings of the griever, and then she may be responding to her own loss rather than the griever's loss. This is often what is happening when the counsellor is finding it particularly difficult to maintain the basic attitudes of acceptance, empathy and congruence. This in turn is one of the reasons why trying to understand these feelings in 'supervision' with another individual is so important in counselling work; for without the maintenance of these basic attitudes counselling is ineffective. The form and function of supervision will be discussed in Chapter 18.

Counselling developed out of Carl Rogers' conviction that the seeds of healing are to be found within each individual (Rogers, 1967). From the first chapter we know that each person's response to loss is the unique product of their own individual experience. Counselling, with its emphasis on listening to the individual, is particularly suited to helping someone through the work of grieving a loss.

In Part II we consider the experience of death and bereavement as a specific example of human loss, before moving on in Part III to consider how counselling attitudes can foster a set of more helpful responses in practice.

Summary

- Babies are predisposed to create intense emotional connectedness with their caregivers.
- This emotional connectedness is the bedrock of the capacity to think.
- Thinking about feelings and managing emotional states are prerequisites for the development of empathy and emotional connectedness.
- Certain attitudes towards feelings are more helpful than others in fostering growth and in healing the wounds of grief.
- Responses that demonstrate an accepting attitude are more helpful.
- Three particular attitudes create the necessary conditions for change in a helping relationship. These are acceptance, empathy and congruence.
- Research indicates that these attitudes are effective in personal relationships.

Part II

Death as a particular form of loss

Chapter 4

Experiences of death and bereavement

Within the course of any human life there are very many different experiences of loss. Some losses, such as birth, weaning and death, happen to all of us and can be called 'necessary losses' (see Chapter 1). Because they all lead to separateness, and are an integral part of development and maturation, they are often also called 'developmental losses'. However, these are only some of the losses we may experience as part of the cycle of life and death.

Circumstantial losses

There are losses that do not happen to all of us and that might not at first appear to lead to personal development. However, these circumstantial losses, as they are sometimes called, can themselves become sources of personal growth and maturity. Some of these losses are listed in Exercise 4.1 (p. 28).

At first glance, some of these events are more obviously associated with loss than others. The less obvious ones may be fire, birth of a disabled child, sexual abuse, rape, impotence, old age, infertility and going into hospital. We have included these because whenever someone feels safe enough to ponder their experience of such an event, the word 'loss' or 'lost' comes in. In recalling, for instance, sexual abuse as a child, many people mention loss of innocence, loss of control, loss of trust, loss of self-esteem, loss of dreams, loss of ideals. In talking of the birth of a disabled child, loss of dreams is mentioned by the parents, as is loss of self-esteem, loss of security, loss of faith. The loss of hopes can be so profound that the name chosen for the child before its birth cannot be used for the disabled child.

By now it is evident that events involving loss and separation may occur throughout our lives. Though many of these other losses are more frequent than we might at first think, the most extensively studied adult loss has been bereavement and specifically widowhood. For this reason, we shall present widows' responses to the death of their husbands in considerably more detail than widowers' responses. We shall then extend these particular responses to other losses.

Exercise 4.1 Circumstantial losses

Separation	Blindness
Divorce	Deafness
Emigration	Loss of speech
Burglary	Disfigurement
Stillbirth	Amputation
Miscarriage	Mastectomy
Abortion	Infertility
Death of partner, close	Death of a pet
friend, member of family	Fire
Ageing	Natural disasters
Moving house	Accidents
Imprisonment	Bankruptcy
Birth of a disabled child	Loss of job
Retirement	Disability
Sexual abuse	Going to school/college
Hospitalisation	Loss of mobility
Serious illness	Menopause
Leaving home	Rape
Adoption	Impotence

You will probably think of other circumstantial losses.

Identify how many of these have happened to you.

One of the major studies was done by Colin Murray Parkes in the late 1960s. He had been so impressed by Charles Darwin's observations on grief in animals that he drew them to Bowlby's attention. From this there followed a fruitful collaboration, with Parkes deciding to focus on human grief and in particular widowhood. He asked a group of 22 London widows under the age of 65 to tell him in their own words about their bereavement. He saw each widow five times, seeing them at the end of the first, third, sixth, ninth and thirteenth months following bereavement. From this he was able to establish a pattern of 'normal grief' in the first year of bereavement and to discover what factors affected the grieving process. After listening to these widows he was able to see that a clear set of feelings usually emerged (Parkes, 1972).

Subsequent work by people such as Margaret and Wolfgang Stroebe, Henk Schut, Robert Neimeyer and Tony Walter have been critical of the way in which Parkes focuses exclusively on feelings in the grief work and aims to reach detachment from the dead person and thus acceptance of the death. Stroebe and Schut (1995) have observed that the griever has to mourn the loss and learn new tasks and roles, thus both emotional and practical work needs to be done. Neimeyer and Walter have focused on the 'continuing bonds' with the deceased that often exist forever in the minds of the survivors, and are actively created and sought by them. In support of Parkes and other people conducting research on bereavement in the 1960s, their focus on detachment may have arisen not only because of Freud's ideas about the need to detach and withdraw energy from the old relationship, but also because they were interviewing groups of relatively young women who had been prematurely bereaved. Parkes *et al.*'s focus on feelings was also understandable at the time, because the vast majority of British people found it hard to express feelings. The stiff upper lip was lauded rather than questioned.

All the researchers must have heard many tales rather like Anne's tale which follows. It is told by a woman about her experience of when her husband died unusually young and just at the point when he was most needed as father of a young child and a newborn baby. It is told verbatim.

It all started one Whit Monday. I was 25 and my husband, James, was 36. Michael was a small boy of two and we were expecting the new baby any day. As we drew into a petrol station my husband casually mentioned that he had found a lump on his shoulder. He sounded casual but somehow I knew it wasn't. My mind raced; was it cancer? A lymphoma maybe? Some of these thoughts were shared as we planned what to do. He must go to the doctor next morning. As a result of the doctor's examination James was admitted to hospital that very Thursday for a biopsy. On the same day I went to another hospital to have our second baby induced. Despite strenuous efforts, labour did not start.

What anxious, nail-biting days those were. I knew something was seriously wrong with James and yet could get no answer from anyone. James was in another hospital, Michael was at home with my mother and I was alone, with my second baby showing no signs of shifting. On the following Tuesday contractions started at last and to my joy James appeared at the hospital about half an hour before Pete was born.

There followed a lovely week at home for us all before 'all hell let loose'. Hell was preceded by a doctor's visit and the casual remark 'Oh, by the way, the growth was not highly malignant'. This seemed good news. But of course I was clutching at straws. What I heard was the 'not malignant', what I failed to hear was the 'highly'.

So sure was I of a reprieve that I did not believe the hospital's letter, which arrived next day, recalling him for more tests. I even phoned and checked with the GP. Yet within 24 hours James looked desperately ill and the night before returning to hospital insisted on taking me out for a meal, even though he couldn't eat much. When he started telling me where his will was and when the gas and electricity bills needed paying, I had to begin to take on board that he knew he was seriously ill and his insistence was his way of making me face things. I tried to stop him talking this way. I just didn't want to believe what I was beginning to realise. Within two days I knew from my GP that he had inoperable cancer, with perhaps only six months to live. He knew that he had 'some malignancy' which would be reassessed in six months. Yet when I approached his bedside the first thing he said was 'Sorry I didn't take out that life insurance policy I've been talking about.' By this stage we both knew, at least some of the time, where we were and that he was dying.

The shock left me feeling sick, with loss of memory and appetite, and an inability to sleep. Each night alone in bed I tossed and turned wondering what would happen. Would he die at Christmas? How would I manage? I had two tiny boys, how would they manage? Would I marry again? What would dying be like? Would he die peacefully or in great pain? Did he know I loved him? Could I get a job? Was it my fault? I didn't sleep much in those weeks and frequently cried for much of the night.

When James came out of hospital a fortnight later it was obvious that he was going downhill rapidly. I asked friends and family to come and see us. After his parents had left he told me he had given them our slide projector. At that moment I was suddenly so furious with him that I didn't know what to do with myself. Rather than hit out at him I rushed out and disappeared down the garden, knowing he couldn't reach me. Later that night I was able to apologise and we were then able to talk for several hours. We had sensible discussions about what I would do after he died and about those mundane things such as insurance, mortgages and electricity bills. We also talked about the unknown future for both of us. Oddly to me, we also talked of the holiday in six months' time which we both knew we would not go on together.

After a few hours' sleep I woke up to find that James was much weaker, he could no longer talk easily. We had done our talking just in time. He was so bad I realised that if James was to be at Pete's christening it would have to be very soon. By noon the christening was arranged for that afternoon. The family all came and the neighbours provided an iced christening cake and the vicar christened Pete in the garden.

All this time James knew he had cancer, but within four weeks we both had to face the fact that death was imminent. Indeed, it was just over eight weeks from finding the secondary and three days after the christening to James's death. In spite of the shock and disbelief eight weeks earlier, I felt immense relief when, eight hours before he died, the doctor suggested that James would not live much longer. He was right. As James died at 6.00 a.m. next morning I kissed him goodbye, feeling a great peace and a sense of rightness. Within hours this had been replaced by numbness. It felt as though there was a great distance between me and everyone else, as if I was cocooned in cotton wool: literally numb with shock, no tears, no feelings, just absolute numbness.

This lasted for a fortnight and was one of the many sensations which made me wonder if I was going crazy. The funeral passed with almost no feeling, and the following two weeks in my parents' house passed in a kind of haze. Tears broke through briefly as I tried to respond to the many letters of condolence. Surprisingly this numbness did not seem to affect my ability to do things. I looked after the children, made curtains for my mother, cooked, and yet everything was far away.

I returned to my own house after a fortnight. It was then I started to cry and my mind began to run in overdrive. I lay in bed at night tossing and turning, sobbing my heart out. My brain chuntered away, but hugging James's old sweater just to recall what he smelt like and to comfort myself helped me fall asleep. Any quiet moment was interrupted by endless thoughts, a non-stop nightmare of searching and recall. I remembered all the weeks before James died in minute detail. I remembered events and conversations. I worried about what I hadn't done and had done. My brain just would not 'shut down' unless I was frantically busy with something else. Of course I was frantically busy because I now had the house and car to run, I had to pay all the bills, and the children to care for. I had to get my head round practical tasks galore and learn new skills. There was no division of labour as there had been when James had been alive. This searching around in my mind lasted about six months and was relieved occasionally by being able to say it all out loud to someone else. As time went by I became more and more unreasonable with everything and everyone. The slightest difficulty and I blew up, cross with everyone and anyone and often extremely catty. Finally, after about three months, as I drove along a winding lane I said out loud to James, 'You have the better deal. Look what you've left me with!' I then thought the answer was to drive into the wall ahead and I would also be fine. Yet almost in the same instant I knew I couldn't. I couldn't do that with the children in the back of the car. This did not stop the anger, but gradually I knew I was angry with James for baling out on me. This was one of many times I 'talked' to James. At other times I was asking him what he would have done, or telling him of the small developments the children had made. I felt a bond to him and a connectedness despite his absence.

Though I always knew James was dead, and seeing him dead confirmed that, I still did not believe it. Many was the time when I heard his car draw up and his footsteps coming to the back door. Over a year after he died I saw him in the street. I knew it wasn't James and yet I had to make that stranger talk to convince myself. Each time I knew he was there and yet I knew he was dead. 'Was I going mad?' was a frequent question. I felt so silly.

I was also dogged by feelings of guilt. 'Wasn't I mean for going down the garden?' 'It was my fault he had died.' 'I deserved that punishment.' 'If only I'd done more for him.' 'If only I'd told him once more that I loved him.'

As time passed I felt increasingly lonely and despairing, though after the first six months my brain was no longer in overdrive. It seemed that every good day was followed by five bad days. I felt like half a person and was very aware of being half a couple. I knew for certain that people only invited me out because they were sorry for me. People didn't really want to see me, or were only being kind, or so I thought.

Another nagging worry was whether I had cancer too. Any odd ache and particularly headaches made me very anxious. Twice I fainted and I had never done that in my life. I also got a septic finger; again this was unusual for me. I seemed to be forever visiting the doctor, either for me or one of the children. Being a hypochondriac is a real 'no, no' in my family and there I was being that!

Of course each 'celebration' was hard. The birthdays, Christmas and Easter made me acutely aware of James's absence. Each time there were family and friends to talk to which eased the pain, because something shifted into place, and yet there was still more to be said. But as the first anniversary of James's death loomed I gradually found that there were now some days which were almost 'normal' with no tears, anger or guilt. I realised I hadn't apparently thought of James for several days on end. I discovered that although I hadn't thought of him, I hadn't forgotten him. In a funny way I seemed to remember him better and could talk about him more easily. And so I moved into the second year with more hope than despair. He was pretty well inside my head and beginning to become a real comfort.

Invited to reflect on her story some 30 years after James's death, Anne writes:

As the years have gone by, James is not forgotten. Occasionally I still weep for him and I have kept the old sweater that comforted me all those years ago. Both Michael and Pete are married and their weddings were joyful, but painful too, because of the absence of their own father. Even though I have married Thomas who has been a very good stepfather to them, it was James who should have been at their weddings and at the birth of our grandchildren. When I see his old friends and family we still reminisce and laugh about those days when James shared his life with us, and even today I learn things about James that I did not know. He continues to live in our minds and memories.

In Anne's story there are actually three adult experiences described: James's experience of dying and leaving a young wife and two babies; Anne's experience of James dying and leaving her alone with two babies; and Anne's experience of bereavement. In Exercise 4.2 we invite you to list as many feelings and beliefs as you can from the three angles.

Exercise 4.2 Experiences of the 'letting-go' process

| James's experience of facing death | Anne's experience of facing James's death | Anne's experience of bereavement |

How many feelings and beliefs can you find in Anne's story for these three different experiences?

We want to highlight some particular feelings and experiences so clearly expressed in this story. The first is how disbelief and denial emerged for both James and Anne when James was dying, and for Anne as she grieved. Anne seemed at one and the same time to deny the severity of James's illness (e.g. 'clutching at straws') and to face the reality of the speed with which James was dying and manage what needed to be done (e.g. get the baby born and christened). James too could deny the proximity of death, and at the very same time face its reality (e.g. talk of the holiday never to be taken, coincident with the discussion of what Anne would do when he died). After his death Anne partly knew that James was dead for ever and yet simultaneously heard his footsteps, even saw him in the street, as though a part of her would not give him up.

Anne's account recognises that she is well aware of the practical tasks she needs to undertake, and is helped by them because it means that she is not endlessly overwhelmed by feelings. We can also see how she has maintained links, both tangible and emotional, with James over a large number of years.

Anger and guilt feature in all three experiences. James's first response to hearing his 'death sentence' was to apologise for not having the life insurance sorted out. This seems to indicate a feeling of guilt that, typically of guilt in response to loss, was inappropriate as he had in fact sorted out adequate life cover. We can also understand his giving away of something precious to both of them without consultation, as an angry gesture towards Anne. She perceived this unilateral decision as abandonment. Anne's much more obvious expression of anger was probably a combination of appropriate anger about the non-consultation and loss of the projector, but also an unconscious expression of the underlying and unacknowledgeable layer of anger with James for abandoning her through his imminent death. We see an expression of her guilt that lonely night when Anne was alone at home and James was in hospital. She kept asking herself 'Was it my fault?' Later, having been angry with all and sundry and having come to the point of suicidal thoughts, she was at last able to recognise her anger with James for leaving her and having the 'easier' solution. Her guilt again found expression after James's death in her constant self-questioning (e.g. 'Could I have done more?' and 'If only I'd . . .'). This kind of self-questioning and expression of a feeling of guilt is completely natural for us all, and may be an attempt to 'try to make things turn out differently'.

In common with a lot of bereaved people, Anne had suicidal thoughts, manifest when she contemplated driving into the wall. Although 'driving into a wall' may sound like wanting to kill herself, it was actually more a feeling of wanting to be dead and not wanting to be alive with her current level of pain. This thought or idea about being dead as a way of ending the inner pain can, in an odd way, be quite comforting and does not necessarily mean that the person wants to kill themselves. The bereaved frequently think that 'there is no point in living', or 'they might as well be dead', or they 'want to join the dead person'. The majority of them do not commit suicide, but a number of longitudinal studies have shown that there is indeed an increased risk of suicide among bereaved people. This is greatest in the first week of bereavement. Kaprio et al. (1987; cited in Parkes, 1996) found that women showed a ten-fold increase in suicidal deaths and men a 66-fold increase in that week.

There is no doubt that bereavement is immensely stressful, which in turn affects the immune system. Anne showed this stress in fainting and having a septic finger. It is so stressful that the life expectancy of widowers decreases by one and a half years, and for widows it decreases by six months (Mellstrom et al., 1982; cited in Parkes, 1996). In his 1960s study Parkes found that the widows' consultation rate with their GPs increased. This was also true for Anne. For people who are alone or who struggle to express things in words, it may be that the only way to express pain is through a bodily experience and they may present to their GP with some form of psychosomatic pain. Sometimes the psychosomatic pain can become quite entrenched in the person's experience of themselves and may need specialised treatment, or it may begin to shift as the pain is expressed in other ways (see Chapter 16).

Anne was lucky enough to have the capacity to express her grief and not deny it, and thus her physical pains began to ease quickly. This capacity to grieve will have been the result of her early environment, where it was possible to express feelings. Her own ability to grieve, together with the consistent support of family and friends, enabled her to survive and very gradually grow through what had initially looked like a completely impossible situation. The support given to her allowed her to express the different feelings at her own pace and to undertake the new tasks that were necessary without her husband. All of this helped her to work through her grief and regain her self-esteem.

When a person has a less developed capacity to grieve and the surrounding community is less supportive, it will be more difficult to get through the grieving process. This is where a counsellor's task would be to recognise the validity of the feelings being expressed and to notice which emotions are being denied. The emotions most likely to be absent are guilt and anger, the ones that are highlighted in Anne's story. We consider ways of working with anger and guilt in Chapters 14 and 15.

We now turn to another story which demonstrates that patterns of grieving are similar, but we shall see that some important differences emerge, many of which are typical of the ways in which men and women tend to respond differently to bereavement. As you read Geoff's story, told verbatim, of Laura's death, you may notice that it is told more directly and energetically. Geoff reacts much more practically; his anger is tangible in the very way the story is told. His story shows his acute awareness of the loss of his sexual partner, Laura, and it also highlights the intensity of his sexual responses.

> Laura had been an asthmatic since childhood, so when we married I was aware that there was always going to be a problem. When our first child, Julie, was being born in hospital, Laura had a protracted labour and also serious breathing difficulties. With Christine, born almost four years later, it had been touch and go due to a retained placenta and much loss of blood. After that experience Laura had opted for stronger stuff and so, except while carrying Gail, had been on a steroid drug for some years. This had greatly improved her quality of life. Her asthmatic attacks, though still occasional, were less intense and not as debilitating. Usually they were confined to times of high stress or monthly periods.
>
> I knew that Laura was a bit below par, so was not surprised when I said, 'I was off for a jog', that she replied by saying, 'I'll have an early bath and go to bed.' On returning from my run I had a drink of water and allowed my breathing to return to normal before going up for a bath.

She was in bed as I undressed and had my bath. As I was towelling I heard her go to the lavatory. Almost immediately there was a bump and I rushed in to find her slumped against the door, white as a sheet and apparently unconscious.

My mind was clear. I must move her up with my shoulder, and get her to the bedroom floor before (a) starting artificial respiration, (b) calling my good friend John from across the road, (c) dialling 999 for help, (d) waking Julie, who was almost 13. As I moved Laura and carried her in my arms I noticed a bruise starting to form on her forehead. I rationalised the priority into: shout for Julie; phone John; start respiration. And so it was. But Julie didn't appear; it was Gail, who was six. She slept in the room next door and came to see what was going on. I got her to go down and unlock the back door for John, all the while counting and mouth-to-mouth resuscitating. I don't know how long it was before John arrived – probably three or four minutes. I was tiring. John took over mouth-to-mouth and I phoned for the ambulance. We continued, taking it in turns. The chest was moving all right, the airways were clear, we sweated with fear and prayed aloud for help, inspiration, anything. Gail was a shadowy little figure in the doorway about 12 feet away, watching wide-eyed – we'd no time to talk and explain – her mother was dying or dead, and we couldn't say anything to her which would make sense.

The ambulance men arrived, complete with oxygen. We knew it was hopeless and so did they, but they tried. They asked when she'd last breathed; it was about 15 minutes earlier. I knew enough to realise that even if they'd managed to get oxygen in now it would be too late to be of use. They said sorry and could they use the telephone. The police arrived, alerted by the 999 emergency, and one of them knocked the dinner gong with his helmet. Julie and Christine slept on unaware. I was angry with them for not waking, but it was unreasonable and I knew that. We left them sleeping. Enough time for tears before breakfast.

We all had a cup of tea while waiting for the undertaker. Laura upstairs, alone. When the undertakers arrived I took them up. They asked me if I would like to take off her wedding ring. I can't remember who did. It is still around somewhere.

Two or three hours after Laura died, it was the middle of the night. John read a story to Gail, inappropriately the one about wolves eating children up. Gail didn't cry but John did. She went to sleep. John offered to stay with me but I declined this kindness, knowing that his wife would be desperate for comfort and intelligence. Laura and she had been good friends. I lay on the bed and thought. I remembered with wry humour the senior colleague in the Forces who had told me years earlier that the way to stop awake while 'on watch' was to rehearse all the horrible emergencies that could happen and what action one would take. Well, this was one such emergency and I did have an outline plan which may have sustained me: I'll never know how I would have coped without it. I wondered who to tell first and when. I thought about how we'd manage over the next few hours, days, weeks, months. I didn't sleep. At 7.00 a.m. I rose and got Christine to come with Gail and me to Julie's room. Then I told them, with Gail joining in the story. It must have been an 'impossible' shock and I did wonder whether, I still do wonder, was I right to leave them asleep? We had a weep, then Christine said it was the school photograph that morning so she must wash her hair. She did and went to school. We have that photograph.

Julie didn't go to school, but helped me with the other two. She made breakfast whilst I phoned Laura's parents, my parents, close friends and set up the chain to inform as many as possible before they would read it in the paper. A lot to do – no time to grieve. Julie came to work with me before we went to the coroner's office and the doctor's. Then the family started arriving. They were more emotional than we were. Everyone was kind. Few knew how to react to the news. We helped them over the first few sentences, then perhaps we would cry a little. The letters started. Some were horrible and commercial. No doubt all were well meant. They kept on coming for weeks, months even. Julie and I would discuss whether we were strong enough that day to read any, in case they were moving, causing either tears or anger. We read them all – eventually.

In those first few weeks after Laura died I kept busy, there was masses to do. I still had a job, a good job, and I didn't want to jeopardise that. We worked out a routine. Friends and neighbours and relations helped us establish a pattern of life, which enabled a few minutes of calm to pierce the frenetic activity. I was secretary of one of the girls' sports club at the time and most of my colleagues on the committee were expecting my resignation: it did not come. The activity was difficult to work into our schedule but (selfishly) good for me. I even took on another activity, which required absence from home for a couple of hours each week. My job was interesting and challengingly difficult and I often brought home projects to work upon when the girls had gone to bed. I also, with self-justifying parsimony, took to growing vegetables with a vengeance. Sometimes there used to be grief and tears, and often they occurred when least expected. Several times in a line of traffic I would have to pull in when an advertisement, a tune on the radio, one of Laura's favourite songs, would fill me up and I would have, with the sobbing, been quite unable to drive. I'd resume my journey a few minutes later, curiously refreshed by the emotion. When clearing out Laura's wardrobe with one of her sisters we decided to keep some of the clothes in case one of the girls wanted them. It was the same with much of her papers, which we still have in the house – somewhere – to this day. Maybe sometime I'll share them out to the family as keepsakes or 'belonging to the Granny you never knew'. Meanwhile they are mine.

Several times I would hallucinate. In bed was worst. One side was cold – so cold. As winter drew on I'd put two pillows where once she had lain. I'd wake up convinced she was next to me, and then I would cry and sob with anger when it was a pillow. More than once I was making love to her, passionately, not waking until after the orgasm – my thighs wet, just as they had been as a fantasising teenager. This was no fantasy. I had made love to her again. I did love her. But I'd not said goodbye – no one had. What a lonely way to die, just falling off the loo.

The sudden ending of this story perhaps reflects the suddenness of Laura's death. This left Geoff with a painfully unfinished relationship and the deep sadness of not having said a mutual goodbye. His sudden bereavement is different from Anne's, but many of the differences in emotional response seem to support an observation made by Beverley Raphael (1984): 'the external manifestations of grief may differ because of sex role differences in behaviour'. Our own observations are that men seem to need to regain control of their world more quickly, are more immediately in touch with intense sexual feeling and are also aware of the threat to their sexuality that loss of a partner can pose. They may describe themselves as feeling emasculated or even castrated. Men more often find it difficult to express the sadness of grief and in most cultures it is the women who do the wailing, while the men do the active and often angry tasks. Sometimes when men are unable to express either their pain or their anger directly, they may use sexual activity as an indirect expression of grief. Sexual activity of this kind is not usually about real intimate contact with the other person, and may be very wounding for the sexual partner. In the West, men seek new relationships and marry much more quickly after a bereavement than women.

Invited to reflect on his story some 25 years after Laura's death, Geoff writes:

I read the original account [above] with much emotion and still the odd tear, even though it had been written many years earlier, and I am now happily remarried for over 20 of those years. Is there something wrong I wonder? I would not say there is, but clearly with the benefit of hindsight, greater insight and much subsequent life experience there are things which I would have done differently – possibly better for me and the children, all three of whom have suffered some distress as child, adolescent and adult. Maybe they would have done anyway but I now understand that it could have been made more tolerable for them. Christine resents my excluding her from the funeral: Gail seems unaffected by that. Julie, who lost her mother at a particularly sensitive stage of adolescence, has probably been most scarred. I handled the introduction of a new 'wife and mother' to the household with perhaps undue bravado and confidence and was then at a loss to know what to do with the resultant tantrums from all three – well into adulthood. It was fortunate that my second wife, a widow herself, is much more aware of the pitfalls and the means of extricating oneself from them than ever I could have been on my own. She recognised for instance the necessity for each of her new daughters to have more positive evidence of their deceased mother, in both material things and less tangible memories and anniversaries. I kept some of the better clothes Laura had and these were offered to each of the girls as they reached their natural mother's size. None accepted anything and I felt a slight pang of disappointment. However, recently I remembered a rather nice tailored jacket which would not fit anyone except our cleaner. So I offered it to her and the palpable pleasure on her face as she tried it on and accepted the gift would, I felt, have pleased Laura equally.

From these two stories we could make the observation that the 'single' event of each bereavement contains multiple losses for that person. James's death meant for Anne, at a practical level, the loss of a partner, a father for her children and much else besides. Similarly there were multiple losses for Geoff. The multiple losses of Anne and Geoff are listed in Table 4.1.

Table 4.1 Multiple losses

Anne's losses	Geoff's losses
1 Partner/companion/helpmate	1 Partner/companion/helpmate
2 Father to children	2 Sexual partner
3 Breadwinner	3 Mother to children
4 Sexual partner	4 Home manager
5 Link with the outside world	

We have chosen the numerical order to signify the priority they gave to the losses. For others the death of a partner might mean the loss of a car-driver, a party-giver, a do-it-yourself expert, a cook, etc. Each of these separate losses needs to be recognised and grieved as an integral part of the total loss.

We have just highlighted some differences between the responses of women and men, but observations show how basically similar the underlying pattern of response to grief is for both. This underlying pattern for women was recorded by Parkes when he studied the feelings of the London widows. He found that there were four phases to mourning with associated feelings, all of which can be found in the stories of Anne and Geoff. In Table 4.2 we summarise the phases and associated feelings and experiences.

Table 4.2 Phases of adult mourning and related feelings

Phase	Predominant feelings
1 Numbness	Shock
	Disbelief
2 Yearning	Reminiscence
	Searching
	Hallucination
	Anger
	Guilt
3 Disorganisation and despair	Anxiety
	Loneliness
	Ambivalence
	Fear
	Hopelessness
	Helplessness
4 Reorganisation	Acceptance
	Relief

These phases do not occur one after another, but overlap. The feelings often associated with one phase are sometimes associated with another phase as well. We can move from one phase to the next and then back again. Thus, when we are grieving we can begin to recognise and take on board the reality of our loss and to experience the associated despair. Then hope seems to spring again and we move back into experiencing yearning, but then back into despair, when all hope of retrieving the loved one is lost. The way in which these phases are experienced is different for each individual and relates to the uniqueness of each person and their personal life-history. In looking back again at Anne's and Geoff's stories, you can perhaps see the interplay of their individual experiences with the basic pattern.

Just as the phases are experienced differently for each individual, the time-scale also varies. As a rough guide, the numbness frequently wears off within a month, the yearning phase diminishes over about six months, and feelings of disorganisation and despair persist for most of the first year. For many bereaved the grieving proceeds so that acceptance gradually occurs, and with this a reorganisation of one's life and beliefs. As a result, by the end of two years the majority of those bereaved prematurely, and therefore younger, will talk in terms of feeling content or settled and able to feel the normal highs and lows of life and of living.

However, this is not true of everybody, nor of older bereaved, who may have spent a lifetime with the same person. For them the term 'acceptance' and the associated idea of relief can be misleading, particularly if it implies that somehow, in working through the grief, one could actually fracture the bonds with the dead person that one had lived with one's entire life in order to re-engage with life itself.

As can be seen from Anne and Geoff, both have maintained strong links with their past, some intangible in their memories and some tangible, such as James's sweater and Laura's coat. The recognition of the need for a tangible remembrance has long been recognised when working with children, and in Chapter 13 we give examples of how to do this using memory boxes and workbooks. It has become increasingly clear that adults also make their own memory banks. Often there is a box containing some small mementoes, or one or two pieces of clothing that have been kept, or significant letters, certificates and photographs. Sometimes, years later, one or two of these items can be disposed of, but it is a long, slow process. The need to make memory banks has been formalised by Tonkin (2001) in her publishing of a memory book. It has blank pages with suggestions on how to fill them in, and a pocket for bulky items. Similarly, Tess Moeke-Maxwell has marketed 'Soulmates' for people of all ages. These are beautifully made 'contoured cushions' in the shape of an upper body, which are comforting to hug; just as importantly, they have a pocket with a see-through plastic front for a photograph and a hidden zip-up pocket for special treasures.

As well as tangible mementoes, there are the private rememberings of the dead loved one at family anniversaries and significant celebrations. This recognition of the continuing bonds has been greatly emphasised by Neimeyer, Silverman and Klass in particular. As with any scar, the original painful loss is always there; it will continue to feel tender and even a small emotional 'bump' will always be perceptible. We can also see from Geoff's later reflections the importance of his second wife's capacity to manage her own retrospective jealousy of Laura, and to help Geoff see the importance for each of his daughters of having more positive tangible evidence of their deceased mother. If this retrospective jealousy is not managed it can destroy the new relationship. Geoff's second wife was a widow, securely attached herself, and could manage not to deny his and his daughters' need for continuing bonds with Laura. Her inner knowledge of the value of these bonds enabled her to manage her jealous feelings.

As mentioned earlier in this chapter, there has been a lot of criticism of the focus on 'phases' and the associated idea that coming to terms with the death of a loved one involves grief work, in which one simply works through the emotions outlined in Table 4.2 (p. 40). This approach might be seen to give a counsellor the task of encouraging the grief work by only facilitating the expression of feelings. Stroebe and Schut (1995) suggest that this alone is not enough, and that more than just feelings (or in some cultures, something different) is required.

Looking beyond Western traditions, Stroebe and Schut have found huge differences in how grief is handled in different cultures and even within them. It is traditional in Japan to have house shrines to the dead, but in the West this is considered to be an example of a complicated grieving. Some cultures, such as Muslim communities in Bali, have non-grief-work strategies in which grief must neither be shown nor confronted, and yet in spite of this hiding of feelings there appear to be no signs of higher levels of abnormal grief or mental illness. This led Stroebe and Schut (1995) to look for an additional component that might have been missed in the earlier research. They suggest that a better way to understand coping with loss is that there are two processes; thus their model is known as the dual process model. The first process, called loss-orientation, is essentially that described by Parkes, involving the traditional grief work of expressing feelings, yearning, searching, etc. The second process is called restoration-orientation and has had much less attention so far. The loss of a loved one not only makes us grieve, but also means that we have a lot to adjust to in a practical as well as a psychological sense. There are new tasks to be learnt because, as Anne and Geoff observed, the dead partner had taken particular roles in the family, and there are many additional tasks to be done when reorganising one's life. Stroebe and Schut (1995) describe this loss- and restoration-oriented coping as a dual process because both processes need working through and they cannot be done simultaneously. You will remember Anne's comment that when she was busy the ceaseless searching in her mind stopped. The idea of two coping tasks also makes sense of the contrary needs to search and to avoid any reminder. In some groups and cultures the bias is towards one process, and so the bereavement work will involve facilitating the missing component and encouraging an oscillation between the two processes. Schut and his colleagues found that in general men who 18 months after bereavement showed a poor adjustment benefited from loss-oriented therapy, whereas women benefited from restoration-oriented work.

Deborah Tannen's (1992) research into the differing ways in which males and females use language to communicate throughout the life cycle may shed light on this difference in adjustment to bereavement. Women are more likely to communicate empathically, with a focus on feelings. This may predispose women towards the grieving aspect of loss-orientation. Men, on the other hand, communicate predominantly through active advisory and competitive modes which may make the restoration-oriented work seem more natural. They are then more likely to struggle with the less active and more feeling-focused aspects of loss-orientation, just as the women may struggle with the more active and potentially avoidant restoration work. John Gray's best-seller *Men are from Mars, Women are from Venus* (1997) popularises the same theory of difference in communicative styles.

In the accounts of Anne and Geoff there are obvious differences in the extent to which feelings as opposed to tasks are mentioned. Complications in grieving occur when there is no oscillation and the processes seem to get stuck in either one or the other, or when the oscillation is disturbed by the searing effects of a traumatic loss. The need to avoid the intrusion of horrific images can stop the natural process.

Anne and Geoff were both young when they lost their spouses. Their losses were extremely painful and lonely for them at the time, yet for each of them the hope, and subsequent fulfilment, of a new relationship was possible. For older clients, that hope is less likely, and the loss of a partner will be taking place in the context of the many losses experienced in old age. Western society is very focused on youth and the experience, wisdom and value of old age are often ignored or devalued rather than respected. Working with older clients is exactly the same as working with any other griever. Counsellors need to recognise that older people may feel intense loneliness and isolation and often feel misunderstood. It is important, therefore, to demonstrate a particular understanding and respect for their situation.

For a bereavement counsellor, it is important to know the phases of mourning and be able to link these with the feelings experienced in a person's story. It is also important to recognise the two processes of orientation and to remember that each individual experiences these at their own pace and in their own way. Each bereavement is likely to contain multiple losses for that person.

Summary

- Circumstantial losses can become sources of personal growth and maturity.
- The most studied circumstantial loss is the loss of widowhood.
- The stories of the bereaved are varied and contain intense feelings.
- Coping with bereavement involves a dual process: loss-orientation and restoration-orientation.
- Men tend to find the restoration-orientation easier and women find the loss-orientation easier.
- Parkes identified a pattern of feelings in the loss-orientation part of the dual process. There are four phases of mourning: numbness; yearning; disorganisation and despair; reorganisation.
- Men and women may have slightly different responses within the four phases of mourning. The phases do not occur in a linear fashion, and both the pace and the overall time-scale vary.
- Bonds are maintained with the dead.
- With any single loss, multiple losses occur.

Chapter 5

The effect of external circumstances and internal factors on the experience of bereavement

Parkes's study of widows, mentioned in Chapter 4, did not stop at simply identifying the four phases of mourning (Parkes, 1996). He also observed that the outcome of the grief is affected by certain factors in such a predictable way that they can be called *determinants* of grief. Some of these determinants make the grief not only more complicated but also more prolonged. In this chapter we shall focus on the determinants themselves, and in Chapters 14–16 we shall consider ways of working with people grappling with some of these particularly complicated kinds of grief. We have split the determinants into two main groups: external circumstances surrounding the death and the personal history of the bereaved, and 'internal factors'.

External determining circumstances

The external circumstances surrounding the death are summarised in Table 5.1 (p. 45).

The place of death will affect the course of grief. For instance, where a person has died far away from home it is easier to deny the death and imagine that they will return, as expected, from their journey. This results in prolonged grief, which will be prolonged further when the dead person's body has not been seen, because then it is even easier to deny the death and so postpone or even inhibit grieving. To try to circumvent this problem with men lost in war, the Forces have coined the expressions 'missing, presumed dead' and 'lost at sea'. These phrases try to encompass the difficult situations of not knowing if someone is dead and not seeing the dead person.

Coincidental loss refers to losses occurring simultaneously, for instance in a car accident where two members of a family are killed and a third injured. Here the survivor's grief is usually prolonged. These coincidental losses render the griever particularly vulnerable, as each loss needs to be individually grieved. Further, the expected sources of support may be severely reduced through injury or even the death itself.

Other examples might be families caught up in a major disaster such as the Blitz or the Holocaust or, more recently, the major disasters that have

Table 5.1 External determining circumstances affecting grief

1	Place of death	When a person has died in a faraway place, the acceptance of the death will be postponed and the grief will take longer.
2	Coincidental deaths or losses	When there are simultaneous deaths in a family or community, grief is more complex and there is less comfort and support available.
3	Successive deaths or losses	When losses, deaths or disaster follow one another in quick succession, the grief over one may be distracted or disturbed by the shock and grief of the next one.
4	The nature of the death	Where a death is untimely or sudden, it is more difficult to grieve. Where a sudden death is also traumatic or horrendous, it is even more difficult to grieve.
5	Social networks	(a) Close-knit and mutually helpful communities and families will be particularly useful at the time of bereavement or loss. (b) For different groups at different times in history, ideas about and attitudes and behaviour towards death and dying are different. Some groups are more accepting and recognising of death and dying people and therefore they are less likely to deny and more likely to facilitate grief (see Chapters 6 and 7).

occurred in Britain such as the sinking of the *Herald of Free Enterprise*, the King's Cross fire, the shooting of school children in Dunblane, and the crushing of spectators at Hillsborough football stadium. If, for instance, people from three generations have died, a survivor might have little support. Taking Hillsborough as an example, a Liverpool woman could have lost her husband, father and daughter. In order to grieve the death of her husband she might need the support of her mother, but her mother has just been widowed and has her own grief to deal with. In order to grieve her daughter, she would need the support of her husband, but he too is dead, and even her sister-in-law is in grief for her own brother. Her own sister is grieving for her father, as is her nephew of whom she was particularly fond, having been unable to have a son of her own. She has to grieve each of the people she has lost, but the resources in the way of family to help her through the long processes of grief are severely depleted. If the whole community is grieving then the complications facing each individual griever may be even more enormous, with both the family and community network unavailable. In this sort of circumstance grieving will go on for many years, and the ungrieved losses can pass from one generation to the next.

Another external circumstance that complicates the grieving process occurs when deaths or other losses happen in quick succession, so that the griever does not have time to grieve the first loss before the second one is upon her. For an individual this might occur when a parent dies a few days after the last child has left the parental home; or when a house move follows within a few weeks of a separation or divorce.

There seem to be reduced resources to begin to grieve the second loss, which is often put aside or denied. It is then difficult to resurrect and grieve this second loss until the first loss has been worked through. This probably also happens at national level when disasters happen in close succession.

The nature of a death or loss will also affect the way in which it is grieved. Where a death is untimely and unexpected or sudden, it is harder to accept that the death has actually taken place and it is therefore harder to grieve. This may well be because the death is 'unthinkable', which makes it harder to believe. It is as though it becomes, at least for a time, 'unfeelable' as well. An example might be of a child dying before her parents. In the natural order of things we expect to die before our children, so a child's death is unthinkable. This frequently results in a prolongation of the grieving.

Prolongation of the grieving process is often even more pronounced where death has been through suicide or homicide. It will be no surprise that the feelings associated with grieving for someone who has been murdered or killed can seem overwhelming. There will be intense anger, vengeful thoughts and fantasies of revenge directed towards the killer or murderer. Where the killer cannot be identified the fantasies may well be greater and the grief more difficult. Often people feel unable to express these feelings and thoughts. Encouragement to express them and recognise their validity is essential.

In grieving a suicide the mixed feelings are frequently very intense, volatile and difficult to bear. One moment there is intense anger at someone killing themselves that way, the next moment overwhelming sorrow that the person felt there was no way out but to kill themselves, and at yet the very next moment, extreme guilt at having not heard the person's cry for help nor having managed to save them. This alternation of feelings can be overwhelming and can make the grieving process considerably more tortuous. The sense of punishment is often all-pervading. The 'survivors' of the suicide have not been able to prevent the death and think they should have seen the signs and been able to do something. In fact, some 'successful' suicides do not ask for help and their signals of despair have been deeply hidden, perhaps because those around found it difficult to respond to such deep feelings of despair. Perhaps this very inability to recognise and show their own needs was one of the fundamental problems for the suicide and their relatives. The bereaved person in this instance will find anger particularly difficult to express. This gives the counsellor an important role in giving permission for the angry feelings to exist and be expressed.

Death through suicide or homicide also falls into the unthinkable category, and again we tend to deny the unthinkable. This denial is complicated when the survivors have not seen the body, either because there is no body to see or because the body is badly mutilated or decomposed. In the latter case the decision as to whether or not to see the body is a genuinely difficult one. On the one hand, the searing images resulting from seeing the mutilated body may be experienced as persecutory, because they will not go away; on the other hand, the fantasies that arise from not seeing the body can also be haunting. In either case, this aspect of the grieving will need considerable attention, for the griever will have to acknowledge the 'unthinkable' death and think about the horrific nature of that death. This task is, of course, not unique to homicide and suicide. Accidents and disasters can be equally horrific.

In considering suicide and homicide we have mentioned the haunting images associated with horrific deaths. These vivid images frequently persecute the grievers and survivors of disasters, as well as the helpers involved with the disasters. These groups may all be persecuted with both nightmares and vivid daytime images for many months, if not years, thereafter. This, together with overwhelming feelings of guilt about being a survivor, often leads to a set of symptoms and experiences now described as post-traumatic stress disorder (PTSD). This is characterised by psychic numbing, which in severe cases can be linked to intractable, repeated vivid recall of the horrific event and to a sensation of 'guilt' that is hard to expiate. There is no doubt that most survivors of major disasters, whether personal or national, will need referral to experienced specialist helpers. Recognition of this need has resulted in crisis intervention teams being formed by social services departments and trauma counselling services being set up immediately following a disaster. At present it is uncertain whether immediate crisis intervention actually helps survivors, though it is often helpful for family members or others caught up in the trauma.

Specialists working with the survivors will help them to talk through what they experienced. Some survivors may seek counselling weeks, months or even years after the trauma when they begin to sense that they need to talk about it. There is now evidence from magnetic resonance imaging (MRI) scans of the brain that talking about a traumatic event results in a processing of short-term memory that moves the recollections into the long-term memory.

The fifth external circumstance mentioned in Table 5.1 (p. 45) is that of the social networks surrounding the bereaved. Where groups remain together and are not separated by the demands of a more mobile society, and where the extended family remains in close geographic proximity, it may be easier to obtain the emotional support required. Immigrants adjusting to new cultures will find it much easier to let go of the old culture and adjust to the new where there are cohesive social networks of support.

Many people nowadays are separated from their families and may well not belong to the community where they live because they come from a different ethnic and cultural or social group. Unfortunately, it is common for families not to know their neighbours. All this means that supportive networks are frequently missing just when they are most needed. On the other hand, social networks may be present, but the griever may be unable to use them because they do not know how to make relationships. The inability to make relationships is, of course, to do with their personal history; hence the inclusion of 'social networks' in Table 5.2 (p. 49) as well. In either case support is unavailable and the griever will be much more prone to prolonged grieving, if not breakdown. This relationship factor will be considered again under the heading of internal factors.

Similarly, the influence of society at large and the whole culture externally affects the course of grief but also interacts with our personal history, thus shaping our inner world. Every culture has mourning rites and ways of handling a death (Chapter 7) that are available to help the bereaved when someone dies. Families vary enormously in whether they will observe the rituals of their culture or use them to facilitate grieving. There are also differences in communities, cultural groups and families in the balance between focusing on the loss and on the reorientation necessary to manage the substantial changes in one's life that bereavement brings (Chapter 4). Some families and groups are prone to denial, so there will be little encouragement to the griever to express feelings. Thus denial may be compounded rather than challenged. This repression of feelings may well eventually manifest itself in physical or mental illness. The more a particular group in society is likely to repress or deny death, the more likely are its members to have difficulty with grieving.

We have specifically highlighted how the social network affects both the internal world of the griever and the effects of the external determinants. It is therefore inevitable that how we respond to external circumstances is conditioned by our personal life history and the related internal emotional world (Chapter 1).

Internal factors

The personal life history and related internal world are the 'internal factors' affecting the grieving process. Parkes's research confirms that the process of grief is indeed affected by these internal aspects built up from one's personal life history (Parkes, 1996). They include early attachment experiences and the loss history of the bereaved. Further, the age and life-cycle stage of the griever, the level of intimacy with the lost person and the complexity of the relationship will likewise affect the grief. This is summarised in Table 5.2 (p. 49).

You will remember from Chapters 1 and 2 and the references to Bowlby's research that early secure attachments provide useful inner resources. Tom had been securely attached to Mary and had begun to assimilate and develop the 'secure base' that he initially experienced in Mary, and then inside himself. He was then able to tolerate her absence. We can predict that, given a

Table 5.2 Internal factors affecting grief

1	Attachment history	Where, as a small child, someone has been 'securely attached' and can cope reasonably with anxiety (as outlined in Chapter 1), their capacity to express feelings and work through grief in later life is greater.
2	Loss and death history	Where previous losses have been difficult to accept and grieve, the current loss may 'reawaken' the earlier loss and render both particularly difficult to grieve.
3	Age and stage of griever	For children and young people and for those passing through particularly vulnerable transition points in the life-cycle, grief may be especially challenging.

The three factors above will affect the individual griever's capacity to grieve any loss. The following three factors will influence the reaction to the loss of a particular relationship.

4	Intimacy level	The more intimate the relationship to the lost person (spouse, child, lover, parent, sibling, etc.), the more intense the grief. This also links with the quality of attachment described in Chapters 1 and 2.
5	Emotional complexity	The more straightforward the relationship, the more straightforward the grief. More complex relationships with many denied feelings or unrecognised ambivalence are more complex to grieve.
6	Social networks	(a) Close-knit and mutually helpful communities will be particularly useful at the time of bereavement or loss if the griever has the capacity to use them. (b) For different groups at different times in history, ideas about and attitudes and behaviour towards death and dying are different. Some groups are more accepting and recognising of death and dying and therefore less likely to deny and more likely to facilitate grief, provided the griever can be helped in this way.

reasonable life history, Tom will be able to express feelings and respond appropriately to grief in adult life, because the attachment patterns formed in early childhood usually persist into our adult lives. While the attachment patterns are persistent, they are not immutable and strong loving relationships can bring a change from an insecure to a secure attachment, as can a therapeutic relationship. We can further predict that the nursery children in Ainsworth's research, who were insecurely attached, would have more difficulty with grief in adult life and, depending on other resources available in their lives, would have more difficulty in expressing the feelings associated with grief (Ainsworth *et al.*, 1978).

It is also possible to predict from Parkes's research that when a person with insufficient external support and/or internal resources suffers a major loss through death or separation, they will find it difficult to accept and recognise that loss, with the result that the grieving process may well be incomplete and even blocked. If a new loss then occurs it may well 'reawaken' the earlier loss, and the response to that loss may seem 'out of all proportion'. In reality they may be doing double 'grief-work', not unlike the simultaneous losses mentioned in Table 5.1 with the similar task of grieving one loss after the other. The following story illustrates just such a blocking of one loss affecting the grieving of further losses.

> Julia (29) was divorced rather quickly, in a flurry of ambivalent feelings. Forced to leave the marital home and with two small children to look after, it was all too easy for her to get caught up with the tasks of establishing a new home, a new career and looking after two children rather than grieving the lost home and relationship. She seemed to be managing well. However, when her mother died a few years later she was plunged into a deep depression. It was only by being helped to recognise the first loss that she was able to begin the long process of grief for her mother.

A further factor that will affect individuals' capacity to grieve is their age and stage of emotional maturity at the time of the loss and whether or not they are going through a period of transition. Children at different ages have different understandings of death and separation. We refer to young children's grief in more detail in Chapter 8.

Adolescence itself is a transition period of loss as well as gain. Adolescents have to grapple with the loss of childhood in order to face the responsibilities as well as the challenges of adulthood. Although some may try to remain Peter Pans for ever, the continual development of their own sexuality will pull them inexorably towards adulthood. This period of adolescence with, on the one hand, its looking back longingly and searching for that which was lost and, on the other, its looking ahead with apprehension to a new world full of unknown challenges is quite like the experience of grief itself. The griever too looks back longingly for that which is lost and fears the inevitable changes that lie ahead. Thus adolescence is a particularly difficult time during which to grieve the loss of a close relationship. In Western cultures at least, the task of adolescents is to separate themselves from their family of origin. Inevitably the loss of a family member through death or separation at this stage will make the task even harder.

Another transition period in the life cycle when individuals are more vulnerable to loss is the time, for adults, when the children have left the family home, and the parents are adjusting to that change in the family group. Women may be particularly vulnerable, both because this period often coincides with menopause and its changes and because women in our culture are still often more involved than men with the lives and welfare of the children at home. They therefore have more adjusting to do when the children leave. The adjustments required at the transition into retirement also render people vulnerable to other losses.

These three factors – attachment history, loss history and age or stage in the life cycle – will affect an individual's capacity to grieve whatever losses arise. In addition, intimacy and emotional complexity, which are aspects of the relationship that is lost, will affect the outcome of grief.

The more intimate the relationship to the person who was lost, the more intense the grief. Of course we know this in a common-sense kind of way; it is much worse to lose a husband than to lose the relatively unknown neighbour who lives three doors down the street. Yet there are often dimensions to this aspect of intimacy that go unseen or misunderstood, leaving the griever particularly vulnerable. Frequently a friend or colleague could be much closer than a brother or sister. Another example of a particularly intimate relationship might be between a child and her grandparent. This relationship could well go unrecognised by other family members, so that the child can be left alone in her unrecognised grief when the grandparent dies, or is effectively lost through a geographic move or marital breakdown. This lost relationship can be felt as keenly by the grandparents as the child, particularly when there is a divorce, because grandparents have no legal right of access. The importance of the death of a child's pet may also go unrecognised.

Where the nature of a relationship is not understood or, even worse, largely unaccepted by society, then the griever is often abandoned just at the moment when they most need the help of others. Particular examples of this are gay relationships and extramarital affairs. The following story illustrates the particular problems.

> Elisabeth and Jane had been living together in an intimate relationship for eight years. They were very close to one another and, although they had a number of friends in the small town where they lived and worked, not many people knew about or understood their relationship. Neither of their families accepted their relationship, and although each one visited her family from time to time, they visited alone. They had agreed not to contact one another at the other's parental home. Elisabeth's parents lived some distance away and she had gone to visit them for a week. She was due back on the Saturday lunchtime. Jane had prepared a lovely meal for her, but Elisabeth did not appear. Jane found ways of making sense of this delay, but by Saturday evening she was pretty frantic. She managed to hold out until Sunday morning, by which time she could wait no longer. When she rang she was shouted at by Elisabeth's brother, who informed her that Elisabeth was dead and that it was no use ringing now! He then put the phone down. When she rang again to try to find out more, she was told that the funeral was next day, but on no account was her presence sanctioned at that occasion. Jane later learned that Elisabeth had been very badly injured in a car accident on the Saturday, had been

taken to a nearby hospital and died a few hours later. Her family had been with her much of the time, but she had been too weak to insist on contacting Jane. Thus Jane was left; not able to see Elisabeth in her dying hours and make her farewell, not able to go to the funeral; feeling both punished in some way for Elisabeth's death and utterly alone in her grief.

The other aspect of a relationship that affects the process of grief is its emotional complexity. Where a relationship has been reasonably direct, loving and affectionate the grief will be relatively straightforward, however long and intense. Where, however, the relationship has been less direct and open, has been more complicated, and where feelings have been hidden or denied, the grief will be more complex. The feelings often most hotly denied are those of anger and resentment, and when these feelings 'go underground' they are often turned against the self. We consider these denied or repressed feelings in more detail in Chapters 14 and 15.

Earlier in this chapter we referred to the possibility that even where supportive social networks do exist, the griever may be unable to use them because their personal history affects the use that can be made of such networks and rituals. Thus, internal factors can influence the effect of external factors as well as the other way round.

It is not possible to say exactly how these external and internal factors will determine the course of the grief for any individual. However, in the knowledge of their existence, it is possible to look out for the grieving that seems to be at the extremes of the spectrum outlined in Chapter 1. Counsellors should be alert to the possibility of referring to more specialist care those who may be denying the feelings so much that they seem consistently immune to the experience (Chapter 16), as well as those showing chaotically disturbed behaviour. In Chapter 17 these factors affecting grief are linked to assessment procedures.

Summary

- Certain factors, known as determinants of grief, affect the outcome of grief.
- The external factors known to affect grief are: place of death; coincidental deaths; successive deaths; the nature of the death; the social network surrounding the bereaved.
- The internal factors known to affect grief are: attachment history; loss and death history; age and stage of griever; intimacy level; emotional complexity of the lost relationship; the social network surrounding the bereaved.
- External and internal factors are interrelated.

Chapter 6

Historical change in attitudes to death and bereavement

We have considered different bereavements and the different factors that can affect a person's mourning. We have also looked at how denial functions to protect individuals from the initial impact of the loss, but can also prevent people from recognising the loss and doing the work of grief before eventually letting go. It is not just individuals that deny death, but whole groups and even societies. By taking a historical perspective it is possible to begin to see how patterns of denial within any one society change over time and also influence the present.

In medieval times death was perceived as a much greater presence than in today's developed societies. This is not surprising given that life expectancy was about half what it is today and people had to be prepared to face death after a much shorter life, and that death was much more likely to be violent, cruel and physically painful.

Death was unpredictable and uncontrollable. People therefore had to live with a much greater awareness of death around them and of their own mortality. Dead and dying bodies were things that everyone had seen and, given the rate of infant mortality alone, everyone was likely to have lost someone close to them through death. With these constant reminders of death in the midst of life, people could not deny the existence of death in the way we do today, and they were forced to be more prepared to meet their deaths.

But having to face consistently the possibility of one's end and the finiteness of human existence is a hard task. This was mitigated in the Middle Ages by a belief in an afterlife. A belief that death is not the absolute end and that the soul moves on to another place, or that we are reborn in another form, has given solace to humans everywhere, probably since they first became aware of their own mortality. Perhaps these comforting ideas evolved as people realised that death was the inevitable conclusion to life. Awareness of death has always been difficult to bear, and human beings have long grappled with the meaning of the end and with the feelings associated with death. Anger and guilt seem to have been the most difficult of these feelings to understand.

One of the oldest stories of our civilisation is that of Adam and Eve.

Freud, among others, pointed out the connection here between the fear of death and feelings of guilt. Adam and Eve were innocent and immortal in paradise. However, once they had sinned and violated the commandment of God they became mortal and were condemned to die. The idea that death is a punishment for evil committed was one way of trying to make some sense of the fact that we die. This notion has probably contributed to the human fear of death over millennia.

Among the strong emotions evoked by death, guilt is almost always experienced. It is an unpleasant feeling, and we often rush to find a 'guilty party' or scapegoat to 'carry' any guilty feelings we do not want. In earlier societies a death was often understood as a killing, albeit by nonhuman forces. Even today in relation to our own disasters we can observe how a 'guilty party' is often sought. Sometimes even the victims themselves can become tainted with guilt, through the blaming by those who can find no better way of coming to terms with their own guilt and fear. Today we can observe this in the tendency to blame Aids on 'promiscuity'. Awareness of the association of guilt and death can perhaps help us to understand the enormous value of the religious sacraments of confession, forgiveness and absolution. In medieval times, when disease rendered death so unpredictable and uncontrollable, the regular rite of absolution must have helped to decrease fear and increase a sense of readiness for death. The sense of guilt and the fear of punishment around death seem to have been more clearly recognised in previous centuries than nowadays. The seeking and granting of absolution went largely unquestioned until the Reformation.

With the Age of Enlightenment, scientific understanding grew. Each wave of scientific discovery was followed by biological and medical discoveries. By the end of the nineteenth century both pain and disease were beginning to be controlled. Fewer women died in childbirth, disease had become less random and more controllable through both prevention and cure, and many illnesses had become less painful. Life had become longer, with greater predictability, and death seemed to 'recede' and be more under human control. Gradually it must have seemed as if death itself was controllable. But these great changes were bought at a price.

The major price seems to be that death is denied and 'forgotten about', at a social as well as an individual level. In other words, death is 'repressed'. In earlier times death and dying took place in the family circle and, for many people, within the single, shared family space, whereas now death has become marginalised. Our dying has been more or less 'banished', either to hospital or some other institution or, if at home, to another room, rather than in the bosom of the family. It is no longer common to see or touch our dead. Their corpses are cared for by others and their graves, if there are any graves, are often tended by public services. Not only do we 'not speak ill of the dead', we are hardly able to talk about death and dying at all.

This discomfort about death seems to have led to shame and embarrassment and an avoidance of talking or writing about the stark facts of death and dying. There are quite common words that are spoken in hushed tones or even avoided altogether. For instance, 'a growth' is used to describe cancer and 'passed away' for died. By contrast, in seventeenth-century love poetry, death was used as a favourite theme to remind the beloved of the brevity of life and human beauty and hence the folly of delaying love's advances. Were today's lover to write a poem mentioning the future activity of worms in the beloved's grave, it would probably meet with considerable distaste if not downright repulsion!

We seem to have this embarrassment not only in talking about death and dying, but in talking to dying people. Out of sheer awkwardness, we may say nothing and keep away. We thus deprive both ourselves and the dying person of physical touch, of words of comfort and the mutual recognition and emotional connectedness we all need. Then the very words the dying need to hear, the invaluable proof of our affection and tenderness, go unsaid and unheard.

It is not only the dying from whom we distance ourselves; we also distance ourselves from those who are ageing and infirm and whose mortality is less easily denied. One way of avoiding both their and our mortality is through banishing them to residential homes. Some homes enable the elderly to grieve such losses as independence, professional role and personal privacy, but most homes seem to find difficulty in acknowledging the transitional phase from active life towards death. Many such homes work on the principle of a firm demarcation of the living from those-about-to-die, as if the former were immortal. They quickly and secretly remove anyone who dies, do not encourage any grieving for their dead, and generally refuse to discuss any fears about death and dying (Hockey, 1990). This denial of death is understandably often most intense among those working with the elderly and with the dying.

At the other end of life we find adults introducing a process of embarrassed denial with young children. In modern Western societies children are rarely given much realistic information about death and, where the topic cannot be avoided, it is often treated in a vague or unrealistic manner. Most children nowadays have not seen a human corpse and we go to enormous lengths to protect them from this sight, often also preventing them from going to an important funeral. Adults, although they talk of 'protecting the children', are, of course, protecting themselves from feelings they find difficult and which the children may express more openly. As we will consider further in Chapter 8, adults' denial is the principal difficulty for children who are trying to grapple with death and bereavement.

Another consequence of not speaking about death is that we learn very little about the rituals associated with dying and death. Indeed, our own cultural rituals to aid the transition from life to death seem to be increasingly lost from common knowledge. Frequently there is no one in our local neighbourhood who knows how to lay out the dead, and only nurses and undertakers learn how to do this. Thus we hand over rituals that would be helpful to us to professionals whom we usually do not know personally.

Not speaking about death also means that there is no common knowledge about the procedures associated with burial and cremation. Thus, for instance, we may not know that we can indicate to the undertaker what should be done with someone's ashes. One of our bereaved acquaintances was recently shocked when the urn containing the ashes was delivered to her house. She simply did not know what to do with the ashes. This kind of 'not knowing' renders us powerless, and we tend to believe that the professionals are the only ones who can manage the transition from life to death. We therefore dissociate ourselves further from the valuable rituals, and this 'ignorance' in turn feeds the general denial of death. The cycle of denial then becomes increasingly hard to break.

There are, however, signs that this trend towards denial is beginning to reverse. During the past 35 years there seems to have been a trend towards a greater openness about death and dying. Writers in the 1960s and 1970s such as John Hinton, Elisabeth Kübler-Ross, John Bowlby, Colin Murray Parkes and Beverley Raphael played an important part in beginning to open up death and bereavement as an important topic to be thought and talked about. In the same period the radical work of Cecily Saunders and the hospice movement, in introducing and supporting greater openness about death and the feelings associated with dying, made it possible for many more people to die in relatively little pain and in an open and supportive relationship with their families and close friends. Since then many have written personally about death and loss, indicating a greater openness in this field; we have listed a few in Appendix C.

A 1990 research study into homes and hospices by Jennifer Hockey describes this openness in hospices. She traces the idea of a hospice to the early Christian attitude of unconditional love, and recognises that it is a form of hospitality that existed well before modern hospitals with their regimented admission procedures. Her exploration reveals how the strict boundary between life and death imposed by most residential homes and hospitals is gradually being eroded within the hospice. This enables each individual to choose his or her own personal level of denial and to manage his or her own transition from healthy adult, through the phase of being sometimes healthy and sometimes ill, to ill person and then to dying person. This more fluid system of recognition and support through the transition period has in turn much influenced the management of death in some hospitals and general practices. There are signs that this trend towards openness is beginning to counter the previous trend towards almost total denial, resulting in a more healthy balance between denial and recognition for both individuals and society.

A number of changes in behaviour may be indications of a trend towards greater recognition of death in society. The place of violent deaths (usually road traffic accidents) is often marked with bunches or bouquets of flowers, often with a poignant message attached and a photograph of the dead person. These vulnerable flowers are normally encased in transparent and protective paper, perhaps symbolising the protection that could not be offered to the one who was vulnerable and who has died. Where children have been violently killed, toys are also left, perhaps expressing the disbelief about the reality of death through giving the children something to play with 'in heaven'.

On a much grander scale, Princess Diana, who was both powerful and adored, could not be protected from a violent death. The quality of the response to her death, unforeseen in its intensity, has puzzled many observers. Alongside ideas about changing attitudes to the monarchy is the thought that Diana struck a chord with so many people through, on the one hand the power that royalty bestows, and on the other, her very ordinariness (lacking royal blood) and patent vulnerability as a human being.

The particular 'chord' that Diana seems to have struck unleashed a veritable paroxysm of grief that reverberated well beyond these islands. The intensity of this grief may well have been the release of the repressed past griefs of the individual members of the whole society and of the society itself. Her funeral seemed to bring a new emotional intensity into a ritual that was partly secularised, but was still also part of an ancient religious traditional ritual for the dead. This particular ritual seemed to bring people from very diverse backgrounds and orientations together into a common, and in some sense communal, activity with both formal and informal elements.

The extraordinary media phenomenon of being able to watch and watch again the unfolding of the deaths of nearly 3,000 people in New York in September 2001, when the World Trade Centre was demolished by terrorists, may have further changed the way we respond to mass trauma. The sense of identity with the victims and the bereaved seems to have been enhanced, making it, again, something more like a 'communal activity'. An example of this could be seen during the service in St Paul's Cathedral to commemorate the first anniversary of the attack, when rose petals representing each one of the victims fluttered to the floor. These petals were both an act of remembrance in London for the families of British victims and a communication to the rest of the world.

The possibility that death is indeed 'getting closer' appears to be reflected in many current gravestones. They too seem to be increasingly informal and secularised in language, shape and style. There are fewer crosses to be seen, often animals are carved into the stone and sometimes photographs and other memorabilia are attached to the stone.

Of course the denial of death is a necessary part of the grief process, but there is also a time for talking. Perhaps these recent changes indicate the beginnings of a wish to have a more intimate kind of conversation about death.

While traditions may be changing and developing, we still need to recognise the value of some system of beliefs and rituals to help the dying, and those who are close to them, through this momentous transition. In the next chapter we look at the range of cultural rituals that exist in Britain today. Multi-ethnic Britain consists of a rich variety of groups, each with its unique history and culture, and each developing in its own way. Many of these may be unfamiliar to us, yet a knowledge of the enormous variety of mourning rituals is essential to any loss counsellor.

About a third of people surveyed in the UK in the 1990s and 45% of those surveyed in 2004 say that they do not believe in God or in an afterlife. There is a corresponding growth in humanism and a trend towards the secularisation of funerals. These areas of change are also considered in the next chapter.

Summary

- In earlier centuries death was more 'present' in people's lives and it was harder to deny its presence. It was also seen as less predictable, and people were more ready for death in the midst of life.
- Death has always been associated with guilt, and blame has been apportioned in different ways. Rituals of absolution help to relieve the dying of burdens of guilt and blame.
- Medical advances in the past 150 years have 'banished' death from our midst, together with an accompanying denial of death and a decreased ability to accept or talk about death, even with the dying themselves.
- Death is unknown and the fear of death leads, understandably, to a denial of death. The recognition and acceptance of death can enhance life and can certainly ease the experience of the dying.
- Patterns of denial and acceptance change over time. The trend towards denial in Western societies seems to have slowed, and there are signs of a growing acceptance of death.

Chapter 7

Cultural variety

The value of mourning

In Chapter 5 we observed how the social network surrounding the bereaved is one of the external factors affecting the course of grief. Different social networks and cultural groups deal with grief in different ways. We also noted that every culture has mourning rites and ways of handling a death, and in Chapter 4 we referred to the way in which the loss function and the restoration function in grieving vary from one culture to another. Families and individuals also vary in the extent to which they are able to use the networks available to them, and to which they observe the rituals of their own cultural background. In this chapter we focus on the value of mourning rituals and on the many different kinds of mourning ritual in Britain today.

Attitudes to death in human societies are almost infinitely varied, as anthropologists and archaeologists have helped us to understand. The inner experiences of loss, pain and fear are, presumably, human universals, but the range of attitudes and ritual activities is vast. Any given individual may be able to express only certain emotions and therefore may not follow the common pattern for their own particular group. It was these enormous variations between cultures and between individuals that led Stroebe and Schut (1995) to propose the dual process model mentioned in Chapter 4.

Bowlby (1980), in his wide-ranging quest to understand more about the human response to death, studied the work of a number of anthropologists. Drawing on Malinowski (1925), Firth (1961) (both cited in Bowlby, 1980) and others, he wrote of the common functions of funerals across a range of societies. Although funerals are 'for the dead', they actually fulfil functions for the living. These include helping the bereaved to recognise that the loss has indeed occurred, and providing a place for the expression of grief. Firth also postulates that the funeral enables other members of the community to take public note of their loss, to say farewell and to express, in a prescribed way, the powerful feelings of fear and anger often engendered by the death. In addition, the funeral and funeral gifts express symbolically the relationship with the dead person, the cohesiveness of the group and their willingness to help one another in times of adversity.

Bowlby reflected further that a funeral also offers an opportunity for the living to express their gratitude to the deceased and to take action felt to be for the benefit of the recently deceased person. The bereaved themselves are recognised by virtually all societies to be in need and in a state of shock and disorientation. This in turn elicits, almost universally, certain responses to the bereaved such as care, feeding, support, comfort or respect.

Bowlby reported from his study that although cultural patterns of grief and mourning differ enormously in their particular ceremonies, and in what is encouraged and what is denied, virtually all of them have rules and rituals relating to the following three elements:

- how a continuing relationship with the dead person should be conducted in the mourning period;
- how blame should be allocated and anger expressed;
- how long mourning should last.

We might assume, therefore, that there is a human need to manage the difficult period after a death. There may be a need to express the anger evoked by death and to try to allocate the associated blame; and also a need to define a period of mourning which, through its ending, gives permission or enables the bereaved to return fully to the community. It also helps to mark the change or transition. Referring to these elements, Bowlby (1980) asserted that 'in these ways a culture channels the psychological responses of individuals and in some degree ritualises them. The origins of the responses themselves lie, however, at a deeper level.'

This short résumé of the anthropologists' findings has been included because it highlights the ways in which beliefs and rituals, however varied, help us to take leave of the dying and the dead, and set a term to the period of mourning.

Sadly, rituals that were helpful and useful to the generation of our grandparents and even to our parents may still be disappearing. Rituals help us through difficult changes. They supply specific words and actions that have meanings of great value to those who share in the ritual, and they can help us to say goodbye, make an end to a relationship and move back into the world of the living. Unfortunately, rituals that may in themselves be helpful to the mourners may also be turned into political acts, thus fuelling the very aggression that may have been the cause of death in the first place. Examples include highly publicised funerals in Northern Ireland, Palestine and Israel.

In general, more personal rituals such as shutting the eyes of the dead person, stopping the clocks, wearing black or a black armband, and drawing the curtains during day and night have helped to acknowledge the death and facilitate the grieving process. Many of these customs have now all but disappeared and have perhaps been replaced by such gestures as flowers placed at the site of death or outside the dead person's house, and books of condolence to sign.

Mourning in different cultural and religious groups

Britain is now a multicultural society where different cultural and religious groups have different rituals. Some groups have retained a much richer set of responses and rituals to help them through the processes of dying and grieving than others. In working with people from a variety of cultural groups whose socio-cultural background may be unfamiliar to us, we need to recognise the value of all mourning rituals and also the range and variety of different rituals within each of the different groups in contemporary Britain.

Where groups remain together and are not separated by the demands of a more mobile society, and where the extended family remains in close geographic proximity, it may be easier to fulfil the rituals available and to offer the emotional support required. But many people nowadays are separated from their families, may not belong to the community where they live and may pay less heed to their own rituals. All this means that supportive networks and the concomitant rituals are frequently missing just when we need them most. Without the support of rituals and emotional connections we are much more prone to prolonged grieving, if not breakdown. What is needed most of all is emotional support, for this enables us to talk. Where the expression of grief is not encouraged and where denial is given priority, feelings are repressed. This repression may eventually manifest itself in physical or mental illness. The more a particular group in society is likely to repress or deny death, the more likely are its members to have difficulty with grieving.

We believe that those working within our multiracial society, particularly in the areas of death and bereavement, will need to be aware of those different beliefs and attitudes to human life and death, and of the great range of rituals associated with death and bereavement. It is also important to recognise the way in which the various beliefs and rituals will have separate meanings for each individual within any given 'group' or religion. It is all too easy to jump to conclusions or make assumptions. When someone filling in a form writes 'Hindu', for instance, there will be as many individual meanings of the word 'Hindu' as form-fillers. For any one individual writing 'Jew' as their 'religious affiliation', there are many things we do not know. We do not know, for instance, whether they are liberal-reform or orthodox Jews, or are from a Sephardic or Ashkenazi tradition. Neither would we know what that person's individual beliefs were concerning the afterlife, nor indeed whether their religious beliefs mean very much to them at all. Furthermore, their feelings about their religion, or their belonging to that religious group, would be unknown to us. It is important, therefore, to develop a sensitivity towards the concerns of each individual as well as towards the possible requirements of their faith. This can be achieved by having some knowledge of the culture and religion from which he or she comes, as well as some awareness of the different sects and varieties within that group. Further, people who have moved to the West may blend traditions from the two cultures and may seek support from different, and what may seem to the helper incongruous, sources.

The anthropologist Paul Rosenblatt puts it very clearly: 'In trying to offer understanding and assistance to people from societies other than one's own, there is no justification for privileging one's own reality over that of the people one wants to understand and help. The more useful course is to become adept at learning, respecting and dealing with another person's reality, no matter how discrepant it is from one's own' (Rosenblatt, 1997).

In a book of this size it is, of course, impossible to give anything but the most cursory description of the great religions of the world, all of which are represented in Britain today. What we have chosen to highlight and to try to summarise are the beliefs about death and an afterlife and about the customs and practices in relation to the dying and the bereaved for each of the major religions.

However, there are many people who profess no religious beliefs and yet who are required by law to bury or cremate their dead. They may or may not seek some ceremonial recognition of the transition from life to death. We have therefore added a short section on some of the procedures available to them, and some of the difficulties that can arise.

Judaism

The fundamental tenet could be summed up as follows: trust in a single, invisible, external God who created the world. Jews can relate directly to God, and their relationship with God is depicted as a combination of defiance and acceptance. Rather than a creed or doctrine, Judaism stresses right behaviour, which includes supporting one another. Views about the afterlife are very varied and often rather vague. Judaism is life-affirming and there is great emphasis on the here-and-now. Life now is highly valued, and there are very strict rules about not shortening a person's life.

Resting on the sabbath (sundown Friday to sundown Saturday) is an important custom for many Jews. Even though Jews are commanded to bury their dead as quickly as possible, a body cannot be moved on the sabbath and, usually, someone stays with the body until the funeral. For orthodox Jews burial is essential, while for some progressive Jews cremation is also a possibility. Kaddish, a prayer affirming life and praising God, is recited by the mourners at the time of death and at any service throughout the whole of the first year until the stone-setting. This means for Orthodox Jews, who pray every day, that the Kaddish is said by those people who have been bereaved during the past year while everyone else just says the amens and other responses.

After the funeral the mourners will 'sit *shiva*', i.e. sit on a low chair in the house of the dead and not be involved in any activity. People who knew the dead person or know the bereaved are duty-bound to visit, bringing food as well as comfort and support. For most bereaved people it is a very valuable experience to have the company of people ready to listen to their agony and talk of the one who has died. It is also psychologically useful, for it encourages people to focus on the dead and to express their grief. A stone is set at the grave on the first anniversary of the death: an important ceremony that helps the griever through this difficult anniversary and is an encouragement to move forward into life without the deceased.

The most intensive period of grief is the first seven days (*shiva*). The next 30 days (*shiloshim*) mark a period of lesser intensity. After a year the bereaved may let go of their grief and remarry if they are ready.

The 'rending of garments' originally expressed the passion of grief. This may still happen nowadays but it is generally more ceremonial, with the snipping of a man's lapel with scissors or wearing a torn garment. Symbolically, this gives expression to the powerful – indeed rending – feelings associated with grief.

Christianity

In common with Judaism and Islam, Christianity believes there is only one God; unlike the other monotheistic religions, Christians believe that God has come on earth in human form through Jesus Christ (Christos = Messiah) and through the Holy Spirit as his spiritual force moving in all people. Christianity has many sects and variations, some placing greater emphasis on a literal interpretation of the scriptures than others.

The afterlife is a firm part of Christian belief, but the way in which it is viewed varies from a belief in a different kind of existence for the soul after separation from the body to a less dualistic idea of bodily resurrection in some form. Some will have a literal view of hell and heaven, while others may understand these words in a more symbolic way. At the time of death there is often a reflection on the life lived on earth, but also a seeking after that other dimension of life that is not terminated by physical death. Some may accept death as part of the will of God, while others will view it with fear, anger and disillusionment. It is important to explore these feelings and to remember that some people can find renewed faith and trust as they approach death, while for others faith does not seem to offer any comfort.

The three main groups of Christians are the Orthodox, Roman Catholic and Protestant. Orthodox Christians usually wish a priest to hear a last confession and give communion before death. There is often a lying-in in the church so that family and friends can pay their last respects and make their farewells before burial. Catholic Christians also lay great emphasis on the 'sacrament of the sick', 'extreme unction' or 'last rites', when confession is made, absolution is given and communion is taken. There is usually a lying-in period for farewells followed by burial or cremation. Within the Protestant tradition there are fewer formally observed 'last rites', although many practising Anglicans may wish to receive the sacrament of the sick before death. Practice varies in relation to the lying-in and saying farewell. Cremation is now more common than burial within the Protestant group, although again practice varies. Christian families of whatever denomination frequently follow the burial or cremation with a gathering of family and friends of the deceased.

The variety of belief among Christians is very wide. For most Christians, however, the belief in an afterlife with a sense of being united with relatives or friends and of a fuller relationship with God can help to ease the pain of accepting death. A strong religious faith is sometimes helpful for people approaching death, but anger with God, about an untimely death for instance, is often particularly difficult for bereaved Christians to bear.

Islam

The fundamental tenet of Islam is also that there is one true God: 'Islam' means 'submission' to God's will. The prophet Muhammad is the messenger of the one true God. The Koran contains a record of Muhammad's teaching which, combined with his sayings and deeds, makes up the Islamic legal system. Thus there is no division between secular and religious law. Faith, prayer, fasting, giving alms and pilgrimage are the duty of everyone within the Islamic community.

It is important before Ramadan, the period of fasting, that Muslims sort out disputes, problems and ill-feelings. Where death comes in or around Ramadan, this is a period of particularly intense personal sorting-out.

Like Christians and some Jews, Muslims believe in life after death as one stage in God's overall plan for humanity. The death of a loved one, therefore, is seen as a temporary separation and part of God's will. However difficult, the separation is to be accepted with a surrendering to his will.

The family pray at the bedside of a dying person, whose head should be turned towards Mecca. After the death, the family wash and lay out the body. It is important to remember that non-Muslims should not touch the body; if moving the body is a necessity, then wearing a pair of gloves is an acceptable solution. Muslims are buried, never cremated, and this should be within 24 hours. The body is taken to the mosque or graveside for prayers before burial in an unmarked grave. The body is normally wrapped in a special cloth rather than placed in a coffin. Coffins and marked graves are a requirement in Britain, which may make things particularly difficult for Muslims in this country.

Although some very pious Muslims may exercise great constraint over the expression of emotional pain, believing protest to suggest rebellion against God's will, most Muslims will display grief openly, crying and weeping in public.

Mourning usually lasts for 40 days, with the imam reading from the Koran for the first three days after the death and then every Friday for the rest of the mourning period. For the first three days the bereaved family stay at home and their relatives and friends are duty-bound to visit them, bringing food, comfort and support. The relatives also have a duty to talk about the person who has died and share the loss. During the period of mourning the grave is visited on Fridays (the Islamic holy day) and alms are distributed to the poor. Relatives of the deceased are not supposed to listen to music, watch television or indulge in any other form of entertainment throughout the 40 days. Photographs and television sets are covered with a cloth. These and other rituals are important, and great comfort is gained by carrying out as much religious practice as possible.

Hinduism

Hinduism is a very ancient religion with many gods and goddesses who are all believed to be manifestations of the one God. This may often seem confusing to a non-Hindu. It is a religion of many forms with many ways of worship, prayer and meditation. It is also a 'way of life' that offers great support and comfort to its believers.

The Hindu design for living suggests that as a person reaches the third and fourth and final part or stage of their life they should be preparing to sever relationships on earth, so that the spirit may be released to unite with the Supreme Being. These stages of life suggest that there is a time for all things, and the Hindu believes in a return to earth in a better or worse form according to one's karma. The karma represents the idea that what the individual does in this world affects what will happen to him in the next. Although Hindus sometimes regard health as a reward for living according to religious and moral laws in a previous life, and therefore regard ill-health as a punishment, most Hindus regard their actual death as insignificant because of their certainty of being with God in the afterlife. Hindu priests or Brahmins (who are top of the caste system) will help those who are dying to accept the inevitable, and it is important that a Brahmin is present, and indeed is fed, as part of the mourning ceremony.

Death is usually accepted without the manifestations of anger that may characterise Judaism, Christianity and Islam. As death draws near the dying person is given water from the River Ganges, and passages from holy books are read out. After a Hindu dies, non-Hindus must wear gloves if they need to touch the body. The family usually prefer to wash the body and lay it out. In the past the body was always covered by a white sheet before cremation, though this custom is changing in Britain, with the dress more dependent on the age, gender and circumstances of the death. It is now not unusual for someone to be cremated in a brightly coloured dress. Cremation is the rule, and should be done on the day of the death. This is impractical in Britain, but in recognition of this rule all bureaucratic procedures should be done as quickly as possible. The ashes are scattered either on the River Ganges or into a river flowing into the ocean. A ceremony called Sraddha on the eleventh day after the death involves certain rites for the dead, usually performed by the eldest son. Relatives, friends and neighbours are all bound to be involved in the showing of respect through this ceremony. Grief is expressed openly, with much crying, and the consolation and support given to the bereaved are regarded as most important. The thirteenth day marks the end of official mourning, after which men may shave and cut their hair again and may eat non-vegetarian food.

Hindu religious practice varies enormously between different groups; what is common is a shared attitude to human life. This accepting attitude to life and death is often seen as very different from that in Western cultures, and it needs to be recognised as such and accepted.

Sikhism

Sikhism was founded in the early sixteenth century by Guru Nanak and his disciples (Sikh = disciple, follower), who were disaffected Hindus and particularly deplored the caste system. They had no priesthood and emphasised each individual's relationship with God and his search for the virtuous life by doing good in this world. Sikhs have developed a strong community sense, and each community runs its own gurdwara. This is the temple as well as a place for hospitality and an advice centre. It is here that the service is usually held after the death. Sikhs hold both to a belief in the value of communal service as part of a commitment to actions in this life, and to a belief in the doctrine of karma, like the Hindus, whereby each soul goes through cycles of birth and rebirth, aiming to reach perfection and be united with God.

Again, the doctrine of reincarnation seems to render Sikhs less frightened of death, unless they feel their next life is likely to be considerably worse than the current one. They do believe in a forgiving God.

When a Sikh is close to death the family pray at the bedside and read from the holy book, Guru Granth Sahib. Once the person has died the family lay out the body, and if the person was a baptised Sikh they ensure that the five signs of Sikhism are worn; if not, the body is clothed in normal attire. The body is viewed before cremation, which is mandatory, and should be done as soon as possible. It is the custom for the heir (usually the eldest son) to light the funeral pyre. In Britain, pushing the button at the crematorium could be perceived as a poor substitute. After the funeral more prayers are said at the gurdwara and, when the whole family returns home for the ten days of mourning, friends and relatives come and visit with comfort and support. After ten days or so of intensive mourning, a special ceremony called Bhog marks the official end of mourning. Obviously some families or individuals may need longer, depending on their experiences around the death and any difficulties they may have experienced with the funeral in Britain.

Buddhism

Buddhism is a unique religion, which does not recognise a God as creator and is actually more of a philosophical system or way of life than a religion. It was started around 500 BC by an Indian prince, Siddhartha Gautama, who became the Buddha after his personal 'enlightenment'. Buddhism teaches that greed, hatred and delusion separate people from the true nature of the world. Buddhists seek morality, wisdom and compassion, culminating in a transformation of consciousness known as enlightenment. This is often associated with an inner 'spaciousness' from which all beings become manifest. Some branches deify certain aspects of this 'spaciousness'.

Buddhism is an open religion and has many different forms and 'schools' which coexist peacefully. All the varieties, however, show a great acceptance of the cycle of life and death. For some Buddhists the moment of death is considered very important. Most Buddhists are likely to want to meditate around the time of death and, although not opposed to pain relief, will wish to be in a state of 'mindfulness'. The period just after death is important too, as consciousness is still departing the body, so it is important not to touch it at this point. The winding sheet for a Buddhist must be without emblems. Buddhists are normally cremated, the ceremony often being conducted by a member of the family.

Humanists and non-affiliated groups

Many in the UK today believe neither in God nor in any form of afterlife. Although not necessarily identifying themselves as humanists, they may still subscribe to the basic tenets of humanism, namely that human beings carry sole responsibility for their behaviour in life and that death is simply the end of life, rather than a transition to heaven, or even hell. Research suggests that those with clear convictions, whether about death as the end or about death as a transition to another life, are less afraid of death than those who are unclear about what they believe.

However, the form of the funeral ritual for those without religious beliefs, whose focus is on the end of life, may pose a problem because they often think they have no choice about ritual. It is true that if they have made no plan for the funeral they may find themselves with no options other than those proposed by the undertaker. Usually, if no other suggestions are offered, the undertaker will propose a Christian service, because the Church of England, being an established church, is obliged to offer the rite of burial to any citizen. It is, however, possible in most places to exercise considerable choice about the form of both the burial and cremation services. The *Dead*

Citizens Charter produced by the National Funerals College (1996) emphasises this choice and gives guidance on how to achieve it. This is also the aim of a charity, The Natural Death Centre (see Appendix A), which was started specifically to give people help in exploring the options available to them and to design funerals that are original and appropriate to the dead person and themselves. Humanists have created their own rituals for the legally required disposal of dead people, and are able to engage the services of a 'celebrant' who can conduct a service without the concepts of God or an afterlife. Such a service will focus on a celebration of the life of the deceased, rather than on the progress of their soul, and is likely to involve the bereaved either in direct participation in the service or at least in the creation of a eulogy read out by the celebrant. This kind of service is clearly more for the comfort of the bereaved than for the soul of the deceased. Interestingly, many 'Christian' services nowadays are taking this sort of shape, particularly in the Protestant community, with the priest or officiant taking a more background role and encouraging a direct involvement of the bereaved and the use of secular songs rather than hymns. The songs are often favourites of either the dead person or of the bereaved. People in distress at the time of a death may find it helpful to be reminded that choice is available. A reference to the British Humanist Association is given in Appendix A.

General considerations

In recent years some ecologically-conscious individuals have expressed concern over the use and abuse of natural resources. When wooden veneered coffins are burnt during a cremation they emit toxic chemicals. Cemeteries and crematoria are often unattractive sites, make a permanent imprint on the environment and tend to be very impersonal. This may be why there is more personalisation of gravestones, as we mentioned in Chapter 6. These concerns have led to the development of eco-friendly or 'green funerals' and the establishment of woodland burial sites. Between 1993 and 2003 about 100 such sites were opened in Britain. The plan is that these woodland sites will blend into the environment and the bodies become part of nature as quickly as possible. The dead are buried in a shroud or a cardboard or wicker coffin, everything used is biodegradable and there are no gravestones or memorials. The plots are leased for a finite time and the whole site ultimately reverts to natural woodland, although held in trust for perpetuity. The Natural Death Centre has published a handbook that assists people in arranging their own funerals, whether a 'green funeral' or a highly personalised one. This important trend enables people to evolve their own rituals, which have meaning for them, and counters the trend in society for specialists to impose a 'right way' of doing things that could carry less meaning for the grievers.

Given the range of beliefs, rituals and possibilities of funerals in our society, it is important to recognise that complex issues of cultural ignorance and racist attitudes may arise. In situations where counselling takes place between people of different cultural and racial backgrounds, there are many ways in which the useful effects of counselling may be hindered or even destroyed by a counsellor who is unaware of these complexities. These might include, for example, inappropriate use of language, differences in non-verbal behaviours, prejudicial and racist attitudes, incorrect assumptions and lack of knowledge about the process of cross-cultural counselling.

Counsellors in the UK have debated these issues at length. One view holds that having the skills and attitudes of a counsellor, which would include the attitude of complete acceptance of the client's world view and the ability to empathise with the individual, would be sufficient to work effectively with a client from any cultural background (see Chapter 3). Further, any specific knowledge about religious or cultural phenomena that was of significance to the client would be supplied by the client. This view implies that there is no need to learn about cultures other than one's own and that racism simply would not occur between accepting individuals. An alternative view is that we are so formed by our race, culture and experience that we simply cannot work effectively with people of different racial origins or cultural or life experiences, whatever our theoretical knowledge may be.

A third view increasingly supported in the counselling profession holds that in order to understand relationships between people of different racial or cultural experience and origin and to work effectively with them, a knowledge of the different groups and of the history between the various groups is essential. However, this knowledge must be underpinned by an understanding of racism and of how contemporary society works in relation to race, the exercise of power and the effects of discrimination. Furthermore, counsellors require a personal awareness of where they stand in relation to these issues and of when and in what ways these issues may influence, and need to be addressed in, the counselling process.

At the beginning of this chapter we recognised some common human needs that may underlie the variety of cultural patterns on which we then focused. It may be useful, therefore, to end this chapter by recognising what may be a universal struggle, which is succinctly expressed by the writer, psychoanalyst and sociologist Erich Fromm (1978). He states: 'There is only one way – taught by the Buddha, by Jesus, by the Stoics, by Master Eckhart – to truly overcome the fear of dying, and that way is by not hanging on to life, not experiencing life as a possession . . . The fear then is not of dying, but of losing what I have; the fear of losing my body, my ego, my possessions, and my identity; the fear of facing the abyss of non-identity, of "being lost".'

Summary

- While in different cultures the patterns of responses and attitudes to death and mourning vary enormously, there are three basic elements that seem to be common to virtually all cultures. These relate to the changing relationships with the dead person, to the allocation of blame and expression of anger, and to the length of the mourning period.

- Cultural rituals are generally thought to be helpful in guiding us through the transition of grief and in managing the often extreme emotions of anger, uncertainty and fear evoked by the death. Emotional connections to a cultural or social group enable people to use these rituals more effectively, although individuals may use these in different ways.
- Knowledge of beliefs about death and the afterlife and about mourning practices in different religious and cultural groups, as well as an attitude of open respect for these other traditions, is essential in our multi-ethnic and multi-belief society.
- People are often unaware of the range of funeral services available. When they are uncertain, Christian services are often imposed on them, but a wider range of possibilities, such as a humanist service, is increasingly available.
- A recent trend is the development of 'green funerals'.
- Awareness of racism in society and in ourselves can enable us to work more sensitively with people of ethnic origins different from our own.

Chapter 8

Children's grief

'Gift of tears'

In Chapter 1 we saw how, after the separation of birth, a baby is 'grappling' with attachment and separation from its earliest days. We also saw how children who were separated from their parents by going to hospital, for instance, cried, protested angrily and then despaired. The angry protest and crying went on to alternate with despair as long as hope for reattachment could be maintained. If, however, a child reached a period of detachment then it was difficult for her to reattach either to the old attachment figure or to a new caretaker. These studies help us to get some idea of the immensity of children's grief when they are separated from their parents or caregivers.

We also saw in Chapter 6 how prevalent the denial of death is in our culture in the late twentieth and early twenty-first centuries. Adults introduce this process of embarrassed denial early in a child's life. In modern Western societies children are rarely given much information about death. Where the topic cannot be avoided it is often treated in a vague or unrealistic manner. What sense can a child make of a remark such as 'Grandad's gone on a journey', when the adult actually means that Grandad has died? This is one form of denial.

Another form of denial may find expression through an apparently protective act. For instance, we often go to enormous lengths to 'protect' children from the sight of a dead body. They may also be 'protected' from going to a funeral. Children should be allowed to see the body of the dead person and go to the funeral if they wish to do so. They must be given the option in an open way. Clearly a statement such as 'You don't want to go to the funeral, do you?' is very different from 'Would you like to go to the funeral? Let me tell you what happens.' Children must be given accurate information so they know what to expect. They can then decide for themselves what they want to do. They are entitled, just as much as an adult, to decide whether they want to see the body or remember the person as they last saw them. They do not need protection; they need information.

This 'protection' starts early in a child's life, and it may be that the protection is more for the adult than for the child. Protecting ourselves in this way, it may then be that the piercing cry of the infant reawakens in us, as adults, the painful experience of our early childhood losses, which have been consistently denied. We avoid the revival of these excruciating feelings by quietening or diverting the child and denying the hurt of her loss. The effect of the intensity of the child's feelings on adults' experience can help us to understand how it is that children's grief is so ignored. How often do we hear 'Oh, but he's too young to understand' or 'She can't be missing her Dad, he left us after all' or 'Isn't she good? We've had no tears at all'? The following story illustrates this point.

> Some years ago, a friend, Patricia, who came for coffee with her five-year-old son, arrived hiding her distress. As soon as the children had gone out to play, she told me that Sam had died that night.
> 'How awful,' I said, 'but who is Sam?'
> 'Sam is Pete's guinea-pig and this will break his heart, how can I tell him? My sister will get us a new guinea-pig by tomorrow. But how can I spare him the pain? I can at least tell him that Sam is in heaven, can't I?'
> 'Is that what you truly believe?'
> 'Oh don't be silly, of course I don't, but how can I make it less painful for him?'
> 'Perhaps you can't. Perhaps you would be unwise to. Perhaps Pete has a right to his feelings and his grief over Sam's death.'
> 'But he's only a child, how can he understand what death means?'
> 'Perhaps this is the way he can find out what death means.'
> Patricia and I argued for a bit until I think she began to realise that Pete would actually endure Sam's death better if she allowed him to feel his feelings and to share his experience of loss with her.

In our efforts to protect children from pain we may deprive them of their own best means of managing pain and overcoming the effects of loss. Children use such life events as the death of a guinea-pig to help them understand death and mortality. If they are encouraged to cry and have their feelings in relation to such losses validated, talked about and understood, this will help them to recognise and deal with the possible griefs of childhood.

Perhaps one of the commonest griefs of childhood in Britain today is the circumstantial loss of a parent through separation and divorce. Divorce is a difficult process for all participants. The parents may be so caught up in their feelings of hurt and anger that the child's pain and confusion goes unrecognised. It is made even more troublesome for children when they are told that one parent is bad. Sometimes this is carried even further, with one parent refusing the other parent access on the grounds that the visits are damaging. This stops the children seeing one parent, which hurts the child, except in rare cases where the child would be in danger. When the separation or divorce is acrimonious, children often get caught up, not being allowed by one parent to love the other and having their feelings misinterpreted. An example follows.

Pauline and Philip had separated and he was living with a new partner, Sharon, but Pauline was still on her own. The break-up had caused a lot of rage and hatred, which was often witnessed by their daughter, Emma. They now spoke to each other only when they had to do so, and Pauline refused to speak to Sharon. Emma, aged seven, saw her father for a week-end once a fortnight. Whenever she returned home to her mother's house she was extremely tearful and bad-tempered: so much so that Pauline decided it was harming her to go to her father and stopped the visit.

It is probable that Emma was reacting in this way because she was upset. She will have been sad to leave her father, possibly anxious about her mother's reactions on her return and uncertain whether she is allowed to love him when her mother does not. Pauline may be punishing Philip, unconsciously, by depriving him of visits from Emma. In a situation like this, Pauline will need a lot of understanding and compassion to help her listen to Emma and realise that stopping access will not help her daughter in the long term.

Separation or divorce of one's parents is only one of the circumstantial losses that some children experience. A small group of children, occasionally as a result of marriage breakdown, and more often if they have had very neglectful and dysfunctional parents, endure the circumstantial loss of going into foster care, changing foster-parent or being adopted. We mentioned in Chapter 2 that some children, who have been severely emotionally abused or neglected, are unable to form normal relationships with others. Their capacity to attach has been damaged and in some cases they are unable to make an attachment at all. This produces characteristic behaviour, evident in both children and adults, called reactive attachment disorder (RAD). Unsurprisingly the more disturbed behaviour is found in those who failed to attach at all. Behaviour observed in children and adults when attachment is disturbed is given in Table 8.1.

The behaviour outlined in Table 8.1 is always much more extreme than that exhibited by their peers. For instance, adolescents are often impatient and

Table 8.1 Behaviour observed when attachment is disordered

- Demanding, difficult and resistant
- Unsure about close relationships and prone to produce conflict in them
- Difficulties in giving and receiving warmth, comfort and affection
- Difficulties in committing oneself to family life
- Evidence of low self-confidence and self-esteem
- Consistent tendency to blame others when things go wrong
- Difficulty in making and sustaining peer relationships
- Difficulty in coping with change
- Indiscriminate in attention-seeking
- Impatient and easily frustrated, leading to anger and rage
- Impulsive, no sense of danger, and little ability to concentrate

easily frustrated, but adolescents with severe attachment difficulties will be excessively so. It is not surprising that the capacity of children with damaged or failed attachments to learn and partake in schooling is severely affected. Commonly they find it hard to concentrate and therefore underachieve academically and are disruptive and difficult to control in the classroom. Other signs of considerable unhappiness can be seen in behaviour that is either self-destructive or destructive of the family or communities who are caring for them. Examples are physical aggression and jealous, possessive and spiteful behaviour, lying, stealing, abuse of drugs and/or alcohol, self-harm and eating disorders. There is no doubt that they are very troubled and unhappy children.

Apart from the abuse and neglect, these children have suffered multiple separations and losses. Some research in the US suggests that approximately half of the children put up for adoption have attachment disorder symptoms. These children are so hugely damaged by unpredictable, neglectful and insecure relationships and mishandled separations that they are extremely difficult to foster or adopt: so much so that the placements often fail and the children enter yet another cycle of separation and loss. They and their foster or adoptive parents need specialist support and help, which is beyond the scope of this book.

Other circumstantial losses that many children experience are: moving house or school; failure at school; loss of health through accident or illness; loss of trust of adults owing to physical or sexual abuse; and, of course, the loss of a parent through death. In many of these circumstances the children's grief is simply disregarded by adults through encouraging the children to think only of the gain. All too often a child is told, when one of her parents remarries, 'Aren't you lucky! You now have a new Mummy [or Daddy] and brothers and sisters.' In this there is no recognition of the child's loss of intimacy with her own parent who has remarried.

It is, of course, particularly difficult for children at the time of loss when the grief goes unrecognised, but the consequences in adult life are profound. We know from working with adults how often their difficulties stem from unacknowledged losses in childhood. A study of depressed women in Camberwell (Brown and Harris, 1978) showed that one of four vulnerability factors, which predisposed women to suffer from depression, was the loss of their mothers before the age of 11. This childhood loss had clearly contributed to these women's depression. Since unrecognised childhood losses can affect adult life in this way, it is useful to consider the experience of grief at the different stages of children's development.

0–2 years

Children's understanding of loss and death changes as they grow and develop. For the baby under six months we can assume that as the attachment intensifies so the experience of separation intensifies, and this loss will be experienced as if it were a death. Should the mother die this will be experienced exactly as if she had gone away, and the quality of substitute care will be enormously important.

For the older infant between six months and two years we can see the beginnings of grief and mourning in a child's behaviour. She will search for her mother, call out for her and ask for her, even though she has no concept of 'death' as such. The notion of 'finality' will come only slowly. She will initially protest, then feel despair and gradually detach. She will be loath to let other attachment figures out of her sight. Her sadness will be almost palpable and it is at this stage that denial of the child's grief may be most intense. Few children in this age group will have conscious memories of parents who have died. When they are older this frequently results in fantasies of a perfect parent. Thus, when told off by their mother, for instance, they will fantasise that their dead Daddy 'would not have been nasty' to them. If this fantasy remains unrecognised it can cause considerable problems for the surviving parent, and step-parent should remarriage occur.

2–5 years

There are few systematic studies of grief and mourning in early childhood. In one study of children in the 3–5 age group, Rochlin (1967) found that they thought a lot about death, were aware that it represented the end of vital functions and were interested in the causality of death. This is the age when children are most likely to ask openly about death and tend to drag home such delights as smelly, dead seagulls! Yet for all the child at this age may be the 'little scientist', she is also highly susceptible to fantasies. Bowlby (1979) points out that for these young children fantasies about death may be reinforced by parental comments before the death such as 'You'll be the death of me'. A child is also likely to be very confused by explanations of death such as 'like going to sleep' or 'not waking up again'. It would hardly be surprising in these circumstances if a child were to become reluctant to go to bed. She may well be associating going to sleep with becoming like the dead seagull. Although she may have some vague concept of death, she may not be able to associate this 'scientific' concept with the actual experience of loss through death, should she be bereaved at this time. Her feelings are likely to be expressed very directly and there is less control or constraint of feelings. She also struggles to find words to fit feelings, and will be enormously helped when adults can give her clear words and concepts. The child needs to know as clearly as possible what it is that has happened to cause her loss. She will probably need to ask again and again as she grapples with these difficult ideas. She will need reassurance that she did not 'make' the person die or, in the case of divorce, 'make' them go away. In addition, in the latter case, she needs to know that both her parents love her even if they do not love each other. This will have to be reiterated many times. Her relationship with the adults around will affect how she manages her grief and mourning. She may find it difficult to put her feelings and memories into words, just at the time when the adults find her reminders of the death, and her painful mourning, unbearable. As they struggle with their own feelings they may not be able to empathise with her feelings and will therefore fail to listen to and understand her.

However, if the adult can listen she will hear the child's message behind the words and behaviour. You will remember Anne's story (Chapter 4). Just as she was wondering how on earth to manage her own feelings and tell Michael about his father's death, Michael helped make the link.

> Anne's two-year-old son Michael had been staying with grandparents over the last couple of days of James's life to enable her to be with James and attend to baby Pete's needs. When Michael returned the day after James's death he didn't go and look for him, which rather surprised Anne, and she, still pretty numb, didn't quite know what to do or say. After lunch Michael helped her:
>
> *Anne:*   Would you like a Polo, Michael?
>
> *Michael:* These are Daddy's Polos.
>
> *Anne:*   That's right, they were Daddy's Polos. But Daddy won't be needing them any more, because Daddy's not here now.
>
> Michael then pensively ate the Polo, had a good cuddle with Anne and returned to playing with his favourite cuddly toy. That was probably enough information for that day, but there were many fears, nightmares and strong feelings to be worked through and the concept of death understood before Michael could be said to have resolved his grief.

Nightmares are common in grieving children of all ages, and are difficult for adults to handle when the child has few verbal skills. In a two-year-old a comment such as 'You are safe here' and a hug accompanied by 'I love you' will probably be sufficient. For an older child it is important to get them to tell you about the nightmare and then try to help them to understand what the nightmare might be 'saying'. For instance, Ruth, whose parents had separated, had a nightmare about being chased by dragons and getting lost between the dragon's and the witches' castles. Her mother was able to comfort her and then to ask whether she thought her lost and frightened feelings might have something to do with feeling lost between the two homes and/or perhaps fearing that she might somehow get lost from one of her parents. Several books mentioned in Appendix C can be a helpful aid to talking about fears aroused by this situation.

From this age on children will explore everything that is happening to them through play as well as through asking questions. It is this capacity to play that is used very extensively in Chapter 13 when we look at ways of working with grieving children.

5–8 years

A child in the 5–8 age-group is developing fast and beginning to get a sense of the idea of the 'future'. She can therefore begin to understand ideas such as 'Daddy won't be living with us *any more*' or 'Grandad is dead and we won't *ever* see him *again*'. At this stage too the child is developing the capacity to feel guilt but is not able to understand the difference between feelings and acts. Thus the child's growing understanding of her own actions will often lead her to think she actually caused the loss herself, e.g. 'it was because I got cross with Grandad that he died' or 'I cried until I was allowed to sit next to Mummy at tea and not Daddy and that's why Daddy's left us'.

Unable to make a distinction between thought and action, they can believe that when they are so angry that they wished someone dead, their thoughts actually killed the dead person. To counteract this tendency children need to be listened to and their fantasies and 'magical thinking' explored, so that they can discover that they were not the cause of the death, the departure or the abuse.

Children of this age group are intensely interested in the world about them and are often very interested in what has happened to the dead person's body. For adults this almost seems a ghoulish interest and can be upsetting, particularly when they also suggest that the body should be dug up now because they do not understand the finality of death and believe it could be reversed. They would also be helped by an understanding that they want to bring the body back to life and thus bring the person back, but that this is not possible. These children, if not understood in this way, will quickly deny their own feelings, either when feelings are difficult for them to handle themselves or when they sense that an adult cannot manage the feelings or might ridicule them. Children will actually protect an adult in this way, particularly in the case of abuse, but suffer in the process by carrying on as if nothing had happened. Usually, however, the child-sensitive observer can see the signs of grief in the hurt child.

Exercise 8.1 Example of a grieving child

Paul was almost seven when his father, Thomas, was killed in a car accident (Exercise 9.1). The accident happened after Paul went to bed and he only knew next morning. He cried for a few minutes, but when encouraged to go to school he went easily. From then on he never cried about his father and rarely talked about him. He always seemed exceptionally good and well behaved. However, the family did notice that from about the time of his father's death he was really clinging with his mother, Susan. Whenever she went out in the evening he would say nothing but she would see his little face, with tears streaming down, glued to the window. This became progressively worse, as did bed-wetting. His teacher noticed that he frequently did not know that she had spoken to him.

About two years later Susan was feeling really anxious about Paul, who was now nine, particularly when she found her favourite scarf, which she wore a lot, hidden in Paul's bedroom. It had been missing for some time and Paul had been asked more than once if he had seen it. He said he hadn't. When she found it, Paul still said he hadn't known that the scarf was in his room. Susan decided at this point to seek help. In talking she realised that Paul needed help with grieving, and that he was showing signs of grief in more ways than she had realised.

What signs of grief can you find?

In the story of Paul's bereavement in Exercise 8.1 we see how his grief was not recognised and his frightening feelings went underground. He then had to try to express his grief indirectly through his behaviour. This behaviour was trying to express what could not be said in words.

You will have noticed some signs of grief in Paul in Exercise 8.1. It was difficult for Susan to notice these at the time as she was, naturally enough, preoccupied with her own grief. In such circumstances adults will often be struggling with their own grief, so that listening to and understanding the children can be very difficult. This leaves the children isolated and much in need of external support. We turn now to look at how Susan came to recognise and work with Paul's grief:

Encouraged by a listener, Val, Susan started talking to Paul about Thomas. Gradually Paul told Susan that his Dad had been really cross with him just before he left for a meeting on the night he died. He had sent Paul to bed and Paul had been very angry with his Dad. Susan also remembered the incident.

Val suggested to Susan that maybe Paul had been so angry with his father that night that he had wished him dead. Paul found it very hard to tell Susan that this was so, but then he blurted out 'It's all my fault, I killed him'. Susan then took Paul on her knee and told him that she understood his reasoning, but that it was not actually true that he had killed his father. She needed to tell him this several times over the ensuing months before he could really believe it. Gradually his clinging behaviour stopped.

Talking with Val, Susan reflected that there were many ways in which Paul was stuck as a 'seven-year-old'. When Susan asked Paul if he felt as though he was still seven, he said 'Yes, that's how Dad remembers me'.

In this example we have thought about the possible meaning of some signs of grief. In Paul's case, his regressing to a 'seven-year-old' seemed to be his way of trying to express his need to deal with something that happened when he was 'aged seven'. He may also have feared that, were he to grow up and become a real nine-year-old, he would be unrecognisable to Thomas. It was almost as if he retained a hope that by his remaining aged seven his father would recognise him 'when he returned from the dead'. His clinging behaviour was his way of saying to Susan 'Please don't go in case my angry feelings kill you as well as Daddy'. His taking the scarf may have been his way of saying 'If I express my badness this way then perhaps I won't have to kill you' and perhaps also 'The scarf means I do have a bit of you, if and when you do die'. Once Susan was able to begin to unravel his fears, his fantasies and behaviour could be understood and his grief expressed more appropriately.

Table 8.2 Some signs of grieving in a child

Signs of Paul's grief	Help required
1 Over-dependence on living parent. Frightened and clinging behaviour. Difficulty with every separation.	Understanding of Paul's feelings of fear about losing the other parent. Recognition of his fear of Susan's death or disappearance, perhaps as a 'result' of his angry feelings.
2 Daydreaming	Recognition of Paul's need to escape, possibly into a fantasy world. This world might be explored.
3 Wetting	Understanding of Paul's need to become a 'little boy again'.
4 Symbolic stealing and 'forgetting'	Recognition of the meaning to Paul of his taking 'something of Susan', enabling him to express his fear of losing her.
5 Excessive fear and compliant behaviour becoming 'bad behaviour'	Recognition of Paul's fear of being punished again. There is then sometimes a period of difficult behaviour, which may usefully express the angry feelings that were denied.

Table 8.2 summarises the behavioural messages Paul used to express his grief indirectly, and the help that enabled him to understand and express his feelings more directly. This list tells us something about the symbolic way in which Paul expressed his grief. Other children will use different ways to express their grief. Some of these, such as over-assiduousness at school, over-cleanliness and over-tidiness, are sometimes encouraged by overwrought parents and not recognised as part of a grieving pattern. Other, more obvious signs such as soiling, school avoidance, nightmares, accident-proneness, breaking up friendships, taking other people's possessions, may be very trying for the other grieving siblings and parent. Children can be helped to express their need for caring in a more appropriate way. The signs of grief outlined above refer to children bereaved by the death of a parent, but children grieving in a divorcing family will behave in similar ways (Kroll, 1996). We consider other ways of helping such children in Chapter 13.

Grieving children of school age often have considerable difficulty with mathematical concepts such as addition, subtraction and division. All these words are especially emotive for a child who has lost someone precious. If the concepts are being taught close to a loss or separation, a child may find it very hard to think about the ideas and therefore be unable to understand the ideas. It will also be no surprise that for many children creative writing becomes very difficult after a major loss or separation. Their fantasies and nightmares may be too terrifying for them to use their imagination at all.

It will not be surprising that saying 'goodbye' is also hard for children who have had a member of the family die or leave. This is illustrated in Exercise 8.2.

Exercise 8.2 Saying goodbye

Josh was five when his parents finally separated, though there had been many vicious rows that he had witnessed before they parted. After they separated there had been two brief periods when his father had moved back in. Josh's mother, Claire, became very concerned when she noticed that every time they met up with friends he played amicably until it was time to leave. At that point he became sulky and bad-mannered, and refused to say goodbye. Telling him off about his bad manners made no difference, so she asked a counsellor for help.

How might you try to help Josh and Claire understand what his behaviour could mean?

In Exercise 8.2, you were probably aware that goodbyes were difficult and painful for Josh because they reminded him of his misery about his parent's separation, and that this understanding would be helpful for both Josh and Claire. 'Goodbyes' are likely to exacerbate his fears because whenever he and his father had come together again, he had hoped that his father would stay. These hopes were dashed each time they said goodbye.

8–12 years

Magical thinking is beginning to diminish in the 8–12-year-old child as she understands the distinction between thought and action. She also has a clearer concept of the future. Thus she has the cognitive ability to realise what the loss will mean to her. The death of, or separation from, a parent threatens her and can reawaken feelings of childishness and helplessness. She may show outwardly coping behaviour but may be denying the feelings inside, not resolving the loss and thus delaying the grieving process.

In Geoff's story (Chapter 4) we have in Christine's behaviour a typical example of this coping behaviour. On the morning of her mother's sudden death, she remembered that it was the school photograph that day and that she had to wash her hair. Outwardly she coped beautifully. It was only in her late teens that Christine was able to experience deeply the pain of grief about her mother's tragic death. A child in this age group may also become involved in symbolic behaviour and, for instance, become obsessed by the dead parent's possessions. This is a way of trying to express a longing to hold on to and continue the lost relationship as it was.

The dawning sexuality of this pubescent period, together with a growing sense of sexual identity, may complicate relationships with parents, sometimes leading to a pulling away from one parent and an increased identity with the other. The 8–12 year-old usually 'identifies' increasingly with the parent of the same sex and will be particularly affected if that parent dies or leaves. When this grief is difficult to express it may be shown symbolically through behaviour patterns not unlike those outlined for Paul in Table 8.2 (p. 79).

It is at this stage of development too that children come to recognise the possibility of their own deaths. Such an identification with death may make the subject particularly frightening for them. This probably intensifies the tendency towards denial, and it may be necessary to be quite firm about talking with this age group to give them the opportunity to share their longing, their feelings and their memories with us. When they do trust us they will usually respond to this kind of encouragement. As they begin to share their memories and feelings, their behaviour usually becomes understandable as a sign of grief.

Adolescence

Adolescence is a period of loss as well as gain. The passing of childhood and the possibility of separation from the first family need to be mourned, just as much as the new sexual possibilities and growing independence of adolescence need to be welcomed. There is much upheaval during the period of adolescence, and relationships with peers, siblings and parents pass through many phases as the young person moves towards separation and reorganisation. An additional separation task such as the death or loss of a parent through divorce coming at this time is particularly challenging, especially in early adolescence when self-confidence may be lowest.

Adolescents' mourning process for the death or loss of a parent, sibling or friend follows the usual pattern, and, if the powerful feelings and the mood swings can be expressed and understood, it will take its natural course. When adolescents identify very closely with a lost person they may take on their mannerisms, behaviours and values. Identification with a more 'adult' person is a natural aspect of adolescence. It is usually short-lived, and may change from week to week (changing allegiances to pop-stars, for instance). If, however, this 'over-identification' with the lost person continues and does not shift, then adolescents may need help to get in touch with their anger with the lost person for 'deserting' or 'abandoning' them at this important stage. With this help they may then begin to let go of the lost person and be able to get on with their own developmental tasks. This will include depressed and aggressive feelings as adolescents begin to experience the pain of the loss and recognise the need to find a new identity without the lost person. This seems to be particularly true for boys who have lost a father (Van Eerdewegh *et al.*, 1982).

Our own experience of adolescent girls is that they too usually have periods of depression in response to loss. Another way in which adolescent girls often try to manage a difficult loss is to deny the grief and become 'the little caretaker'. This pseudo-adult, 'bossy' and powerfully controlling behaviour then masks the girl's own need for comfort. This role also serves to protect her from feeling the pain and emptiness that the loss has caused.

In Geoff's story (Chapter 4) his eldest daughter Julie, who was 12 when her mother died so suddenly, seemed to slip almost effortlessly into the 'little mother' role. It was she who stayed off school the following day to 'help with the other two'. It was she who accompanied father to work before going to the coroner's office and the doctors. It was she who discussed with her father whether they felt strong enough to read the letters that day. In some sense she 'couldn't be a child' any more, for there was no mother, and she 'managed' this by becoming a 'little mother' herself. But as others worked through events and feelings, she needed to maintain her role and tried to control everyone by behaving in a 'bossy' and controlling manner. This meant that although people said 'Isn't she wonderful?', Julie was not getting the comfort she needed and her feelings of anger and sadness were increasingly denied. It was many months before Julie's increasingly angry and controlling outbursts were recognised as her attempt to deny her grief rather than experience the pain of her great loss. Once she could risk recognising her own pain she swung back to being a 'very little girl', refusing all age-appropriate responsibility. This may have been her way of trying to get the comfort she had refused before. Eventually, though not until her late 20s, she was able to be her own 'real age', appropriately caring for others and being cared for herself.

Late-adolescent girls may try to 'fill the gap' left by the loss of someone important to them by becoming pregnant. If the pregnancy leads to abortion or miscarriage, then the grief over the lost child, who might have filled the gap, is likely to be intense. However, it often goes unrecognised, with people suggesting that the abortion or miscarriage was 'for the best', and the 'original' grief remains unseen. If the child is born, the young mother may find enormous difficulty in letting the child find its own identity, perhaps because the baby is treated as if it were the lost person.

With children of any age who have been sexually abused, the loss of innocence is a severe wound, which usually remains deep inside and unrecognised because of the pressures towards secrecy. Often these wounds remain secret into adulthood, only emerging if the person is lucky and forms a loving relationship. If such a relationship cannot be established, then the wound may go unrecognised for decades. The inappropriate guilt and appropriate anger of those who have been sexually abused will be considered, albeit very briefly, in Chapter 16.

Table 8.3 summarises some signs that young people give when grieving.

Table 8.3 Signs of grieving in young people

• Over-dependence	• Difficulty with saying goodbye
• Nightmares	• Cognitive difficulties with maths
• Daydreaming	• Withdrawn behaviour
• Wetting	• Inability to do 'creative writing'
• Soiling	• Symbolic 'stealing' and 'forgetting'
• Over-industriousness	• Precocious maturity
• Regression to younger age	• Changes in behaviour ('too good'/'too bad')

In this chapter we have seen that children do indeed grieve, but frequently mask their grief. Carers need to become aware of these many signs.

When these signs are recognised and children are encouraged to express their true feelings, then they can be helped. The following quotation from Beverley Raphael (1984, p. 138) illustrates just such an interaction.

> Jessica was five. She showed her mother the picture she had painted. There were black clouds, dark trees and large red splashes.
>
> 'My,' said her mother. 'Tell me all about this, Jess.' Jessica pointed to the red splashes. 'That's blood,' she said. 'And these are clouds.' 'Oh,' said her mother. 'See,' said Jessica, 'the trees are very sad. The clouds are black. They are sad too.' 'Why are they sad?' asked her mother. 'They are sad because their Daddy has died,' said Jessica, the tears slowly running down her cheeks. 'Sad like us since Daddy died,' said her mother and held her closely, and they wept.

In families that have developed their relationships with openness and shared feelings, a child can usually express her grief directly and can receive comfort. She is, of course, hurt by the loss but there will be healing and she will not fear life because of it. She will be able to integrate the loss into the 'story' of her life, however painful. Families who find difficulty in expressing feelings openly will often need help with grief.

Children who have developed the sort of 'narrative competence' described in Chapter 2 will be able to make some sort of account of their lives in the form of a coherent story, however distressing the actual events. This competence is more likely to be achieved in families who are able to express feelings and talk about things in an open, accepting manner. Where children's grief is not expressed, they may need special kind of help.

We will look at some practical examples of working with grieving children in Chapter 13.

Summary

- Children do grieve if adults recognise this and allow them to do so.
- Frequently adults deny children's grief, in the guise of 'protecting' the children. Children subsequently mask their grief.
- Some circumstantial losses that children experience are: being fostered or adopted; divorce or separation of parents; moving house, community or school; failure at school; loss of health; disability.
- The experience of grief for children has specific features linked to their emotional development.
- Severely emotionally abused children express their distress about loss through extreme forms of behaviour.
- Sexually abused children can carry a deep wound of loss into early and sometimes late adult life.

- Children often express their grief symbolically through altered behaviour or through dreams.
- Children's direct grief, often their gift of tears, needs acceptance and understanding from adults.

Chapter 9

Personal and family experiences of loss

Up to this point we have looked at bereavement largely through the eyes of the researcher and through our own personal experiences. As loss counsellors we need to be able to apply this knowledge to bereaved people, and we also need to know whether what has been said about bereavement is true for other losses. If that is indeed the case, then we will be able to extrapolate from bereavement to other losses, whether natural or circumstantial.

The aims of this chapter are twofold: to enable you to apply knowledge about bereavement to specific families and situations, including your own; and to see whether the response to loss has similarities to bereavement. In thinking about how bereavement will affect a particular family we have to look at the individuals who are bereaved, their family network and their past history. An example of such a family is given through the family tree outlined in Table 9.1 (p. 87).

Introducing you to so many people in this family at this stage may seem rather unnecessary. Yet any one loss within a family will undoubtedly affect others, particularly those who themselves are still in the process of their own grief. Grief has been called a social process, and this is nowhere more true than within the wider family circle. The ways of handling grief, or indeed denial of grief, tend to be reflected or repeated from one generation to the next. It is often the case that the more we can understand the feelings, relationships and griefs in ourselves and our own generation, the more we can understand those of past as well as future generations.

Members of the family represented in Table 9.1 have experienced loss through death, emigration, divorce, disability and miscarriage. No doubt other losses such as going to school, moving house and losing jobs have also happened to them. In Exercise 9.1 (p. 88) we invite you to think about this extended family, in particular about Susan and Thomas and their families.

In thinking about each member of the family, consider both the external determining circumstances surrounding them and their particular personal history (see Chapter 5). We cannot draw conclusions about their attachment history, capacity to be intimate or the network of support surrounding them, but we can deduce their loss and death history and the impact of these,

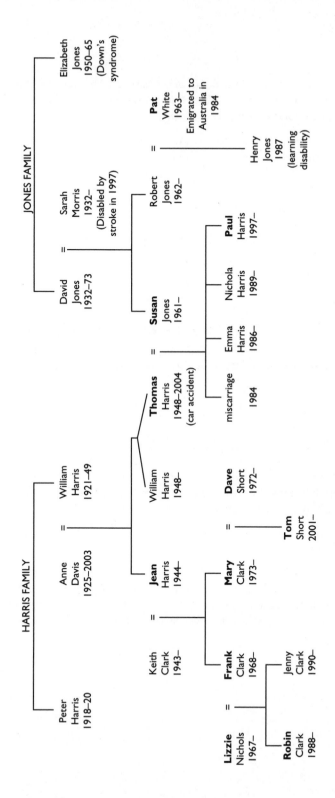

Note: Names in bold refer to the people we have used to illustrate points in the text.

Table 9.1 Family tree

Exercise 9.1 Use of the wider family tree

1   **Consider Susan Harris in 2004 when her husband Thomas was killed in a car accident. At that time Emma was away at college and Nichola and Paul were at school locally.**

(a) Think about the support sources that might exist for Susan. The families' experiences of loss will be particularly relevant.

(b) What about the position of William, Thomas's identical twin brother?

(c) Paul's seventh birthday was five days after Thomas's death. Should Susan let Paul have the planned birthday party? When should Thomas's funeral be? Does Paul have special needs?

(d) How might the death of Susan's father when she was 12 affect the current grieving? Susan had one bout of depression soon after Paul was born. Though she has recovered, might this previous post-natal depression be a significant factor now? Might her miscarriage in 1984 affect her grieving now?

(e) Thomas's and Susan's marriage was fairly rocky when Thomas was killed. He had said more than once that he was thinking of leaving. How might this affect Susan's grieving?

2   **Consider Robert Jones and Patricia White, now in Australia.**

    (a) What position might they have found themselves in when Henry was born?

    (b) How might they have been affected by Thomas's death?

3   **In what ways might the Welsh origins of the Jones family affect the rituals of grief?**

4   **Have these families experienced exceptional numbers of losses?**

5   **There are many other losses in this family tree. You might like to focus on other members and, given the information you have, consider what determinants would affect each of their losses.**

depending on their age and therefore their developmental stage when these events occurred. This will give you ideas about how each individual's grief might be expressed, whether the grief process could become blocked and the likelihood of their needing extra support.

The family tree is one way of looking at what factors affect grieving throughout a whole family. By drawing a lifeline (as in Table 9.2) for a particular member of a family, we can highlight all the losses in one individual's life and focus in on their 'loss history' more clearly.

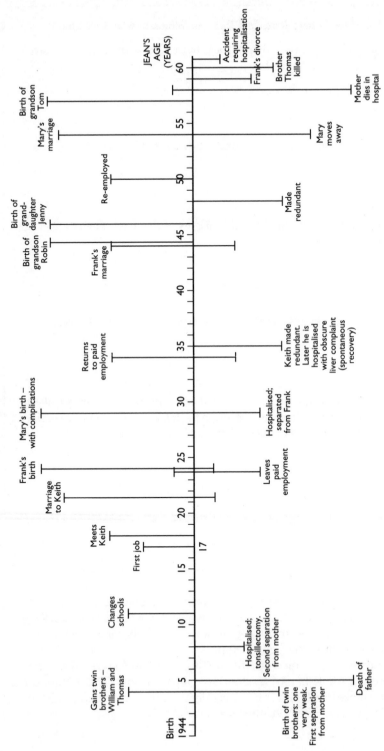

Table 9.2 Lifeline of Jean

Let us try to illustrate this by looking in more detail at Jean Clark, Tom's grandmother. Jean, aged 60, has just had an accident and this loss has been influenced in various ways by her earlier experiences. We can use her lifeline to focus on important events in the past that may be influencing present circumstances. In the example of Jean's lifeline in Table 9.2 (p. 90) we see that she has marked some of the events in her life. She has indicated the relative importance of the event by the length of the line away from the central lifeline, and also the meaning by deciding whether the line goes above for a happy event or below the central lifeline for a sad or difficult event, or both.

Jean was four years old when her twin brothers were born. This experience was mixed for her, with the sense of loss and sadness being greater than the gain. This may be because her mother was away in hospital for a week and may have been very preoccupied with the twins when she returned from hospital. Jean probably missed her mother a lot and turned to her father for reassurance, so his death a year later would have been very difficult for her, as the length of the line indicates. We do not know the details of Jean's attachment history, but we do know that the quality of her secure or insecure attachment to each of her parents will have affected how she managed both her mother's hospitalisation when the twins were born and her father's death one year later. Then, in turn, the handling of these two events will have affected how she grieves and copes with all future separations and deaths.

We see that the births of her two children and her three grandchildren were happy events for Jean. Separations from her mother and her children were sad or difficult events; the death of her mother was particularly sad for her. This happened fairly close to her brother's death and her son's divorce; both difficult and sad events. Some events, such as the birth of her twin brothers, have been both gain and loss simultaneously. She experienced her marriage mainly as a gain, but she was also aware of the loss of freedom that marriage signified for her. The birth of her daughter Mary, and later the marriage of Frank, also contained these mixed elements. We notice in comparing Jean's various losses that, for her, many of these were linked with periods in hospital. When Jean is hospitalised it is possible that any one, or indeed all, of these previous experiences may be influencing the way she is feeling now. As we indicated earlier, a lot will depend on how her earlier losses were experienced at the time and on what these previous losses still mean for her. Jean has a life story with losses, as we all do, but she will also experience multiple losses when she goes into hospital. By completing Exercise 9.2 on the following page you can reflect on the losses Jean experienced in hospital.

Some of the losses and changes Jean is likely to have experienced are loss of freedom, loss of health, loss of safety, loss of sexual intimacy, loss of expectations (she may well not be able to walk for some time), loss of hobbies, loss of comfort, temporary loss of job and associated interests and loss of routine. These multiple losses can have profound effects on people. For some the only way to cope with being looked after is to become compliant and in

---

Exercise 9.2 Multiple losses

Tom's Gran, Jean, and her husband Keith live 40 miles from their daughter, Mary, and her family, and 200 miles from their son, Frank, recently divorced. Jean has a job and she and Keith have enjoyed holidays and outings since the children left home. She was recently knocked down and seriously injured by a drunken driver and is now in hospital.

Can you list some of the losses which Jean experienced while in hospital?

---

some ways childlike, if not childish. Others seem to find their greatest maturity at such times of crisis. Studying the lifeline of Jean's loss history can help us to understand more about her likely responses to the multiple losses she experienced in hospital.

Drawing your own lifeline

Jean's lifeline in Table 9.2 (p. 90) shows her life history and the weight she gave to the losses and gains associated with various events in her life. In Exercise 9.3 (on the opposite page) we give you the opportunity to look at your own life history in the same way.

As you look at your lifeline now, think about any picture or pattern of feelings that emerges and take time to reflect. You might also like to think about whether some events have left you with unresolved or ambivalent feelings and thoughts. Also take time to reflect on your own personal history. The counselling attitudes of acceptance, congruence and empathy are firmly based in self-knowledge, and counsellors need to be aware of their own life history and learn to accept their own feelings and vulnerabilities. Many people find it difficult to share their personal feelings, and yet in a counselling relationship it is what we expect others to do. It would, therefore, be important for you to share some of the feelings you know to be associated with events in your life

Exercise 9.3 Your lifeline

Using Jean's lifeline (Table 9.2) as an example, create your own personal lifeline from the line printed below.* Mark off your current age and put a cross on the line at each age that a significant event occurred in your life. (These might be events such as the birth of a brother or sister, leaving home, marriage, death of someone special, birth of children, job loss, etc.) Then for each event draw a vertical line either above or below the central (horizontal) line, or indeed both above and below. Lines above the central line indicate a happy event and below the central line a sad or difficult event. Some events may be both sad and happy. Indicate the relative importance of the event for you by the length of the vertical line.

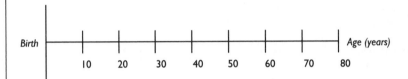

Once you have completed your lifeline as indicated, go back in your memory to these events and see if you can remember the feelings associated with the events or the period of the events. As you remember the feelings, write them down.

* You can, of course, create your own size of lifeline on a separate sheet.

with someone else, preferably someone you do not know too well. This will give you the chance to experience what it is like to share your own personal feelings with a near stranger. It will also give you the opportunity to discover more about your feelings in relationship to past losses.

Table 9.3 Feelings associated with loss

Shock	Guilt	Hopelessness
Searching	Fear	Helplessness
Disbelief	Ambivalence	Anxiety
Anger	Isolation	Loneliness
Hate	Frustration	Acceptance
Bitterness	Despair	Shame

Table 9.3 summarises the feelings of other people who have used a lifeline to discover the feelings they had associated with losses in their lives.

Compare your feelings associated with the losses in your life (Exercise 9.3) with those of others. It is likely that many of your feelings will be similar to those of others experiencing a loss, as shown in Table 9.3. If this is the case, it will make sense to you that when loss occurs certain feelings can be

Table 9.4 Comparison of loss reaction in adults and young children

Phases of mourning (C.M. Parkes) (Table 4.2)	Adult loss (your feelings) (Table 9.3)	Childhood loss	
		(Tom's feelings) (Table 1.1)	(Children's attitudes) (Table 1.1)
NUMBNESS	Shock	Shock and	Disbelief in loss
	Disbelief	Anger	(Still hope of recovery of lost person)
YEARNING	Searching	Angry longing	
	Frustration		
	Anger		
	Loneliness	Despair	Belief in loss
	Hate		
	Love		
	Ambivalence	Hopelessness	(No hope of recovery
DISORGANISATION and DESPAIR	Guilt		of lost person)
	Bitterness		
	Isolation		
	Fear	Emptiness	
	Anxiety		
	Despair		Denial of needs
	Hopelessness	Ultimate	
	Helplessness	despair	
REORGANISATION	Acceptance	Reattachment	
	Relief		

expected. These feelings will vary in intensity for different people at different times, but they are the natural response to loss and an inevitable part of being human.

If you then compare the feelings from Table 9.3 (p. 94) with a child's response to a sudden 'longer' loss, as summarised in Table 1.1 (p. 10), you will notice similarities. Looking at these two tables with the phases of mourning and associated feelings outlined in Table 4.2 (p. 33), you will be able to make further links.

We have tried to simplify these three patterns and brought them together in Table 9.4 to show how they interconnect. We have also indicated how the feelings associated with adult loss link in an overlapping pattern with Parkes's phases of mourning and feelings associated with grief. From these links we can conclude, first, that the response to bereavement is a specific and a particularly intense example of the generalised response of human beings to loss. Second, bereavement fits into a well-established pattern of response to loss. We have outlined the ways in which external and internal factors can affect the response to bereavement. Such factors will also affect other losses, whether natural or circumstantial. As loss counsellors it is important that we know about loss in all its ramifications. It is equally important to know our own pattern of grieving and be aware of our own personal loss history, for this will markedly affect how we grieve and how we listen to others' grief. If there are feelings that we as counsellors have never expressed or perhaps do not even feel, then it is unlikely that we will be able to empathise with these feelings in others and help them to think about and express them. We will almost certainly inhibit their expression.

Summary

- Drawing a family tree can help us become more aware of the range of losses affecting a family, of the different ways in which different members are affected and of the interconnectedness of different losses.
- Within any single loss, multiple losses occur and these are in turn affected by that person's loss history and attachment pattern.
- Drawing our own lifeline can help us focus on gains and losses in our lives and on accepting the feelings associated with these events.
- Certain feelings can be expected in response to all losses, including bereavement and childhood separations. The way in which these feelings are experienced and managed is affected by personal loss history.
- As loss counsellors it is important to know these feelings and their history in ourselves and to be able to accept and think about them so that we can empathise with those feelings and experiences in others. Once feelings can be experienced and thought about, ideas and sense can begin to emerge.

Part III

Working with the grieving

Chapter 10

Basic loss counselling skills

'Give sorrow words'

We have now looked at different aspects of loss and bereavement. In Part II we focused on research into bereavement in general and also experiences of bereavement, which can bring us more personal insights about human loss. Recognition of loss in our own lives (Exercise 9.3, p. 93) and the feelings associated with these losses enables us to think about loss so as to accept and listen to those who have recently suffered a loss. Therefore when using counselling skills or when functioning as counsellors we can listen more effectively because we draw on our knowledge of ourselves and the natural-ness of our own mourning process. We also have a confidence in the function of grieving and are not surprised that any one loss is experienced as multiple losses or that it evokes feelings from previous losses. Rather like the anthro-pologists mentioned in Chapter 7, our role is to observe, accept and value the experiences of others, trying to understand this experience at many levels yet without wishing to change it in any way.

The particular attitudes of care, nurture and non-judgemental acceptance mentioned in Chapter 3 will enable others to talk to you. Then they are more likely to tell you not only their stories and memories of the person who has died but also their feelings. This putting of sorrow into words will help the bereaved to stop fearing and condemning their own feelings, to accept their loss and experience their grief to the full. Throughout this chapter we focus on ways to enable people to talk about their feelings, but this is always done in the context of the client telling you about life with the person whom they have lost. It is in the telling of the story that the feelings emerge.

Attitudes alone are not enough. They have to be conveyed through responses. Responding skills need to be recognised, separated out and learned. As these learned skills become integrated into the flow of the rela-tionship, they become counselling.

The difficulty of learning how to integrate skills into a relationship has many parallels with learning how to ride a bicycle, where the mechanics of learning to ride are like the skills, and the balance is like the attitudes. At first you need someone to hold on to the saddle and help you keep your balance as you struggle with the mechanics of keeping the pedals going round; learning you cannot freewheel going uphill; remembering to look ahead and not down at the wheel; thinking about which gear is which and which brake to use; remembering to look behind and give signals. As you begin to get your balance and go off on your own you start to forget about the mechanics, and miss a corner or a gear, or don't brake in time and may even fall off. But, gradually, with practice, your sense of balance grows, you begin to integrate the separate tasks into your overall behaviour, and you discover you're actually riding a bike. However, you can have all the skills in the world, yet if you do not have balance you cannot ride. So the skills in this chapter need to be learned in their own right, but without the appropriate attitudes it will not be counselling.

In a book of this size we can provide only a brief introduction to skills and attitudes and what you can practise from a book is but a pale reflection of the real thing. It is, of course, in the practice of skills in a real relationship that you learn how to use them. But to aid this transition from the written word to the relationship 'out there', we have designed some exercises to be done on your own and, wherever possible, subsequently discussed with a friend or fellow counsellor. On a loss counselling training course these exercises could be adapted by the trainer for skills training work. In the design of some of these initial exercises we have drawn on ideas from Mearns and Thorne (1999) and also from the Truax and Carkhuff (1967) study mentioned in Chapter 3.

For some of these exercises we have introduced the word 'client'. While we are well aware that the listener may not be working as a 'counsellor', nor may the grievers define themselves as 'clients', none the less we have used the terms 'counsellor' and 'client' in most instances as a kind of shorthand to avoid confusion. The examples are, of course, enormously simplified and assume that the external determinants and internal factors are such that the grief is relatively uncomplicated and that this level of counselling is appropriate. Advanced skills for working with more complicated grief are outlined in Chapters 15 and 16.

In this chapter the basic skills will be outlined and discussed. Four further chapters will take us through the development of the skills in relation to other theoretical ideas. In Table 10.1 (p. 101) we have summarised the most important skills for loss counselling and indicated the chapters in which they are considered. We have divided them into three levels to indicate that the further and advanced skills cannot be practised without a solid grounding in the basic skills. When the skills are integrated in practice, this rather artificial division disappears.

Active listening and distractions

This skill is not so much a skill of doing as a skill of being. When humans are faced with a crisis, the 'urge-to-do' can be extraordinarily powerful. Being with a person who is expressing strong feelings can sometimes feel like a

Table 10.1 Skills necessary for loss counselling

Basic skills (Chapter 10)	A	Active listening and distractions from listening
	B	Reflecting experience and feelings
	C	Reflecting with deeper empathy
Further skills (Chapter 12)	D	Setting limits or boundaries
	E	Normalising disturbing experiences
Ways of helping children (Chapter 13)	F	Immediacy about information and feelings
	G	When feelings get lost
	H	Techniques to explore relationships
	I	When information is lacking
	J	Maintaining links
Advanced skills (Chapters 15 and 16)	K	Working with anger and guilt in complicated grief
	L	The 'stuck' patterns
	M	Knowing when to consult
Assessment and referral (Chapter 17)	N	Assessment skills
	O	Referral skills

crisis, and the 'urge-to-do' can tempt us into rushing to 'make it better' with a platitude or other unhelpful response. But it is, of course, not action but reception that comforts. It is a counsellor's task to help clients 'give words' to their sorrow.

It is not easy to find the words to express grief, and the listener can easily react to her own anxiety, letting it get in the way and thus prevent the words being found. There is a special quality of reflective silence within a relationship, however, which can enable grievers to find their own words. This silence is not an empty silence but contains acceptance and understanding. This lets the bereaved know that you value them and what they have to say about their experience of loss. It also tells them, without words, that you know they must struggle to find their own words. As you listen and give attention they will begin to trust you not to rush in with the useless platitude or controlling question and will be able to risk sharing more of their feelings with you. It is then possible to begin to think about their inner world and allow possible meanings to emerge.

When you consider this aspect of 'being-with' another in their search to express their sorrow, you need to pay attention to a number of ways in which you or the client can be distracted. These are listed in Table 10.2 (p. 102).

External distractions

You may need to use your confidence as a counsellor to make sure that the environment of counselling is conducive to the work, even if there is no alternative to being in other people's homes.

Table 10.2 Distractions to good listening

External distractions	–	things in the world, in the room, outside the room
Distractions in your own behaviour	–	posture, eye contact, facial expression
Distractions from your attitudes	–	some of your own personal attitudes and judgements may get in the way of listening
Distractions in your feelings	–	your own unresolved losses; your own fears and anxiety; unexpressed anxieties in you about the relationship between you and the client

Telephones, televisions, radios, cooking, callers, active animals or small children can be distracting and it is necessary to arrange for these things not to intrude, whatever the situation. If the client is reluctant to remove distractions you may be picking up their unconscious avoidance and fear of their own feelings. You need to pay attention to this fear.

Distractions in your own behaviour

An open and relaxed posture (not crossed arms or legs) is generally perceived as more accepting and trustworthy. Eye contact is important: not intermittent or staring, but gently sensing how much eye contact can be tolerated. Facial expression is also important; raised eyebrows or grimaces can be understood as expressions of disapproval even though not intended in this way. A smile may be reassuring as a welcome, but would be inappropriate as a response to feelings of sadness. It is worth remembering that fear, helplessness or sometimes anger may lurk behind a smile that is 'stuck', both in yourself and in your client.

Attitudinal distractions

In Table 3.1 (p. 23) we summed up the basic attitudes of counselling as the attitudes of real acceptance, empathic understanding and genuineness. People are more likely to reveal themselves to counsellors who demonstrate these attitudes and are perceived as trustworthy. As humans, we seem to be more comfortable with and ready to trust people who we think are like ourselves. People are less likely to trust those in whom they detect prejudices.

It is important for counsellors to find out as much as they can about their own prejudices and reactions to those who are different from themselves. Exercise 10.1 (on the opposite page) offers you a chance to find out more about your reactions and attitudes to people whom you perceive as either similar or different to yourself.

Exercise 10.1 Listening to your own reactions and distractions

Imagine you are entering a counselling relationship with each of these nine people and try to conjure up a picture of each person in your mind's eye. Think through your feelings and reactions to each one. *Do not analyse the situation* **but focus on your own feelings and think about them. Then try to rate each situation according to the difficulty you might have in really listening to that person. Rate them according to the following scale:**

0 = No problem in listening
1 = Slight problem in listening
2 = Considerable problem in listening

Sketches   *Rating*

1   Jean (60) is a grandmother who was recently knocked down by a drunken driver. Her daughter Mary and family live 40 miles away, and her son Frank is out of touch after a difficult divorce. Jean was quite badly injured but insists she cannot stay in hospital and seems fearful of all hospital routine.

2   George (55) is a successful businessman whose wife died six months ago. He implies that he was a bit of a 'woman-iser' and goes on to tell you that he had a mistress until six weeks after his wife's death. He broke off the relationship out of guilt about his mistress's perceived contribution to his wife's death. He is now lonely and remorseful.

3   Josie (27) is a beautiful young woman whose common-law husband, Dean, the father of two of her four children, recently disappeared without trace. She constantly com-plains about him and about living in a situation where she feels her rights are frequently undermined. She is angry and resentful.

4   Joe's mother, Katherine, died 18 months ago from cancer. He was an only child and his father, Joseph, left when Joe was two. Joe is now 22, single, unemployed and says he can't see any reason to work; the state owes him money after all his troubles. He seems listless and lifeless.

5   Oliver (24) has just been told that he has an incurable form of leukaemia and is dying. He has just graduated in phil-osophy and was hoping to train as a social worker. He is engaged to Angie (also 24), who has just graduated in French. He seems numb.

6   Fatima (19) has just been told of her father's decision that she should marry Ismail. She tells you that she loves

Rahindra but that she cannot marry him for he belongs to the wrong religious group. Her father's will must be respected, she says, without rancour. Her sadness seems to fill the room.

7   Alice (44) is the mother of Brendan (22), who died six weeks ago from Aids, contracted as a result of using infected needles to inject heroin. Her husband Fred had expelled him from their home three years ago when he had learned of the addiction. Fred cannot cope with Alice's grief. Alice seems on the verge of hysteria.

8   Clive (52) is an 'upright' bachelor who recently retired from the armed forces. His dog, Matilda, who was his only companion, had become lame and was run over and killed by a bus when running out of Jubilee Park next to his house. He keeps talking angrily about how awful the weather is.

9   Lizzie (37), now divorced, married Frank just before the birth of their first child. They were both 18 when they married. Frank is a workaholic and Lizzie looks after him and their two children. She's been depressed off and on for most of their marriage but now is feeling so low that suicide seems the only option.

Having rated each person for ease of listening, write down your immediate attitudes to each person in this exercise and, for those rated 1 and 2, think of the reasons why you would be distracted from listening accurately to that person. What assumptions might you be making about the kinds of people you think you know least?

Are there any other characteristics you can think of that might distract you from active listening?

What assumptions have you made about the ethnic origins of the people described here? In what ways might a person's ethnic origin and/or colour of skin influence your listening?

You might also try to 'get inside the skin' of the people described here and see how closely you can identify with them. See if you can get inside them enough to experience what they might be feeling. These feelings might be different from the feelings you identified in your own reactions to the individuals.

Wherever possible, discuss your answers with a colleague or fellow counsellor.

Having done Exercise 10.1, it is worth thinking about what you discovered about yourself and what steps you might take to enlarge your experience of human beings who are different from you. You may then be able to identify things that distract you from maintaining the counselling attitudes. If you discover attitudinal distractions in yourself it is worth thinking about your particular prejudices. Discussing these with a non-judgemental friend may help you understand which attitudes can be changed. If some seem unchangeable you may want to think about what this might mean for you, and also about how to refer such a client to someone less prejudiced in that area.

Distractions in your feelings

This distraction is somewhat different from the other three. Distracting noises, behaviour and attitudes interfere with our capacity to listen, and it is important to find ways to lessen them. Distraction caused by our feelings usually has two components. One of these can, like the other distractions, interfere with the counselling relationship, while the other can be a useful source of understanding.

The first component of a feeling distraction relates to feelings in us about our past life and losses, and it is in this area that loss counselling can be especially challenging. When you really listen to a grieving person it may stir up painful feelings from your past or current losses. These feelings may also evoke fear about things that could or might happen in the future to you or those you love. Listening to bereaved people, for instance, may heighten your awareness of your own mortality. It is for these reasons that it is important that you come to terms with your own fears and feelings about the losses in your own life and about your attitudes to death, so that these feelings do not interfere with your listening. Understanding your own losses will also help you to determine your limitations in terms of whom you can help at any particular time. In Exercise 10.2 (oppposite page), the feeling distraction in Penny is related to her own personal feelings about her husband, Christian.

The other component of the feeling distraction may be a feeling experienced in the counsellor, but not actually originating in the counsellor. This feeling from the client is neither experienced nor recognised by her. The client unconsciously 'projects' this feeling into the counsellor and is unable to feel it herself. When the counsellor recognises that this feeling does not belong to her, she can use the experience as a useful message in understanding the counselling relationship. This process is discussed further in Chapters 12, 15 and 16. Actually letting yourself experience the various feelings and thinking about the two different components is a very important part of counselling training and counselling supervision.

Skill of reflecting experience and feelings

When we are able to listen openly to another person and to enter their world without judgement and with acute sensitivity to their experiences and feelings, then we could be said to be offering empathic listening (Table 3.1, p. 23). Another way of expressing empathy can be found in reflecting the client's words. Reflecting happens at many levels. At its most basic it means restating in your own words the literal meaning, as you understand it, of what your client has just said. At the beginning, this idea of reflection may seem highly artificial. It may also seem very difficult when faced with choices about how to understand all the messages coming from your client, as well as choices about how to formulate your response. As with the bicycle, in the early stages you are acutely aware of these choices, but as you practise, the conscious choices recede from awareness and are made on a less conscious level. This seems to allow balanced and more natural or spontaneous responses to develop.

Exercise 10.2   Interfering feelings

Penny (49) is a counsellor at a voluntary counselling agency associated with her local church. Her children have recently left home and her husband, Christian (50), has recently fallen in love with a much younger colleague of his, Jennifer (29). He is full of soul searching, pain and guilt in the process of trying to decide whether to leave Penny to live with Jennifer. He says that their marriage is 'dead' and Penny knows that there is some truth in this, but she desperately wants to renew their marriage vows and be given another chance. She is trying to keep this painful situation secret and separate from her work

One day Jackie (27) comes for counselling. She tells Penny that she had been totally absorbed in her research work till about six months ago, when she had fallen passionately in love with Cameron, a much older married colleague. He says he wants to marry her. She loves him deeply and feels sure that at last she has met someone who is right for her, but feels deeply guilty about his leaving his wife. She asks Penny what she should do . . .

As you can imagine, Jackie's situation will touch Penny in a variety of ways. Take a few minutes to reflect on:

(a) **the range of feelings you might expect Penny to experience, and**
(b) **the ways in which Penny might find it difficult to think about Jackie's world and therefore be present and available for her.**

A good reflection does not mean just the mechanical repetition of the words you have heard. It means finding your own words to reflect back to the person the sense of what they have said, at the level of both the content and the feelings expressed. If you also use an intonation that is tentative, this allows the client to disagree or put you right or, indeed, put themselves right as they begin to understand themselves more clearly. In Exercise 10.3 we give you an opportunity to practise accurate reflection.

Exercise 10.3 Accurate reflection

Restate in different words, and in clear and simple language, the literal meaning of the client's statements.

Try them out loud, paying attention to voice quality (gentleness, tentative style, etc.) as well as to intonation (the rise and fall of the voice).

Example

Susan: My husband was a fine man. His sudden death was a great shock. I still miss him terribly.

One of many possible responses from the counsellor might be:

Counsellor: Your husband's unexpected death really shook you to the core. You still miss him terribly.

Reflect in your own words the sense of the client's message.

1 Joe: I thought I was prepared for my mother's death but ever since she passed away I've been thinking that life is not worth living.

Counsellor:

2 Robin: Ever since my parents' divorce I've been feeling angry and resentful but at last I'm beginning to see that not having them together is not necessarily the end of my life, I suppose.

Counsellor:

3 Lizzie: I'm feeling so depressed. Just getting through the day is an enormous effort. I don't think I'll ever get on top of things now that Frank's gone.

Counsellor:

4 Josie: Since Dean disappeared my mother says 'do this', my father says 'do that', and my sister says 'do something else'. Now I'm feeling totally confused.

Counsellor:

In the examples in Exercise 10.3, the clients have all been able to express fairly clearly what they were feeling using the feeling words themselves. People are not always so articulate, lucid or helpful, and it is sometimes up to the counsellor to find the 'feeling-word' that expresses the sense of what is being communicated. Having one's feelings understood, accepted and tentatively put into words can be a very affirming experience. This non-judgemental attitude to feelings can be expressed:

(a) by voicing the feeling-word in a warm tone and with rising intonation
(b) by linking the feeling-word with the situation that appears to have given rise to the feelings. This gives a 'sense' and rightness to the feelings in their context.

In order to feel at home in the language of feelings, you need a wide range of feeling-words at your disposal. For a preliminary list of such words, see Table 10.3.

Table 10.3 Feeling-words

Angry	Fearful	Excited	Frantic	Lonely
Sad	Frustrated	Loving	Helpless	Happy
Furious	Warm	Desperate	Accused	Listless
Anxious	Tense	Hating	Numb	Injured
Frightened	Terrified	Cold	Tentative	Battered
Resentful	Annoyed	Icy	Hurt	Pierced
Hopeless	Relieved	Despairing	Guilty	Valued

You can add to this list from your own experiences of counselling, television, sport, music, theatre, books, films and of life itself. Exercise 10.4 gives you the opportunity to find the feeling-words hidden in the statements.

Exercise 10.4 Reflecting feelings

(a) **See if you can guess the feeling-word that the statement might be trying to express. Reflect it back out loud with a warm tone and rising intonation just to experience this for yourself. It may help to make a tape-recording of yourself.**
(b) **See if you can link the feeling to what you have heard in a way that 'makes sense' for the client.**

Example
William: I said some awful things to Thomas the day before his accident. I can't get them out of my mind.

Counsellor:	(a) . . . guilt? or . . . remorse? (b) It sounds as though you've been feeling guilty about the things you said to Thomas and you can't get them out of your mind.
1 Alice:	What could I have done to deserve having my son die?
Counsellor:	
2 Joe:	I can't go on like this . . . I've been thinking of chucking it all in.
Counsellor:	
3 George:	The doctor who operated on my wife was an incompetent fool.
Counsellor:	
4 Oliver:	Everything is in a muddle. I can't seem to make any decisions.
Counsellor:	
5 Christopher:	Just how do you think you can help me? Do you know what it feels like to have your lover die? Can you give him back to me?
Counsellor:	
6 Jean:	What could have pushed Lizzie that far? Was it a cry for help or did she really *mean* to die? Why did she do it? What can I say to her?

Counsellor:

7 Fatima: I love Rahindra deeply but he is not one of us. A girl must obey her father. I expect I will manage.

Counsellor:

Listening and sensing the feelings behind the words is sometimes called 'listening for the music behind the words'. Of course, dry words on a printed page give you very little sense of the music behind them because we pick up the 'song' not only through words but through intonation, voice quality, gestures, facial expression, posture, dress and other features.

We cannot create the 'music' in this book, but we can try to listen for the music behind the words with real people. Take time to pick up the signals and sense the feeling state of those around you from time to time. You can always check it out with them!

Skill of reflecting using different levels of empathy

As well as the music behind the words, there is often a different tune we begin to hear or sense. Sometimes this tune may seem to be at odds, or out of harmony, with the main music. There may be, for instance, angry feelings lurking under the sadness, or a discrepancy between gesture and word, or even a discrepancy between the meaning of the words and the way in which they are expressed. When we notice this, we are sensing a different tune behind the main theme.

This sensing of the different tune of which the speaker may be only very dimly aware is sometimes called 'empathy at the edge of awareness' (Mearns and Thorne, 1999). In grief, the feelings at the edge of awareness may be those that are the most frightening or most painful to experience. Sensing these feelings and allowing their expression is very helpful to the grief process. It is wise, however, to approach them with gentleness and care, as they are the feelings that have 'needed' to be hidden and of which the griever may be afraid.

We shall call this kind of reflecting, 'reflecting with deeper empathy'. In our next example we give possible responses, at four so-called different levels of empathy. Again these responses can seem artificial out of context, and they can only begin to indicate what is meant by deeper levels of empathy in the whole context of a counselling relationship. There is a real danger that these minimal context examples give an impression of ease and simplicity to a set of responses, which in practice are much more complex.

They can, for example, give no indication of the importance of pacing in the flow between counsellor and griever. Nor can they demonstrate the inestimable value of receptive silence, which forms such an intrinsic part of the empathic response. For all their shortcomings, however, these examples offer a way of starting to look at the complex response we have called deeper empathy.

Example of empathy levels

Susan: He left so suddenly, leaving me with the children, the bills and the house half painted. Why did he leave me all on my own? . . . Well, I suppose I'll manage . . . (grits teeth) . . . I will cope then. I'll have to. I'm strong enough.

Counsellor's response

Empathy 0:   It's God's will and there's no explaining it!

Empathy 1:   What a shock for you!

Empathy 2:   You must be feeling really abandoned through his sudden absence, and I expect you're angry because you're having to deal with so much on your own.

Empathy 3:   You must be feeling really abandoned through his sudden absence, and I expect you're angry because you're having to deal with so much on your own . . . but I see you're gritting your teeth as though perhaps you were frightened of something else?

In this example, the empathy level 0 response shows no empathy at all and we could understand this response as meaning something like, 'I think I hear pain and I don't want to feel pain so let's change the subject', or 'I think I hear anger or even envy and I don't want to know about them either'. Whatever it does mean for the counsellor, there is no sense of understanding the client's perceptual world.

The empathy level 1 response indicates some understanding of the sense of shock that is being experienced, but it could be expressing the counsellor's shock, with the 'for you' just tagged on at the end. The tone of voice would make a big difference to the way these words were understood.

The empathy level 2 response shows a recognition of the possible feelings of abandonment and of anger, and links them with the experience. It is a good empathic response and the most basic counsellor response.

The level 3 response adds to the level 2 response the sense, presumably picked up from the client, that she might also be frightened by what had happened, and this extra level of understanding may enable her to recognise and face her further fears about, for instance, surviving on her own.

In Exercise 10.5 (p. 113) you can assess the different levels of empathy shown by the counsellor.

Exercise 10.5 Levels of empathy exercise

Rank the jumbled empathic responses into their most appropriate levels.

Square brackets [ ] denote aspects of voice quality such as tone, intensity, feeling etc.

Joe: I thought I was prepared for my mother's death, but ever since she passed away I've been feeling down and thinking that [getting louder] life's not worth living.

Responses   *Rank*
(a) You'd thought you were ready for her death but since then you've been feeling really low and wondering if you want to go on living . . . But I wonder . . . whether you're per-haps a bit angry that things haven't gone the way you expected, the way you were prepared for . . .?
(b) It was a shock all the same.
(c) You thought you were ready for her death but since it actually happened you've been feeling low and not sure if life is worth living.
(d) Death comes to us all, doesn't it?

(Key: a = 3, b = 1, c = 2, d = 0)

Robin: Ever since my parents' divorce I've been angry and resentful. Why should I have to suffer just because they can't manage to get along with one another and quarrel all the time? But I suppose I'm beginning to see that their being apart is not necessarily the end . . . [rising intonation].

Responses   *Rank*
(a) You have to get on with your life.
(b) Since they divorced you've felt angry and resentful about their inability to get on with one another. Now you're thinking that their being apart may not be the end for you.
(c) It must be very difficult for you now.
(d) Since they divorced you've felt angry and resentful about their inability to get on with one another. Now you're thinking that their being apart may not be the end . . . and

perhaps . . . there's a ray of hope that things may eventually start to feel easier now that they're apart and not quarrelling all the time?

(Key: a = 0, b = 2, c = 1, d = 3)

Josie: Since Dean left me my mother says 'do this', my father says 'do that' and my sister says 'do something else'! Now I'm feeling totally confused.

Responses   *Rank*
(a) Since he jilted you, everyone's been saying something different and now you're feeling totally confused.
(b) He wasn't much use anyway.
(c) That's upsetting for you.
(d) Since he finished with you, your mother's been saying 'do this', your father says 'do that' and your sister says 'do something else' again. Now you're feeling totally confused . . . and, well, you look so sad. I wonder if there are some really sad, painful feelings behind all the confusion?

(Key: a = 2, b = 0, c = 1, d = 3)

Angie: I feel so angry that Oliver should have got leukaemia. What a waste of a life! And he is going to die – why do they have to keep giving him more and more treatment at the hospital? I wouldn't stand for it – why couldn't it be me who got leukaemia?

Responses   *Rank*
(a) You're feeling really angry that Oliver should have become so ill.
(b) Life's not fair, is it?
(c) It sounds as though you're angry that Oliver is ill, and angry with the doctors who seem not to accept that Oliver is dying. You wish that he could be left in peace.
(d) You are angry that Oliver is ill and can't understand why it's him . . . I wonder if you think it should have been you and . . . perhaps you feel guilty . . . even helpless that it isn't you who has got leukaemia.

(Key: a = 1, b = 0, c = 2, d = 3)

Empathic listening is the bread-and-butter work of loss counselling and is likely to facilitate the main grief work of a session. When these skills are 'practised' separately like this, 'in a box', they can feel quite artificial. However, with practice they gradually become more real and genuine and begin to integrate themselves into the way you would normally speak. It is important to find your own natural way of integrating the skills so that they feel more 'normal' for you. They will then also feel more normal and real for your client. In the next chapters we shall consider the tasks of mourning and related skills.

Summary

- The counselling attitudes can enable grievers to be less frightened and less condemning of the feelings they experience as part of grief.
- Counselling skills, learned separately, are later integrated more naturally into practice in a way that is responsive to the grieving person.
- Reflective listening can enable grievers to find their own words to tell the story of their relationship with the dead or lost person, to share the memories, good and bad, and to express their feelings of loss. It is easy to be distracted from this reflective listening, particularly in the area of feelings arising in the listener.
- Reflecting the client's experience and feeling in words of your own can be very affirming. It can help clients to accept the validity of their own feelings.
- More deeply empathic responses pick up feelings at the edge of awareness. The griever may have 'needed' to keep certain feelings out of full awareness; their recognition and reflection will require care and consideration.

Chapter 11

Tasks of mourning: meaning and internalisation

In the previous chapter we described ways of developing the empathic and responding skills for bereavement counselling. We saw how deeper levels of empathy can enable feelings at the edge of awareness to become more conscious and hence more available for thought and processing.

In this chapter we shall look at the ways in which counselling can help grievers actually to recognise the loss that has occurred and to undertake the tasks of mourning. They will then be in a position to integrate both the event of the loss and the reconstruction of its various meanings into the narrative of their lives. Any new relationship is then forged within the context of the recognised loss of the earlier relationship, whether it be the death of a child or a marriage partner, or the loss of a partner through a separation or divorce.

J. William Worden, in his book *Grief Counselling and Grief Therapy*, picked up and applied Freud's theories on 'grief work' and 'detachment' (Worden, 1983, 1991). Drawing also on the work of Bowlby (1979, 1980), he developed the concept of grief as an active process in which various intellectual, psychological, moral and even spiritual tasks needed to be completed. He outlined these very practically in what he called the 'four tasks of mourning'. For him, mourning, the adaptation to loss, is a process that needs to be completed. If this is not done at the time, then the 'incomplete grief tasks can impair further growth and development' (Worden, 1983).

Between the first edition of Worden's book in 1983 and the second edition in 1991, Freud's idea of a 'detachment' was challenged by a number of researchers who observed that, rather than 'detaching', successful grievers seemed to 'internalise' the memory of the lost person and make them a part of their continuing internal world as well as having tangible representations in the external world. Living in the presence of a consciously remembered continuing bond seems to have been a source of strength for most people rather than a burden.

This idea of continuing bonds was incorporated by Worden into the 1991 edition of his book, and resulted in some major changes to the titles of his 'tasks' between the first and second editions. Thus, his description of the third task originally was 'to adjust to the environment in which the deceased is missing'; in the revision it became 'to adapt to a world in which the deceased is missing'. And the fourth task, 'to withdraw emotional energy and reinvest it in another relationship', became 'to emotionally relocate the deceased and move on with life'.

The tasks

The tasks as described by Worden (1991) are outlined in Table 11.1.

Table 11.1 Tasks of mourning

- To accept the reality of the loss
- To experience the pain of grief
- To adapt to a world in which the deceased is missing
- To emotionally relocate the deceased and move on with life

In examining these tasks in more detail, we shall begin to see how important it is to consider notions of 'meaning' when thinking about the grieving process, as well as linking it with the creation of a narrative.

To accept the reality of the loss

Worden (1983) recognised that even when a loss is expected, there is always a sense at first that it has not really happened; 'the first task of grieving is to come full face with the reality that the person is dead, and will not return'. Not accepting the loss is one aspect of the denial, which we have mentioned in a number of chapters. Denial of the facts of the loss is natural and happens when the loss is anticipated as well as after the loss. It also happens in various ways and to different degrees.

You will remember that Anne (mentioned in Chapter 4) took time to grasp that her husband James was seriously ill, even though she knew that he was more ill than she had ever known. She remembered 'clutching at straws' when she first heard the diagnosis. She heard the 'not highly malignant' as 'not malignant'. Thus, reality was distorted by her need 'not to know' yet. Similarly, Geoff carried on with artificial respiration and also allowed his friend, John, and the ambulance men to continue long after he partly knew it was hopeless. After James's death Anne heard his footsteps at his 'coming home' time. She did not want to believe he was dead.

Where the death is sudden, and particularly if it is in a faraway place, taking the reality on board will be even harder and the distortion slightly greater. In both these cases counselling can help by reminding the client that the dead person 'will not be coming home alive', as well as recognising how difficult it is to take this truth on board. Counsellors can encourage clients to remember the events leading up to the loss; when and where they heard about the loss; what they were doing at the time; who told them; what happened then; who they spoke to at that point; and so on. Anything that triggers the memory of the feared moment of loss can usually help people back into the recognition that the loss has actually taken place, even if this reality can only be taken in one bit at a time.

Where there is an enduring total distortion of reality and the loss simply cannot be accepted, then a more intensive form of therapy may be called for and the client may need to be referred to someone more specialised.

To experience the pain of grief

Worden acknowledges that frequently there is literal physical pain as well as the emotional and behavioural pain associated with loss. All these levels of pain must be experienced in order to work through the grief. When a person continually avoids the pain of grief, then mourning is generally prolonged. However, the 'subtle interplay between society and the mourner' (Worden, 1983) often results in just such a suppression or avoidance of pain, thus rendering the completion of Task 2 more difficult. We have seen in Chapters 6 and 7 how societies help or hinder this task in different ways at different times. While this may be beginning to change in the West generally, there is still an enormous amount of societal denial of the pain of loss in early twenty-first-century Britain. If we add to that the lack of close family networks nowadays, we can see how people are often left to face their pain alone, thus enhancing the urge to deny and not face the necessary pain. We described how these external factors are known to affect grieving in Chapter 5.

The empathic approach of counselling will recognise the isolation of many mourners – whether caused by death, estrangement or termination of a relationship – and will understand the urge to deny and avoid, but will nevertheless keep returning to the pain whenever the mourner is able to do this. Talking about the lost person in a detailed and wide-ranging way is an important part of the process. After the recognition that the loss had taken place, the counsellor would encourage an exploration of the whole history of the lost relationship, remembering the small details and idiosyncrasies of the dead person. Exploring the pain of grief means recognising the whole range of feelings – sadness, regret, bitterness, anger and lost hopes never to be achieved – as well as recognising the love and connections that have now been broken and lost. The increasing awareness of the inner reality results in a reorganisation of past experiences and enables the future to be faced with all its new losses and new possibilities. This remembering will need to be done many times, some of which will involve repeating the story, but each time new thoughts and feelings will arise as well.

This method of going through the story again and again creates a narrative that begins to make sense and finally succeeds in making meaning, albeit painful meaning, out of what has been unbearable, chaotic and meaningless.

Experiencing and thinking about the pain of grief enables understanding to emerge and helps the mourner to come to see themselves as someone facing the challenges that life brings rather than being a victim of life's vicissitudes.

To adapt to a world in which the deceased is missing

Worden's use of the word 'adapt' rather than 'adjust' in the later edition may be indicative of a general change in thinking, in which the idea of letting go was moderated to take account of the process of internalisation and the recognised continuing bonds. Closely associated with this is the importance now given to meaning and narrative in the grief process. Worden, drawing again on the research done by Parkes (1972) with widows, outlines the task of adapting to the new situation. For example, he mentions the time it can take for widows to realise what it is like to live without their husbands. He also emphasises that multiple losses are associated with any one loss, which have to be recognised and adapted to. You will remember from Chapter 4 how the loss of a partner signified a number of additional and quite different losses for Anne and Geoff (see Table 4.1, p. 39). The process of adaptation is highly individual, relating to each individual's own special circumstances and to the particular meanings of that loss for that person. Counselling can be helpful in relation to this task in the many ways already outlined in this book, and includes a recognition of the slow and painful steps towards what at first looks like a very 'empty' world without the lost person. The task of adapting to a new world with different challenges and possibilities takes time, and may need to be revisited as new events touch the loss again.

To emotionally relocate the deceased and move on with life

As this title clearly suggests, this task is to recognise the emotions related to the lost person, and to locate them as part of the past narrative of one's life. This is in contrast to Freud's first ideas about mourning. In 'Mourning and Melancholia' (Freud, 1917) he stated that 'Mourning has a quite precise psychical task to perform: its function is to detach the survivor's memories and hopes from the dead'. This seems to imply that one should eventually lose one's attachments to the loved ones who have died. Later in his life he discovered that he was unable to cut off old attachments, detach and reinvest in new ones. He never got over the death of his daughter Sophie or of her four-year-old son, whom he considered to be 'the most intelligent child he had ever encountered' (Jones, 1962). Writing to Marie Bonaparte after this grandson died, he said that he 'had never been able to get fond of anyone since that misfortune' (Jones, 1962). Thus when in 1923 Freud wrote a letter of condolence to Binswanger on the death of his eldest son, he recognised that, 'Although we know that after such a loss the acute state of mourning will subside, we also know we shall remain inconsolable and will never find a substitute. No matter what may fill the gap, even if it be filled completely, it nevertheless remains something else.' Freud not only could not detach, but in his deep pain he seems to have been unable to make a meaningful adaptation to the loss of his loved ones so that he could not integrate these events into the narrative of his own life.

Not just Freud's life, but all our lives have narratives, as we saw from reflecting on our lifelines in Chapter 9. The events of our histories cannot be rewritten; loss is always loss, and grief does not have a 'final ending'; it simply becomes part of the story of our lives. But in order to get on with life, there needs to be this 'emotional relocation' of the lost person into an inner representation or image in the mind.

What now needs to be added to such a theory of grief is a greater understanding of the nature and extent of the changes that occur in the relationship between the living individual and the dead or absent person, who is represented only, or largely, through images in the mind. These images or inner representations are not rigid but open to change and modification. In Chapter 3 we suggest that counselling attitudes will foster trust and self-acceptance. This may well change the way the person listens to and thinks about themselves and their inner representations.

Many models of counselling suggest just this, and that a counsellor who is accepting, empathic to the experiences of others and genuine in her responses will enable the client to 'internalise' such attitudes so that they can be used towards the self. This idea of an inner representation, amenable to change, could also be applied to the inner representation of the deceased within the mourner's psyche. What often happens in counselling is just that; as the client becomes more accepting of themselves, their attitude towards the deceased begins to change, often becoming more flexible, and the 'emotional relocation can proceed'. Processes of adaptation and narrative creation are an important aspect of the development of the continuing bonds that are so important for the progress of grief.

The development of continuing bonds

The process of adaptation

'Adaptation' here refers to the complex and often painful psychological processes that move a person gradually towards a meaningful inner representation of the lost person; a representation that is not carved in stone, but changes with time and further experiences. This idea allows for the possibility that people can actively respond to life's challenges, can experience their own personal response to loss and can react in a variety of meaningful and passionate ways to loss. They will, of course, be marked for life by one or more losses which, when things go well, will become an integral part of the story of their lives.

Narrative creation

We all love stories: not just stories in books, but on TV or in the theatre. We share stories with one another all the time. People share stories of their day with their families, and some share stories of their families with their work colleagues next day. Those who live alone become very dependent on the telephone or email system in order to share stories with friends or family. We seek an audience for the stories of our lives through our social networks. These stories may often appear quite mundane and repetitive, but when the stories become gripping, as in the case of loss, then we most certainly need an audience. We try to make sense of random events by turning them into a story, and we sketch ourselves into existence through the stories we tell about ourselves and others.

Our narrative competence (see Chapter 2) helps to give us a sense of ourselves and our history, as well as binding us into a social network. Loss disrupts these narratives in various ways. In the case of trauma, for instance, the disorganised disruption to the narrative destroys our biological sense of continuity and dislodges us from the sense of who we are. We then struggle desperately to integrate this new and unwanted experience into the continuity of our lives. Sometimes the narrative of a person's life may become stuck and constricted so that the 'script' cannot be changed as new events occur, thus leading to increased depression and fatalism.

The development and maintenance of continuing bonds

If the various disruptions and constrictions can be managed so that a way can be found to continue the narrative, then the relationship with the lost person will be able to continue, although of course in a different form to when they were around or alive. When things go well, the bereaved maintain bonds with the deceased and thus remain involved and connected to the deceased and actively construct an inner representation of them. This is part of a normal grieving process. Death ends a life, but it does not end a relationship. The continuing relationship, which appears to be largely conscious, has an inner interactive part as well as a social aspect, which includes talking about the deceased person. There is also an inner and largely unconscious process whereby features of the dead person are gradually integrated into the bereaved person's inner world as if they were their own. This is described as 'internalisation'. Sometimes there is a more tangible aspect in which such things as photographs, mementoes, conversations, amusing episodes, and shared memories of events (e.g. birthdays) all become part of a shared history. Once the shared history can be made conscious, and usually shared with someone else, it in turn contributes to the inner representation of the lost person.

When the tasks of mourning and the internalisation of the lost person get stuck, then skilled counselling can enable people to face feelings and understand their grieving in a way that facilitates a return to the mourning process. In the next chapter we shall consider these skills in more detail.

Summary

- The process of grief entails four basic 'tasks of mourning'.
- The internalisation of the lost person requires an adaptation to life without them.
- The adaptation requires energy, courage and time as the person gradually incorporates the loss into the narrative of their life.
- These processes of internalisation and adaptation strengthen the sense of a 'continuing bond' which becomes part of the narrative of that person's life and can function as an inner resource of comfort and self-esteem.

Chapter 12

Further skills related to the tasks of mourning and ending counselling

In the previous chapter we saw how important it is to be able to accept the reality of the loss and to experience the associated feelings. These feelings are often extremely painful and may be very frightening. If counsellors are going to be able to help people with these tasks and the associated feelings, they need to be able to provide the kind of listening that is reasonably free of fear and offers some genuine safety.

Earlier we saw how non-judgemental attitudes of acceptance and empathic responding can offer an environment of relative safety where the often frightening feelings associated with loss can be understood, validated and contained. 'Contained' here means two things. First and foremost, it means that the feelings find a place or container in which they can be safely held. Counsellors can do this only if they are able to create a boundaried space in which to listen and not be shocked or disturbed by what they hear. A second meaning of containment here is that misconceptions and fears, through lack of knowledge or information about the mourning process, are clarified and explained. Without clarification these misconceptions can cause the kind of fear that blocks the grieving process. First we shall consider the 'container' as a safe place, which includes the management of the beginning and ending of sessions and the specialist use of time in time-limited counselling.

Setting limits or boundaries

Containers, like counselling sessions, need limits or boundaries. The enclosed space of the counselling session, safe from intruders either in person or on the telephone, constitutes one aspect of the 'container'. The stretch of time between the beginning and end of the session is a further aspect of the container. Time, and meanings associated with time, are often particularly significant for those who have suffered a loss. Time-past was the time which contained that which was valued and then lost, time-now (in the session) is the time in which the feelings about that loss are allowed to emerge, and time-future has to be faced without that which was lost.

When a person has suffered a loss they also suffer a distortion in their perception of time and space. This distortion varies in intensity from being merely unnerving for some people to chaotic and frightening for others. Setting clear time limits or boundaries can contribute greatly to a feeling of safety and predictability, even though it can feel a little odd or even 'heartless' to an inexperienced counsellor. Of course boundaries need to be negotiable in certain circumstances and flexible in others, but they need to be clear and to be openly talked about. This is not in order to exercise power over the other person, but in order to create a framework within which power can be shared and safety enhanced. The safety and predictability create clear time and space within which strong feelings can be shared and contained.

Beginnings: sessions and relationships

Sometimes the first encounter with the bereaved is the beginning of the loss counselling relationship, at other times the work of grief emerges into an already established professional relationship like nursing or acting as a solicitor. The pain of grief may also erupt at the beginning of a meeting within an established counselling relationship.

First session of a new counselling relationship

The beginning of the first session is, of course, nearly always the beginning of the counselling relationship and the openings of further sessions take place within the context of this relationship which has already begun.

Harry has arranged to see you for the first time at 11 a.m. Each new client brings an entirely new world into your work. You may or may not have information about Harry, but in one sense you know nothing about his world nor about his expectations of you. So you do not even know what questions it might be appropriate to ask. Even 'How can I help you?' implies that 'help' (whatever that means to Harry or to you) is what he's expecting, and implies also that 'I' might be able to supply that from a position of power or 'superior' knowledge. Counselling may indeed be a very helpful way-of-being with someone in distress and grappling with strong feelings, but offering 'help' only exacerbates the already unequal power relationship in counselling, and might imply that you were going to do the work.

At this point we do not know anything about Harry. We have no idea where Harry is in the mourning process, and we don't even know whether he has been able to take his loss on board, that is, whether he is yet engaged on Task 1. But what we do know is that if we are prepared to be there with him, uninterruptedly, for a certain time period, he may than feel safe enough to take the opportunity to get started. Let us say, for instance, that you are able to give him half an hour. We are also assuming, for the moment, that he wants to be with you for that amount of time. You will, of course, find your own personal way of opening your first sessions, but here are some possible opening phrases.

Possible openings

- Hello Harry. We have 30 minutes together . . .
- Hello Harry. We have 30 minutes together . . . I wonder what has brought you here?
- Hello Harry. We have 30 minutes together . . . Where would you like to start?
- Hello Harry. You are free to start when you are ready . . . we have about 30 minutes together.

In the first example, simply setting the time boundary in a warm and confident manner, with its implication of a predictable space and time, may be enough in itself to allow Harry to get started where he wishes. If he wants or needs more encouragement, then any of the other examples would probably help him get started and also recognise and put into words the fact that the time is for him. It also indicates that you are not in the business of trying to control him; your limit, as opposed to control, is the time boundary. Getting straight down to business and avoiding social chat about the weather or his journey indicates to Harry your recognition of the seriousness of what he is bringing.

This first session opening can set a pattern for future session openings. As Harry gets used to the amount of time he has with you, whether ten or 50 minutes, it may be enough simply to say 'Hello Harry, where would you like to start today?' and, as trust grows, you may find that 'Hello Harry? . . . [with rising intonation]' is all that is necessary. It may be especially useful for him to have a consistent amount of time with you on each occasion if this is manageable.

In the next examples of 'openings', different counsellors use their empathy and 'gut feelings' to sense what the clients are feeling in those first minutes and then try to put this into words.

Dan

Counsellor: Hello Dan, we have 30 minutes together.

Dan: [Seems to shrink down inside his coat, which he has kept on. He says nothing.]

Counsellor: [After a few moments, sensing his apprehension and struggle for words] I suppose it's not easy to begin . . . some things are really difficult to put into words.

Sharon

Counsellor: Hello Sharon, we have 30 minutes together.

Sharon: Yes, I know! [falling intonation]

Counsellor: [Sensing her discomfort and possible rebellion] I expect it feels pretty uncomfortable having to come along and see me like this, and . . . well, I don't know, but perhaps feeling you're expected to do what I want?

Andy

Counsellor:	Hello Andy, we have 30 minutes together.
Andy:	Yes [softly and obligingly with rising intonation].
Counsellor:	[After a few moments, sensing his shyness and apparent expectations of something] I guess it feels pretty odd coming to talk to a strange person like me and not knowing what to expect – mmm?

In all these examples of beginning a session, the counsellor tries to convey to the client the wish to take part in an exploratory process with the client and to try to understand more of the client's world without imposing her own will. She also does not know where in the grief process the client might be, and which tasks may or may not be started yet.

The grief emerges into an already established professional relationship

Sometimes feelings of loss emerge within the context of a more or less established other professional relationship such as nursing, care working, medical practice or legal work. In whatever way the loss material is signalled, it is worth establishing and contracting the time boundary to ensure containment of the client. This is illustrated in the next example.

> Sonia is a worker in a children's home. Mrs Murphy, who visits her son Seamus in the home on a regular basis, has always been punctual, competent and cheerful, if anything perhaps too cheerful. Sonia noticed that recently Mrs Murphy has been forgetting her son's special food. When Mrs Murphy started to tell Sonia about the accident that led to Seamus's disability, Sonia could sense that Mrs Murphy was beginning to be ready to tell her of her grief and face her feelings. She suggested warmly and firmly that they should go to a nearby office for half an hour. Having arranged for someone else to cover for her, Sonia knew that she would not be interrupted and would be able to give Mrs Murphy her undivided attention for the half hour she knew she had created. This 'safe container' helped Mrs Murphy to get on with what she needed to share. Mrs Murphy, in facing the feelings of pain and rage about the accident, was beginning the work of Task 2.

The grief erupts into the start of a session in established counselling

For some people the start of Task 2 may come quite suddenly and the accompanying feelings are so strong that they are expressed almost before the session has started. Let us consider the start of a counselling session with

Angie (Exercise 10.5, p. 113) who, you will remember, is engaged to be married to Oliver (Exercises 10.1, p. 103 and 10.4, p. 109). Oliver is dying of an incurable form of leukaemia. He is still in hospital but is being allowed home to die. This session opens very abruptly, with Angie's feelings so near the surface and ready for expression that she breaks in before the counsellor has finished speaking.

Example of a tricky opening

Counsellor: Hello Angie, we have 30 minutes togeth . . .

Angie: [angrily] So what use is that going to be? All the time in the world won't bring Oliver back! You can't bring him back, can you?

Counsellor: [Gently and slowly] No, you're absolutely right, I can't bring him back. What I *can* offer you is some time to look at your very frightening situation.

The counsellor's response arises out of the attitude of genuineness, which recognises his helplessness in facing the reality of Oliver's imminent death. The slow and gentle tone also recognises the sadness and untimely nature of Oliver's death. This tone will also have a calming effect on Angie, who is caught up in anger and panic. The clarity of the time boundaries means that Angie can have at least some control over how she uses the session. It also means that if she chooses to talk about and feel her fear and anger about the approaching death, it will be contained by the time limit. By choosing the word 'frightening', the counsellor brings an appropriate feeling-word to the situation. This gives Angie a sense of recognition and perhaps enables her to face her frightening feelings. Under the anger may well be helplessness and despair. This 'sense of recognition' may help Angie to begin to trust her counsellor, even at a time when trust of anyone must be difficult for her.

Endings: sessions and relationships

In writing about beginnings we could treat the beginning of the session and the relationship as one broad topic. We cannot do this so readily with endings, for a number of reasons. Usually the end of the first counselling session is not the end of the relationship. Therefore session endings will be different from relationship endings, although there will also be similarities. In addition, most of us have much stronger and more complex feelings associated with endings than with beginnings. You only have to watch farewells at railway stations or airports to see examples of this. Less obvious perhaps is that the ending of the counselling relationship, and the consequent loss of intimacy, may reflect the very loss that the person has come to grieve. This 'reflected loss' may also be present towards the end of each counselling session, and sometimes makes bereavement counselling sessions particularly difficult to end. This reflected loss is, of course, not the same as the 'original loss', and the counsellor may need to remember that the end of the session does not 'make the loss worse'. On the contrary, it may be the one ending over which the client is able to express feelings and think about them. What is important is to recognise, validate and contain such feelings re-evoked through the ending of the session.

Session endings

Let us return to our sessions with Angie. After the rather tricky beginning, Angie realised that her anger was acceptable to the counsellor after all. As her panic subsided she was able to face and experience strong, angry feelings about Oliver's death and the way his death seemed to make a mockery of her health and liveliness. She also gained more understanding about Oliver's mother's anger and her apparent resentfulness of Angie's blooming health. Gradually she was able to become involved with the plans to allow Oliver to die at home.

The end of the first session had been relatively straightforward. The counsellor had reminded Angie of the time about ten minutes before the end of the session. Angie had expressed surprise that the time had passed so quickly, and became aware of how relieved she was to have shared her angry feelings. She also felt she had laid down a burden of guilt about her anger. She seemed quite pleased to finish that session.

However, during the sixth session, when considerably more trust had developed with her counsellor, Angie started to talk about her rather perturbing feelings. She was beginning to wish that it could all be over for Oliver, yet at the same time desperately wishing that Oliver would not die and leave her. Angie was still struggling with this conflict of feelings when the counsellor pointed out, as was usual, that it was ten minutes to the end of the session. Angie did not seem to notice this and went on without stopping. The counsellor again reminded Angie of the time after a further five minutes, while recognising verbally that Angie was struggling with something very important. Angie ignored him. The counsellor, wondering briefly how he would ever end this session, reflected on this feeling of slight panic in himself. He began to realise that Angie's mixed and ambivalent feelings about the end of her relationship with Oliver were probably being experienced in the ending of this session. He thought to himself that perhaps in Angie's world out there with Oliver she had no control over the ending of the relationship; but that in here she was going to exert all the control she could muster and see how long she could put off the dreaded ending. It was difficult to stop Angie's flow and the counsellor was not sure that he had understood what Angie was experiencing, but he sensed it must be about 'endings'. An example of how he might use this idea is shown next.

Example of a difficult session ending

Counsellor: Angie, [louder] Angie! Perhaps it feels uncomfortable when I interrupt you like this but I have something important I want to say to you . . . It is difficult to finish this session at the time we have agreed. I am wondering whether some of the difficulties of ending the relationship with Oliver are making it particularly difficult to end our session today? We don't have time to pursue this now, but it might be very useful for us to look at this difficulty early on in next session. As we finish today [eye contact] I recognise that I am leaving you with a lot of very unresolved and difficult feelings . . . I will see you on *Friday* at the usual time.

It takes energy and planning to make a response that cuts in on a client who is preoccupied. The suggested response in the example focuses on a number of issues. First it recognises Angie's discomfort in being interrupted. The counsellor accepts that it is difficult to end, and recognises that this 'difficulty' has a meaning. This allows both the counsellor and Angie to consider the difficulty without either of them being burdened by it. Then the counsellor confirms the agreement about the time of the ending. This reminds Angie of the agreed and predictable nature of the sessions, thus offering her something secure, which is particularly important when she cannot predict how or when Oliver will die. Finally the counsellor highlights a possible parallel between the difficulty in ending the session and the difficult and painful ending of the relationship with Oliver.

Note that the counsellor does not extend the session any further. It is perhaps tempting to offer more time when we sense that someone is very needy. However, this has to be weighed up against the burden of disorganisation and stress for the counsellor and, even more importantly, the burden of unnecessary guilt for the griever, who may feel she 'stole' time from the counsellor. Another reason for stopping the session on time is that the counsellor suspects that Angie may want to take control of the session just as she wants to control Oliver's dying. Letting Angie wrest the control of the ending might lead her to imagine that she can actually control Oliver's dying. Allowing her to take control would not be useful to her, but it might well be useful to explore her desire to control the ending in words during the following session. From this exploration Angie will discover that endings cannot necessarily be controlled, but the feelings about the endings can be worked on before the ending of the relationship takes place.

During the following sessions Angie did recognise her mixed feelings. She began to face the meaning of Oliver's death and the fact that she would have many months of grief ahead of her. She then became able to think about how she might say 'goodbye' to Oliver. This included thinking about and planning what she wanted to do and say to Oliver while he was still alive.

Ending the relationship

Clients usually raise the question of ending the relationship with a counsellor when they feel ready for it. Raising this question may, as already mentioned, remind them of loss in general and, in particular, may reflect the very loss they are trying to grieve. This recognition often seems to set them back as they go through a separate process of grief for the loss of the counsellor. However, this very grieving for the counsellor can be enormously healing, and in working through this loss together the 'old wound' will also be grieved.

This was indeed what happened with Angie. After Oliver had died and many months of grief had passed, Angie began to think of doing things for herself again and to meet new people. But just as life seemed to be going much better for Angie, and the counsellor was wondering about raising the question of the ending of the counselling relationship, so the sessions again began to get more difficult to end. This time Angie herself noticed the difficulty and then remembered a dream she had had of seeing the counsellor off on a large ship and waving white handkerchiefs. On waking she had felt terribly sad. She herself made the connection between the dream and the session. Inside herself she felt ready to end the relationship with the counsellor, but the sadness of ending reminded her of her grief and longing for Oliver and left her feeling almost overwhelmed.

The counsellor recognised Angie's sadness but also pointed out that they shared the sadness at the ending of the relationship. Finally the counsellor reflected on how the sadness about Oliver's death would always be a part of Angie's story and would be something she would share with other people in her life, both now and in the future.

We can see here how Angie had largely adapted to her life without Oliver (Task 3) and was beginning the emotional relocation, which enables a moving on with life (Task 4). Indeed, in grieving for Oliver she had found new depth and sensitivity. She and her counsellor parted company aware of both sadness and excitement as Angie faced the world again. We shall pick up Angie's story again in Chapter 18.

Sometimes the counselling relationship does not end naturally because the work is finished but has to end because the counsellor is leaving, perhaps because of a change of job or a house move. If a counsellor absolutely has to leave a job before a counselling relationship has ended it is, clearly, important to give the client as much notice as possible. Sometimes the counsellor faces the dilemma of whether to bring information about her own departure into the counselling relationship at a time when the client may be grappling with her grief from long ago. Generally speaking, the longer the client knows, the more time is available to talk about this new loss with the very person who is going to be lost. Helping the client to face up to and grieve the impending loss is an extremely important part of the work.

The sudden death of a counsellor would be one of the most difficult experiences for a client, particularly when the main focus is on loss. It is most important that another experienced counsellor or supervisor should inform all clients and potentially be available to help them with the complex feelings arising out of a further unplanned loss. All counselling agencies or counsellors should have arrangements in place for such an event (Syme, 1994). This is discussed further in Chapter 18.

Time-limited counselling

A specialist use of time has been developed in time-limited counselling, where the limited amount of time available is a conscious feature of all the work. When a client is in a position to receive independent counselling or to receive help from a well-endowed voluntary agency, then longer term counselling may be a practical possibility. If a person has many and/or intense griefs to be worked through, this may also be the method of choice. Certainly longer term work used to be regarded in some sense as 'better' than time-limited work.

However, as counselling has become more recognised over the past 15 years as an important intervention across a range of interpersonal activities, demand for counselling has grown and there has been greater pressure for organisational provision. Marriage Guidance, as it was then called, was the first organisation to supply counselling. Subsequently universities started that provision through student counselling, which rather later was followed by counselling provision in general practice, in other medical settings and then in the workplace, either through 'in-house' counselling or through EAPs (Employee Assistance Programmes). In order to enable a larger number of people to get at least some bite of the finite cherry of counselling provision, these organisations all started offering time-limited counselling. More recently research has been funded into the efficacy of time-limited counselling, and the results under certain conditions have been very encouraging.

In general they indicate that when there was a clear assessment of counselling need and aims, where a clear focus had been agreed between counsellor and client on the nature of the work to be done and a contract agreed about how this might be achieved, then time-limited counselling could be very effective. Effectiveness was also enhanced when a clear and mutual ending had been achieved, with a recognition of the feelings associated with endings. Counsellors trained in time-limited work need to have training and thus develop specific skills in contracting, making a rapid connection with the client and managing the ending.

Contracts are made at the beginning of counselling after the initial assessment session. This aims to establish, among other things, whether time-limited or longer-term counselling would be more appropriate. For those suitable for time-limited work, a designated number of sessions with dates would normally be agreed at the assessment stage. The reality of the ending of the counselling would therefore be recognised right from the beginning, with an end-date usually agreed in advance.

It is important in time-limited counselling to make as quick and intense a connection as possible so that there is the opportunity for a real relationship to be developed and then grieved within the short time of the counselling relationship. This opportunity to work more consciously and constructively towards an ending from the very beginning becomes one of the most potent tools of all brief work. It helps the client to tackle and resolve issues of loss and unfinished mourning as well as the issues consciously agreed in the assessment.

In bereavement counselling, when the focus itself is loss, the loss presented may be touching deeper losses as yet unrecognised. If a counsellor senses that exploring one 'layer' of loss might unleash a Pandora's box of many and deeper losses that have occurred over a long period, then longer-term counselling might be the chosen method of working. If, none the less, the decision is to offer short-term work, then the two issues of loss – that of the presenting loss as well as the brief relationship itself, with its clear ending – become a joint focus for the work.

We mentioned earlier that one of the common difficulties in loss counselling is the ending of the counselling relationship. This can be even more challenging in time-limited counselling. As we know, everyone unconsciously fears loss, and many consciously as well, so that it is all too easy for the focus to slip, leaving 'no time for the ending' of the counselling work. Counsellors need to be constantly aware of this pull, both in themselves and in their clients, towards avoiding the ending and not recognising the importance of the loss of the counsellor at the end of the work. When counsellors are aware of the importance of significant losses in their own lives, this gives them the confidence to encourage their clients to approach the ending.

Counsellors' expectation and understanding of some of the more frightening experiences in grieving are another way in which clients are given confidence to continue with the counselling.

Normalising disturbing experiences

You will be aware from Angie's (and also perhaps from your own) experiences that certain reactions to loss can be very frightening. The fear and accompanying isolation can then block the process of mourning, often at Task 2.

Usually fear can be lessened through the counsellor's acceptance of its expression. Sometimes lack of knowledge or lack of information exacerbates fear, in which case some form of clarification of the client's misunderstanding or a piece of relevant information may be very useful. This is an extremely delicate task, as it can threaten the exercise of shared control and power and can make the client feel powerless. None the less, there are certain kinds of information related to bereavement and other kinds of loss that can reduce fear and isolation, thereby actually empowering the client to proceed with the expression of feelings, which is necessary for the grieving.

Hallucinations

We mentioned in Chapter 4 that the disbelief that someone is lost often manifests itself in a kind of hallucination. Anne, you will remember, thought she saw James in the street almost a year after he had died. Angie's counsellor, knowing of this kind of experience, provides us with an example of how a counsellor might give information to a client in order to clarify and understand a similar experience.

Giving information about a hallucination

One day not long after Oliver's death, Angie arrived trembling with fright, and told the counsellor what had happened.

Angie: I was on the bus going along Victoria Road and just waiting to get off by Central Library. I was not thinking of anything in particular when suddenly I saw Oliver walking along the pavement. I shouted and leapt off the bus. Fortunately it was slowing down or I'd have killed myself – as it was, I nearly got run over and hurt my ankle quite badly. I knew I'd seen him but as I sat there on the pavement of course I began to realise that he was dead. An old lady came and asked me if I was all right. I must have been crying and I told her I'd seen Oliver. She didn't seem particularly surprised about Oliver but more surprised that I'd leapt off the bus. I must be going mad. I'm so sure I saw him. Perhaps I'm crazy. It was such a shock seeing him like that. Am I going mad?

Counsellor: Angie . . . [gently and slowly] people who've lost someone close to them sometimes do 'see' them suddenly like that . . .　$\left\}\begin{array}{l}\text{Clarifying through} \\ \text{information-} \\ \text{giving}\end{array}\right.$

It can be very frightening and disorientating.　$\{$ Link with feeling

Angie: You mean I'm not the only one?

Counsellor: [Shakes head]

Angie: Then perhaps I'm not going mad – yes, it was very frightening and I feel quite shaken up by it . . .

The task of the counsellor is to find a way to make it clear that the event is perfectly 'normal', while not denying the particular experience of the individual. In this example this is done by using the word 'people'. The counsellor then recognises the metaphoric use of the word 'see'. Having given the information it is important to link back into the person's feelings evoked by the experience. It might also be important to recognise the ankle pain!

'Irrational' behaviour

This 'carrying around in our head' of something familiar is, of course, not restricted to the bereaved and can occur while awake or in dreams. We are all familiar with waking up at the normal workday time when on holiday and wondering where we are, or with carrying on a routine when it is no longer necessary. This may seem irrational, but probably we are still carrying around the comfort of the familiar routine until we can tackle the change. The next example illustrates this, and demonstrates one way of helping someone recognise what is happening.

Understanding 'irrational' behaviour

Sheila was visiting her GP with lower back pain shortly after her youngest child, Ruth, left for university. Her GP could find no obvious organic cause for the back pain and, noticing Sheila's apprehension about leaving the surgery, asked her what else was worrying her.

Sheila: Well you see, I keep dreaming that Ruth's still here and then I wake up as usual at 7.30 a.m. and I go straight into her room and shout 'Ruth, time to get up!' It's quite dotty, but I do feel as if she's here when I wake up and just can't seem to remember that she's gone to university.

Doctor: Of course you feel as if she's still at home, that's quite natural. Many people feel as if the person who has gone away is still there. [Seeing relief on Sheila's face.] I expect you miss her enormously.

Sheila: Yes, I keep worrying about whether she'll be all right, whether she'll make friends, whether she'll manage on her grant, whether she's happy . . .

Doctor: I understand your worries. Ruth has a lot of new challenges and new experiences to savour . . . But you have the challenge of learning to live without Ruth, of how to live without waking her every morning. You must be feeling very sad and empty without her.

Sheila was thus able to feel surer that she was not going mad and to recognise that she too had a big challenge ahead; that of managing and enjoying term-time life without Ruth. Her feelings of sadness and emptiness were also recognised. This helped Sheila to recognise and grieve her loss and enabled her to adapt to her new world and find more resources in herself.

Understanding dreams

The desire for a return to a former time so as not to have to bear what is happening in the present can also manifest itself in dreams. In the following example it is important to recognise the feelings evoked by the dream and those evoked by the information being given.

Normalising a dream experience

You will remember Robin Clark (Table 9.1, p. 87 and Exercises 10.3, p. 108 and 10.5, p. 113), whose mother Lizzie was severely depressed and whose parents Frank and Lizzie had subsequently divorced. The divorce was hard for him to accept.

Robin: It seems so silly. I had this dream ... it was so realistic. My parents had got together again and were reconciling their differences. My father had come back ... we were a family again sitting round the table ... Then when I woke up I really believed it. I just could not believe it wasn't true. I felt so bad about not wanting to let them separate, or let him go off to a better life. I must be crazy ...?

Counsellor: Robin, many people whose parents are divorcing feel like that and, naturally enough, dream of the reconciliation they had longed for. Of course you don't want them to separate but you have very little power to alter that situation ...

         { Information to clarify (a) Robin not crazy (b) Robin powerless

Robin: [Reflectively] I suppose so.

Counsellor: Indeed, you might perhaps find yourself feeling angry as well as quite helpless about your situation?

         { Recognition of angry or helpless feelings at the edge of awareness, possibly covered by the more 'acceptable' guilty feeling.

In this example it is likely that when Robin heard from the counsellor that he was in reality powerless to change the situation, he would have felt recognised, understood and validated. He could then begin to see that his wishes were quite natural and that he was not guilty for his feelings and longings. This might allow him to feel the natural anger that an adolescent would feel towards divorcing parents, which in turn would enable him to start to accept the real separation. After that the dreams of reconciliation would begin to fade.

'Irrational' beliefs

It is quite common for someone coping with an unacceptable situation to construct incorrect beliefs to help them cope with the loss, as the following example illustrates.

Challenging an 'irrational' belief

Valerie had come to you soon after she had discovered that not only did the discovery of a lump in her breast mean she would have to have a mastectomy, but many lymph nodes would need to be removed as well. She would also have to undergo radiotherapy and chemotherapy. In her shock, she was trying to make sense of all this and became convinced that her cancer was a punishment from God for the termination she had undergone ten years previously.

Valerie:	It's clear, there's no other way to make sense of it. I should never have done what I did . . . it was wrong and this is my punishment. There's got to be a reason for it.
Counsellor:	Valerie, women often feel this way in your situation and I can understand you're trying to make sense of something that seems out-rageously unfair. ⎰ General information
	Perhaps that belief, though indeed painful, is less painful than accepting the awfulness and randomness of your cancer, the loss of your breast and the challenge of working out ways of accepting your new body. ⎱ Recognising feelings Challenging beliefs
Valerie:	Er, well, possibly . . .
Counsellor:	I guess that's a new and painful thought. ⎰ Recognising feelings again

When Valerie was able to recognise and work through her own pain and helplessness about the cancer, she was then in a position to begin to grieve the termination of ten years previously and to feel less guilty. This led her to be more able to adapt to the loss of her breast (Task 3), and she was able to let others help her in a way she had never done before; a kind of 'emotional relocation' (Task 4).

Persistent thoughts or images

Another experience that is common after a loss is that of persistent thoughts that simply will not stay away or images that keep returning, unwanted, to the mind's eye. Usually these thoughts and images return with aspects of the loss that still need to be confronted. The counsellor may need to support the client in facing the fear of the thought or image as well as the image itself with its half-hidden message.

Giving information about repetitive thoughts or images

Pat Jones (Table 9.1, p. 87) in Australia had discovered from the doctor's investigations sometime after the birth of her first-born son Henry that he was mentally disabled. About the time of his first birthday she found that she could not get the powerful image of Henry-at-birth out of her mind.

Pat: It's so silly, Henry's *birth* was an easy first delivery. Well, there were no complications and I was able to be wide awake when he was born and Robert was there too, it was wonderful . . . but now this picture of Henry still all tiny and wet, but perfectly formed, simply keeps coming back to me at all times of day and night. I can't keep it away. Am I going mad? Do I need tablets?

Counsellor: This image . . . it seems to be linked to an important memory with feelings of . . .? delight, I guess, about your perfectly formed baby?

Pat: [Wistfully] Yes, yes it was delightful. He was so beautiful, so perfect, so tiny, so full of potential. I had *such* dreams for him . . .

Counsellor: [Carefully] And now?

Pat: [Angrily] *Now*? Now it's so terrible, now my dreams are all gone [breaking down into sobs]. Now it's all so awful I can't bear it [sobs deeply for several minutes, gradually the sobbing begins to subside].

Counsellor: Your feelings of pain make a lot of sense to me. You have had a most terrible shock and disappointment. I expect you are wondering how on earth you are going to live with this different Henry now? The image of the original Henry seems to be a bitter reminder of the Henry you have now lost.

Once Pat really began to hear her counsellor's affirmation of her loss and hear that her 'image' had been accepted and linked with feelings, she could start to take on board the enormity of her loss. She could then hear the counsellor's 'And now?' for the reality that it represented. She allowed herself to experience her pain at that moment. She was then able to begin the long and often arduous process of grieving for the original Henry and all the hopes she had lost. For Pat this process could well be more difficult being so far from home and support from her family (see Tables 5.1, p. 45 and 5.2, p. 49 and Table 9.1, p. 87). Gradually she could identify and express her feelings and move through Task 2. Other people may not let themselves experience feelings so quickly, and it may be useful for the counsellor to invite the client to describe the 'thought' or the 'image' in greater detail. If the counsellor can reflect back her picture of the thought or image, linking it tentatively with any feelings she may have perceived, then the client can usually begin to experience the feelings more fully and make sense of the image, thus moving through Task 2.

It is worth remembering that the tasks are not usually completed in a linear fashion. For instance, while Task 2 may be largely completed, it may take considerable time and frequent returning to the story for someone to have experienced enough of the feelings of grief to be truly able to adapt to a world in which the lost person is missing.

Returning to Pat, as she began to gain more acceptance of Henry as he truly was, she was already moving into Task 3 and adapting to the reality of her world without the original 'perfect' baby. The images then began to disappear. The more she adapted to the new situation, the more she was able to open herself to others again, and in particular to her husband and then to the other children who were born some years later.

Once people have truly adapted to the world without the missing person, the process of 'emotional relocation' (Task 4) has usually already begun. The work of grief can usually proceed through personal and social networks and without further need of counselling.

It is not just adults, but children too, that can be helped to face their feelings (Task 2) and work through their grief. In the next chapter we shall consider ways of working with children who have suffered a loss and with children who have buried their grief. Then in Chapters 14 and 15 we shall took at ways of understanding and working with adults who have buried their feelings and whose grief has become stuck, but who are still able to become 'unstuck' with the help of a skilled counsellor. In Chapter 16 we shall consider instances where counsellors must consult with their supervisor and consider the possibility of referral to more experienced counsellors or psychotherapists.

Summary

- If a counselling session is to offer safety and containment it must have clear boundaries. In loss counselling in particular, firm boundaries are important in creating a safe enough place in which to recognise the loss and experience feelings (Tasks 1 and 2).
- Beginnings are often marked by fear or anxiety, and it is useful to offer clear time boundaries and to focus on the feelings the client is experiencing.
- Endings, both of sessions and of the counselling relationship, may re-evoke feelings associated with loss and separation. These need to be recognised, while still holding a firm boundary, and may enable the griever to move on to Task 3.

- Time-limited counselling is suitable for some bereaved and depends on specialist skills in contracting, making a rapid connection with the client and managing the ending.
- Clarity and simplicity of language is useful when trying to clarify and make sense of hallucinations, behaviour, dreams, incorrect beliefs, repetitive thoughts and images.
- Recognising the associated feelings usually enables the grief work to continue.

Chapter 13

Ways of helping children

There may be fewer children nowadays who lose a parent through death. There are, however, many other circumstantial losses that children need to grieve. A particularly common loss for children is the breakdown of their parents' marriage. In Chapter 8 we recognised that children do grieve and that their grief may often be denied by adults in the guise of 'protecting the children'. Children will hide their grief in different ways according to the stage in their development and their family patterns. However, just as adults can be helped with grieving, as outlined in Chapters 10, 11 and 12, so can children. In this chapter we describe ways of working with children who have suffered a loss.

If children have had a secure relationship before the loss takes place, then specific help will enable them to resolve their grief. Ideally this specific help will come from the children's families; but the parents, guardians and adult carers will almost always be grieving themselves. Even if they are overwhelmed by their loss, they will usually want to do the best for their children. It is easier for them to do so if they are treated as colleagues collaborating to help their children. This means discovering what they know and then supplying them with the necessary information to fill in the gaps. Much of this information will be given by helping the parents imagine the possible conversations with their children. This can be backed up by some excellent leaflets and workbooks published by support organisations for bereaved children (Appendix A) and by a number of websites (Appendix B).

We mentioned in Chapter 4 that there is a dual process in grieving. The practical act of getting information about the children's needs, for instance, could be seen as part of the restoration-orientation process, and as such is helpful to the grieving parent. Adults often seem unaware of how powerful a model they are to their children, and that their silence, withdrawal or disapproval of feelings will actually encourage the children to behave in the same way. Despite adults' attempts to hide things, we know how much children 'read' the situation and the emotional climate. Grieving adults, therefore, need to know that children will:

- read emotions round them;
- respond to body language;
- overhear conversations, and if forbidden to do so will find a more covert way to do so;
- ask questions both directly and symbolically, the latter obviously being the more difficult to 'hear'.

Further ways in which adults will need support are in helping them to manage the views of other people, who are encouraging them to 'protect' the children from the reality. For instance, the bereaved child may have decided, supported by their parents or a counsellor, that they would like to go to the funeral; but other members of the family may have very strong views that children should never go to a funeral because it is 'too upsetting for them'. They often will express these feelings very forcefully, making it hard to hang onto the original decision (Chapter 8).

The specific help that children need in order to grieve was identified by Bowlby (1953). First, they need information and their questions answered immediately, honestly and as factually as possible. Second, they need to be allowed and enabled to participate in the family's loss, which they can only do if their parents share their feelings. Last, but not least, children need a continuing relationship where they can rely on the comforting presence of a parent or another adult and feel the reassurance of a reasonably ordered routine. We consider first how this kind of specific help can be given to the reasonably secure child. We then go on to consider some extra help that less secure children may need.

Of course not all parents can give the specific help identified by Bowlby. This is frequently not available because the adults around a grieving child are overwhelmed or embittered by their own loss, and find it hard to be warm, congruent or empathic when they feel so hurt themselves. In addition, the child's reaction can be disturbing and painful and the child's questions, which do need answering, can be infuriating for the hurt adult. This means that other adults, such as relatives, doctors, teachers, priests, friends or counsellors, have an important role to play, in which they will be more effective when they can enlist the trust of the parents, guardians or other supporting adults. Without this trust it will be harder for the child to feel safe and the work could be undermined. Treating the children's carers as colleagues in the work is essential to build trust. Once trust is established it is then possible to help the parents with their guilt about letting someone else help their child(ren). This can be done by encouraging them to be kind to themselves and appealing to the common-sense idea that there is so much pain that each person needs their own support. An important spin-off of this contact with the adults is also being able to learn something of the family's belief system, which must be respected when working with their children.

Any adults, whether the parents or a supportive outsider, helping a grieving child will be more effective when using the basic attitudes and skills described in Chapters 3, 10 and 12. This enables a relationship to be built up which the child can rely upon for understanding and comfort. In creating such an environment the adult can also help the child explore her feelings, though it is important to remember that the ease with which a child can identify and give words to feelings depends on her age and her family's attitudes to the expression of feelings. For some children identification and expression of feelings is very difficult and so more direct, active and playful ways of responding need to be found.

Immediacy about information and feelings

In this section we look at how adults can respond to 'secure enough' children in ways that recognise their specific need to have immediate and honest answers, and that allow them to share in the family grief. Above all else, the child needs to know the truth and be responded to warmly and immediately. Children respond best to clear and simple language, and obviously will need medical terms explained. When in grief and turmoil oneself, it is very easy to give children confused ideas about death by being vague or using euphemisms. If they are too young to understand the finality of death, statements like 'Daddy has gone to heaven', or 'Daddy's with God', are muddling. You will remember Michael and his mother Anne from Chapter 4. She said both these things to him. Weeks later he asked her 'When is Daddy coming back from heaven?' He thought heaven was a place like Madrid or Stockholm, two places his father had gone to on business. Months later, when in a church, he said 'Where is Daddy?' This puzzled Anne until she worked out that Michael, using the logic of a child, assumed that because church was 'God's house' his father should be there. Other expressions such as 'passed away', 'gone before', 'returned to his maker' and 'left us' are equally confusing.

If the child's feelings or questions are postponed by the adults around, then the child may decide that such feelings are unacceptable and push them underground. In this case children may need extra help. We will discuss ways of helping children with denied feelings later in this chapter.

In a secure enough setting children will usually try to get the information they need. In Chapter 8 we gave an example of how Anne's son Michael used the Polo sweets as a way of questioning Anne about his father's death. When he received an immediate answer that made sense, and a cuddle to help recognise and contain the feelings inside him, he was quickly off to play again. That was probably as much grieving and understanding as he could do for that moment. However, over the next months he came back again and again to the same questions, as well as asking many others. All his questions needed to be answered straight away and his feelings recognised, often with physical closeness, so that each issue could be resolved and the grief could proceed.

Children need reassurance. One way is to return to the previous routine, or to establish a new one as soon as possible and thus give them some security, and life some predictability. Older children often have additional worries about such things as what people will say and who knows what's happened to them. These anxieties need to be met and the head teacher and form teacher involved if the child is of school age. Children may be very anxious about any illness, theirs or others'. The reassurance about the likelihood of another death or loss has to be realistic and not misleading; in most cases illness does not lead to death.

In general it is useful to make physical or at least eye contact with children who are grieving; not to give false reassurance, to deny feelings, or to change the subject, but to help the child feel safe enough to express and contain the feelings that may be raging inside. As we mentioned earlier, children are particularly prone to fantasies or magical thinking, which results in their believing they caused a loss. They need to feel reasonably safe in order to share such fantasies. Only then will they be able to begin to let go of the fantasy and take reality on board.

It may be very difficult for adults, who themselves are grieving, to accept and respond to a child's feelings and questions. This is particularly so when the questions are shocking, critical and hurtful to the parent. It can be tempting to turn the angry or frightened feelings into blame of the other parent, as illustrated in the following anecdote. This can result in the child's sad feelings, evoked for her by this separation from one of the people she loves, being totally ignored.

The Campbell family were going through a difficult time. Peter and Ruth had decided to split up and the children, Philip (aged nine) and Sally (aged seven), were still rather confused about what was happening. Peter had failed to return Philip's anorak, which he had left in Peter's car. It was lashing with rain and they were late for school. Ruth was getting frantic about the anorak and her anger became focused on Peter's carelessness.

Mum: Your Dad's a beast leaving us like this . . . he doesn't love us any more!

Philip felt hurt and confused at this, but his mother suddenly saw his hurt expression and knew it was most important to be able to stop and apologise.

Mum: I'm sorry Philip, I didn't mean that. Of course Dad's not a beast! . . . Daddy and I weren't able to work things out between us. What I meant was, he doesn't love me any more; but of course he still loves you and Sally and will do always, even if he lives somewhere else.

Philip could then forgive her and was able to make more sense of his situation.

It can often be difficult for divorcing parents to keep the child or children separate from their own angry and bitter feelings. But whatever bitterness exists between the adults, each ex-spouse continues to be the child's other parent. It is important to recognise and accept the child's own separate feelings about the loss of his or her other parent. To illustrate a way of handling this problem, we return to the Campbell family.

Ruth Campbell had tried to help Philip with his own feelings of grief about his father. Although at first he had appeared to accept the separate arrangements, some months later he seemed particularly cross about the timing of visiting arrangements. One day when he was being particularly uncooperative his mother, sensing that this was a sign of grief, tried to respond by telling him that both she and his father were concerned about him. She suddenly found Philip shouting 'I hate you! I hate you and I hate Daddy too!', rushing to his bedroom and slamming the door. Ruth realised, just, that his onslaught was not personal, and she was able to be patient about his difficult behaviour. Later she was able to talk to him about his angry feelings and his sense of abandonment.

She had to face many more angry outbursts before his feelings of fury and abandonment were to abate and she could feel reasonably sure that he was not harbouring fantasies of his own guilt. It was important that she treated him consistently with empathy and respect. This was particularly hard for her to do as many people around her, caught up in denial of the child's grief, could only see the child's or indeed the father's bad behaviour. They did not understand the importance of listening to his hurt and angry feelings. Fortunately she had one or two good friends who supported her in the long and often excruciatingly lonely task of helping him and Sally through their sad and angry feelings to an acceptance of their loss without turning Peter into the 'bad guy'.

When feelings get lost

Unfortunately, in our society, children's feelings about a loss often become buried. Their reactions are then delayed and can turn into complicated behaviour patterns. A child who is helped to grieve will normally be relatively free of pain on a day-to-day basis within 18 months to two years. When circumstances are favourable, children may be able to work through their grief at about the same rate as adults; and, like adults, they will continue to have bonds with the dead person forever. They are never forgotten. However, children who 18 months to two years after a loss either show excessive feeling in response to frustrating experiences or show no signs of distress at all to everyday setbacks, have probably buried their grief and may need extra help to gain access to the denied feelings. Children who are less secure themselves, and who have a less secure relationship to a parent or other adult, are more likely to think that they have to bury grief and subsequently to need extra help with their feelings.

As with adults, the feelings most likely to cause difficulty for a child are helplessness, sadness, anger and guilt – particularly when expression of these feelings has previously been criticised. Returning to Philip and Sally, if in the past Philip's feelings of sadness had led to taunts of 'cry baby' or statements such as 'big boys don't cry', then he might have associated feelings of sadness with vulnerability or helplessness and might try to avoid this by repressing his sadness. If his sister Sally's feelings of anger in the past had brought counter-attack or punishment, then she might associate feelings of anger with retribution or even destruction. She might then try to avoid such consequences by repressing her anger and perhaps 'making sense' by deciding she was the 'bad one' and had to 'be good'.

When working with children whose natural responses to grief have indeed been repressed or cut off in this way, it may be necessary for a helper to use a more direct approach than when working with an adult. An example of this is given in Table 8.2 in Chapter 8 (p. 79). Susan was helped to understand more about the meaning of Paul's behaviour in relation to his dead father. With her new knowledge she was able to ask him directly and clearly about these angry feelings and his misunderstandings. Once his behaviour had been understood as a symbolic communication, it was possible to help him understand and express the feelings underlying this behaviour and to give him the information he needed. The difficult behaviour then stopped, he returned to normal development and his self-esteem improved. For Paul, understanding his behaviour helped him to express his true feelings, and grief could proceed.

However, it is very difficult for some children to express their feelings directly, especially in response to questions. If asked a question about mood or feelings, a child will often answer 'I don't know'. This could mean something like, 'I don't know about feelings', or 'I don't know how to talk about feelings', or 'I don't know the words . . .' or 'I'm confused', or 'I just don't want to be bothered at the moment'. At this point some activity that uses methods other than words can be very useful. In particular, techniques involving play are useful to help such children make more direct contact with their lost feelings.

Feelings are experienced within the physical body and are also associated with sounds and images. This association offers a wide range of methods to contact feelings in children and then to enable them to express the feelings and begin to unravel the confusion. Many of the methods for helping children to contact feelings and grieve can be found in publications supplied by Winston's Wish and The Child Bereavement Trust (Appendix A). The following five methods are ones we have found useful and can be used by a worker, or by parents on their own or supported by a worker. If it is a worker, then the handling of confidential information has to be discussed with both the parents and the child and an agreement reached about how information is exchanged. Almost always both parents and their children can be encouraged and supported to tell each other about difficult feelings or thoughts. It is never helpful for a worker to divulge confidential information except in the case of physical or sexual abuse, and even then this should only be done after consultation with a more experienced counsellor.

The use of drawing

Most children are used to drawing and feel safe doing something familiar, and therefore this is often the best way to start communicating with them. If encouraged to draw what they want, they are more likely to tell you about their drawing. Drawings are inevitably static and most children are not skilled enough to convey movement or a series of events, so a good question to help explore the picture is 'What is happening in your picture?'; then a story can be told (Kroll, 1996). Sometimes the child draws herself, but often one of the characters in the picture represents the child, so if they feel small and unsafe they may represent themselves as a baby or a small animal that is seen as vulnerable. Examples of the latter are a ladybird, a mouse, a kitten or puppy, or a small bird. Kroll describes a child who was so worried that he felt sick. He drew fierce tigers, all of which felt sick, and were trapped by fences or forests. An exploration of this picture led Kroll to understand that the boy was finding it difficult to be fierce and wanted these feelings to be managed, understood and made less dangerous. By the end of the exploration he no longer felt sick.

Children think symbolically and frequently use size to convey power and vulnerability. Very large people may be powerful, strong, comforting and protective but they may also be frightening and suffocating. Small people, particularly in contrast to a large person in a drawing, may be very vulnerable and no good as a protector, indeed might need protection. If a person has no eyes, or ears or mouth, does this mean they are not seeing, hearing or speaking to the child? Colour is also used very creatively by children, with dark and heavy ones conveying gloom and red often conveying anger. Sometimes children laboriously make a picture and then scribble all over it, conveying their feelings in the colour they use or the manner in which they blot out the image.

The topics children choose to depict are also informative. Sometimes they draw idyllic scenes, beautiful gardens and happy families, which indicate some of their longings and wishes, whereas scenes of war and devastation can give a sense of the chaos and anger they experience around them or within themselves, or might be an expression of their fears.

A rather different use of drawing was first developed by Winnicott (1971) and is another method of getting in touch with children and their thoughts and feelings. It is known as the squiggle game. Both you and the child have a piece of paper and a pencil and then you take it in turns with the child to make a squiggle, which the other has to turn into something. This builds up a relationship but also gives a rich field for exploration, with both the pictures and the associations to talk about. Kroll tells of one child who, when she played this game, drew a squiggle each time, which she said was a worm. She asked Kroll to turn it into a snail. Kroll suggests that the child felt very unsafe and vulnerable and wanted to be given a shell to protect her and in which she could hide like the snail.

There is no doubt that children's drawings are a rich vein with which to explore their inner worlds. This exploration will call for imaginative skills on the part of the worker. It is a powerful way of working because great sadness may be found and expressed, but it can be made fun for the child and result in the release of pent-up feelings, which will give great relief. However, some children are so unhappy and withdrawn that they cannot draw, and other techniques need to be used to help them find their feelings.

The 'faces game'

As humans, we express feelings through sound, movement and facial expression. One way to contact a feeling is through known depictions of a 'feeling face'. This visual medium can lead on to further possibilities of expression through sounds, movements and words. Our version of the 'faces game' is based on one described by Claudia Jewett (1984). Another version can be found in a workbook for grieving children written by Marge Heegaard (1992).

The basis of the 'faces game' is to find a playful way to get children to draw faces showing six different feelings. These are happy, sad, scared, angry, lonely and bored. We have added the bored face to this game because children frequently introduce 'bored' as if it were a feeling. It is usually a way of protecting themselves against another more difficult feeling, or else a way of 'not feeling'. Once the faces are drawn they can then be used to help the child identify her feelings or those of adults around her. Sometimes adding sound can free the feeling. The following example illustrates how the 'faces game' can be used.

Use of the 'faces game'

Take a large card and with the child cut it into six equal pieces.
Then:

Adult: Now we're going to make some different faces on the cards –
            you know how people often tell you what they feel through
            their faces?
Child: Mmm.
Adult: Do you ever do that?

Child:	Don't know.
Adult:	Well, let's think about this . . .
Child:	Mmm.
Adult:	Supposing your teacher said something like 'It's such a beautiful day I think we should all go to the park and play and have ice-creams' . . . what might your face look like then?

You might copy the child's face with your face.

Adult:	I see, your mouth would go up and your eyes would look 'smiley'. Would you draw that for me?

Offer a piece of card.

Adult:	Thank you. Can we find a word to describe that face? Let's write the word underneath the face. Now let's think of another face.

The child may be able to name feelings, demonstrate and draw them. More often their feelings are cut off and they will need some guidance and encouragement.

Adult:	What if . . . everyone else in your class was taken out to the park and bought ice-creams and you were left to tidy up the classroom?

There are, of course, different feelings that might be expressed in response to this. The feelings could be anger, loneliness, sadness, fear; the expression on the child's face will give you the clues. Help the child explore what feeling is uppermost.

Adult:	I see, that certainly looks different. The corners of your mouth would go down.

Imitate the face. Then offer the child a different coloured pencil.

Adult:	Perhaps you can draw that face? What sort of face is that?
Child:	It's sad.
Adult:	Let's write that underneath that face.

If the child has not identified any anger, then recognising the 'unfair' nature of this situation may help get in touch with angry feelings. The child may still not relate 'anger' or unfairness to this situation. This may be a clue to you about her difficulty with feeling anger.

Having pictures for two feelings and the words to describe them, either you can give the other 'feeling-words' to write on other cards and then add the faces; or you could describe further situations to evoke the facial expression, then move towards drawing and naming as before. Your choice will depend on such factors as the time available and how easily the child can link a feeling expression to the situation described; also, to some extent, on the knowledge you have of the child's life. Either way you will end up with the six faces looking something like:

HAPPY   SAD   SCARED   ANGRY   LONELY   BORED

As we mentioned earlier, children often use 'bored' to describe 'not feeling'. The bored face will need special attention; perhaps the teeth are clenched; perhaps the eyes are closed. Exploring with the child what would happen if the teeth were unclenched, or the eyes opened, and even encouraging the child to clench and unclench her teeth or shut and open her eyes, can lead to a shout of anger or a cry of pain and then sadness.

Once you have the five or six faces on cards, there are different ways in which they can be used. Asking the child to choose a card and then talk about the last time she had that feeling or she 'had that face', and affirming the response, can help the child recognise the validity of a feeling response to a life situation. She may also be able to use that to grieve. She may, however, avoid certain cards. This is another way of knowing which feelings she is finding hardest. If, for instance, she had difficulty making a sad face and/or a sad drawing (e.g. without tears) and avoided that card, you might begin to focus on that card and, as you add the tears, say:

Adult: A lot of people I know do this when they are sad. Do you ever look like that?

She may be able to use a sad story or a sad song to help make a sad face. As she comes closer to sad feelings she may want to take another card and make a 'better sad face' or a 'sadder sad face'. It should then be possible to link sad feelings in herself to the loss happening in her life. This technique can also be followed for angry or scared or lonely feelings. In this way the five cards can be used to explore the range of feelings a child is prepared to experience.

When playing this game the child may become 'stuck' because she is experiencing more than one feeling. The 'faces game' can be extended by encouraging the child to convey the two feelings on one face. An example would be to draw a face with sadness on one half of the face and anger on the other.

One of the uses of the 'faces game' is that it helps identify the feelings a child is avoiding or finding difficult. The problem then is to find other ways to connect and release the feelings. Other media that can be used are sounds, movement, sculpting, drawing, acting and stories in books, films or on TV.

The use of sound and stories

Stories, in a book, play or on video, may enable a child to identify with a person or an animal who is in a similar situation or whose feelings come close to her own. Seeing a child involved with sadness in this way could be the moment to help her into deeper experiencing of that feeling. Examples of storybooks and videos that particularly help children are given in Appendices C and D.

If a child has a problem with sadness, for instance, then making the sound can sometimes connect up the feelings and lead to real experiencing. To do this, encourage the child to make a sad noise. If perhaps this is difficult then friendly competition can help with the inhibition.

Adult: I wonder if I can make a sadder sound than you? – Do you want to try? [start softly, working up as she joins in] Waa-a . . . louder.

As soon as her eyes begin to water and she is in touch with real feelings then the 'competition' is immediately over and you move into the sharing of what may be intense pent-up feelings.

The 'boxes' game

Movement can also free pent-up feelings. The 'boxes' game, again adapted from Jewett (1984), is a movement game that children enjoy.

Have a number of cardboard boxes, which can be stacked up on one another to build a 'tower'. You can introduce the game by taking the 'angry card' from the 'faces game' or making an angry face yourself and saying something like:

Helper: Can you copy my face? [Child copies face.]
             Great! Now I wonder what kind of things make you angry?
Child: Don't know.
Helper: Hmmm . . . some children I know get angry when things are unfair . . . did that ever happen to you?
Child: S'pose so.
Helper: I have a funny game I sometimes play with children when they have those feelings using these boxes. [Take first and largest

	box] This is for the first unfair thing you can think of . . . Come on. Give me one . . . It's not fair when . . .
Child:	I have to stay in at playtime.
Helper:	[Banging down box] I have to stay in at playtime. [Holding second box] And it's not fair when . . .
Child:	I don't get my sweets.
Helper:	[Banging second box on top] I don't get my sweets. [Holding third box] And, it's not fair when . . .
Child:	I get the blame.
Helper:	[With the next box] And . . .
Child:	It's not fair when Jimmy [his best friend] left for America and nobody told me.

. . . and so on.

The helper continues to produce more boxes for each of the child's known complaints, or the helper's hunches based on what he knows of the child, or such things as 'other kids tell me it's not fair when they have to go to bed early . . . yes?'

Helper:	And now what's fun is to kick them all down, *hard*, like this.

Give a good firm kick so that the boxes really fly around, usually leading to:

Child:	I want a go, me now.

The child may build the tower again on her own in her delight or may need help. She may need encouragement actually to go at it. Her movements should accompany her words of 'It's not fair when . . .', thus giving vent to her anger and real expression to her stored-up resentments. It is important at the end of such a session to find words for the feelings and to recognise the excitement and energy involved in such work. Such a session should be ended with something calming before the child leaves.

After a few sessions of such games the child will be more able to express appropriate emotions to life situations and the behaviour masking the angry feelings will begin to change. It may be around this time that the helper or parent can recognise with the child that 'It's not fair when someone you love goes away' (or dies, or gets taken ill, or whatever fits the child's situation). These situations may include such things as the child's best friend leaving the area, the child being hurt or burned and having a permanent scar or injury, or the child being abused.

If the helper is not the parent and the child's family is one where feelings are not easily expressed or recognised, it may be important for the child to tell a parent or parents in your presence that 'We were angry today' or for you, with the child's prior agreement, to let the parents know this in the child's presence. This helps to legitimise the child's angry feelings and thus counter the pattern of hiding angry feelings and creating fantasies of guilt.

The use of drama, play and music

Obviously the methods we have already mentioned indirectly use play-acting and sound, but there are more specific ways that you can use children's enormous creativity. Children need little encouragement to use anything in a room to enact or re-enact something, if you do not have dolls, stuffed toys, puppets, doll's houses, play houses, bricks, jigsaw puzzles, play telephones, etc. With or without these there are endless possibilities. First, children must be allowed to choose what they want to use and to 'invent' the game or situation. The following examples are of ways in which children have used the toys around them. But of course the variety is endless and calls on the imagination of the carer to get maximum benefit from the re-enactments and fantasies that the children create. Kroll (1996) gives many examples.

Dolls, stuffed animals and puppets will be used by the children to speak on their behalf, but remember that any inanimate objects will also speak for them. Puppets are particularly useful to ask difficult questions of children. Kroll often makes the puppet whisper the question in her own ear, to decrease the anxiety, and then asks the question indirectly. For instance, 'Lion wonders what you do when you stay with your mum', and 'the lion says he is a bit confused – can you explain to him why you don't want to see your daddy?'. The lion puppet acts like a third party and makes the child feel safer. We have found that frequently it helps children if they can whisper the answer.

Telephones are an excellent way to get children to 'talk' to anyone they choose, and perhaps even you, to say things that need to be said. Sometimes it is safer to use the telephone than to say the words directly to someone. Kroll describes one small boy, whose parents were separated, who kept ringing home, but each time found he had done something 'wrong'. Perhaps this conveyed both his desire to return to home as it used to be, and that he could not get through to either of his parents. Kroll is careful always to be tentative when exploring ideas because it is absolutely essential to find the child's meaning rather than impose an adult's interpretation.

Playhouses and dolls' houses allow enactment of domestic scenes and desired happenings: the people or animals living in the house often say what the child cannot say. Even without dolls' houses or playhouses, houses can be created out of such things as bricks, floor cushions, and furniture in the room. Children who have moved house as a result of a bereavement, parental separation, adoption or fostering will often create two houses to explore what has happened or is happening. Emily, whose parents had separated, lived with her mother. When she built two houses, she explained that her father's house was a fort with a drawbridge whereas her mother's was in the country and up a windy lane. Of course, neither parental home was like this but she was exploring her feelings about the difference between the two. For a bit she moved furniture from one to another before destroying both houses and talking about how everything had been spoilt and destroyed, thus giving expression to the sense of helplessness and disturbance she was experiencing, while trying terribly hard to manage the two-house situation.

Puzzles are a good way of exploring how things fit together. Kroll describes a small girl, Rachel, aged three and a half, who had been separated from her mother. She played with a simple, five-piece puzzle of a large wooden elephant with a baby elephant which fitted underneath. She was unable to fit it together, which seemed to match her current situation. Instead she used the puzzle pieces, plus other pieces lying around, to make a house in which she placed a small animal, which she referred to as a baby and had her name. This baby, Rachel, lived all alone though surrounded by lots of objects for company. Kroll suggests that Rachel's current position was exactly this, with the family giving her lots of presents but not explanations and comfort. The baby in the house was really frightened by a blue dolphin, which menaced her. Rachel was also able to say she was frightened. This game suggests that she felt that she had been left all alone to deal with a nameless anxiety.

Most children love music and songs. Made-up songs to the tune of a known nursery rhyme or song can get difficult things said. It is often fun and helpful to take it in turns to sing the made-up verses, so that a sort of conversation is taking place. Music creates mood so that feelings can be accessed by moving to the music and expressing what is evoked. Music-making with drums and other percussive instruments is another way of accessing feeling. Anything can become a percussive instrument, and again the ingenuity of the child can be enormous fun for both the child and the helper.

When feelings become very stuck, much more specialised help may be required. One group of professionals, available to children and adults, are drama, play, art and music therapists, all of whom have highly specialised training to develop the ideas mentioned in this section to help children (and adults) who have great difficulty in expressing feeling.

Techniques to explore relationships

When children have been separated from people they love, it is often very hard for them to talk about their feelings and about what is happening or they would like to happen. This is particularly true if people around them are not talking about who has died or what has happened for fear of 'upsetting the child'. Many of the techniques already described are helpful, but there are additional ways that focus specifically on issues such as closeness, family relationships, reliability, safety, trust and loyalty.

We used a family tree in Chapter 9 to explore the different losses that happen in a family. These can be used by older children to explore such things as their family relationships, their support network, where they fit in and the strength or closeness of different relationships. The family tree, or genogram, can have pets and friends in it and the task of working out how to do this will help the exploration. Lines of different length and boldness can be used to signify closeness and strength. You may notice significant people who have been left out, and gently pointing this out may help you to understand why they were not included. This might be for reasons such as that they were not being mentioned by the family or because the child did not like them and therefore did not want them there. For a child with parents who have divorced, putting this in the genogram may help them face and accept what has happened.

A variation of the genogram suitable for younger children is to have a box of assorted buttons: big ones, small ones, highly decorated ones and of every colour possible. Let them choose a button for each person, animal or object in their network. It is not only people and pets that are a support, but a very favourite teddy too. The child can then place these buttons at different distances from one another and from the button representing herself. This gives a forum in which the child can talk about different people, how safe with or close to them she feels.

An alternative to buttons is to cut out circles of different sizes and colours from paper and then invite the child to choose one for each person, pet or toy that is important to her. If the child can write or likes drawing, then invite her to draw a little picture and label each one. If she cannot write or draw you may do it for her, carefully following her suggestion of how to represent them. Ask the child to put the one representing herself down and then place the others round her. This can be explored in the same way as the genogram and buttons game. As with the genogram and buttons game, if a significant person is left out this can be gently explored. Kroll mentions Martin, a boy of 12, who had found his mother's body after she had been murdered by her boyfriend. A number of family members wanted to look after him and a fierce custody battle had been fought through the courts. Neither Martin nor his new family had talked of his mother for six months. When he made the circles he left his mother out until gently reminded of her. He then put her very close to him, an indication of how important she had been to him and how she had been 'left out'.

A further sophistication is to pretend that the child is flown by rocket or a magic carpet to another planet, and 'fly' the 'child' circle out of the pattern. This can then be used to help the child imagine who she would like to come with her, who would rescue her if she was in trouble, who would be worried if she was missing, to whom she would like to send postcards (Kroll, 1996). In this way the child builds up a clearer sense of her support network.

The circles can also be used to reveal angry feelings because they can be scrunched up, torn, stamped on, scribbled all over or 'thrown away'. These destructive feelings can be explored safely this way. If the child does any of these things it is important to retrieve the damaged circles and keep them in a safe place, so that if the child wants them back later they are there, and can then be used for reparation and the resolving of the angry feelings.

When managing loss, through whatever cause, children have very difficult situations with which to come to terms. Kroll (1996) suggests the holiday game to explore this. Ask the child to imagine she is going on holiday, and let her decide what sort of holiday and where. Will it be a camping holiday? In the country? At the seaside? And will they stay in a tent? A boat? A hotel? A castle? A tree house? And so on. Then get the child to list down the centre of a piece of paper all her favourite people, who will come on holiday with her, making sure that she puts her name on the list. It she cannot write, then list them for her. Off they all go. Again, let the child decide the means of getting there. Unfortunately, when they get there the tent, house, castle, or boat is too small for them all to fit into, so instead of one there are two. Get the child to draw the two. The problem then is who is to stay in which house. Get the child to draw a line from each person in the central list to the place they are going to stay. Children whose parents have separated or divorced frequently put their parents together. It takes a very long time for children to stop yearning for their parents to come together again. This game is particularly useful because it enables children to think about the way it used to be, the way it is now and the way they would like it to be. It also helps children talk about unfairness and conflicting loyalties, and it often frees up the expression of anger so that it can be talked about.

The holiday game works well with children managing loss or change, but particularly when they are coping with two houses or a change in houses when moving from one family to another, which can happen because of remarriage of a parent or because of separation, fostering or adoption.

When information is lacking

When a loss has occurred, some children have considerable confusion over exactly what happened, when it happened or in what order things happened. Sometimes remembering is too painful and they refuse to do so. Here again particular techniques can be useful, such as making a life-strip or a life-story book. Both are ways of ordering information, removing confusion and beginning to create a narrative of their lives. The life-strip is made by taking a long piece of string and pinning on to it, with the child's help, information about herself, photographs of herself, her family, houses she has lived in, people or animals who have died, drawings, maps of journeys, written memories and such like, all dated and in chronological sequence. The life-story book is similar, with the same sort of information about the child stuck into a scrapbook, again in chronological order. In both cases, doing such an activity with the child may enable events and their associated feelings to be recalled and ordered. Starting with 'easier' events can initiate the process, which can then lead on to talking about more 'difficult' events.

Maintaining links

Both the life-strip and life-story book give children a chronological sequence and therefore help prevent the breaking of the thread of their life history. They can also act as a bond with the lost person that the children can keep for the rest of their lives. It is important for all children to have a memory bank, in which they can store important mementoes, photographs, perhaps a tape-recording or a video film, their drawing of the dead person or of something they did together. One example is the 'Soul Mate', mentioned in Chapter 4. An alternative idea is to get the child to make a box, which they decorate and then fill with the objects that connect with the dead person. A more sophisticated version of this can be bought from Barnardo's (Appendix A). Barnardo's also publishes a Memory Book, which can be used to store vital information. *Muddles, Puddles and Sunshine* (Crossley, 2000), published under the auspices of Winston's Wish, helps children explore their memories of someone who has died. If a child's parent(s) die when she is young it is important for her to know, and to have written down somewhere, information such as where her parents met, where they were married, how her name was chosen, the first words she spoke, family jokes and traditions, the houses the family lived in, and so on. Sometimes a parent can compile this; other times members of the family need to do it, and as soon as possible so information is not lost.

Another useful way of helping a child remember the dead person is to create a sand sculpture. First of all, make five or six different coloured sand piles by grating chalks and mixing them with sand. Then give the child a small jar such as those used for baby food (125g) and invite her to put layers of sand into it, each layer representing a particular memory. It is important to talk about each memory and to remind them to include layers of sand for difficult times as well as good ones. The jar is small enough for a child to carry it in a pocket or a bag as a tangible memento.

These memory boxes, books, life-strips and stories and sand sculptures all become part of the 'first aid' for bereaved children when they are feeling particularly lost. They are something they can turn to as a reminder of the person they loved. They all help to give a true picture of that person and maintain the bonds.

Further considerations

All the games and exercises we have mentioned in this chapter are designed to help children express their feelings but, of course, they have feelings all the time. They may become pent-up because they are not being expressed, and then may burst out unpredictably, which may feel extremely unsafe both to the child and often to the adult(s) involved. One of the excellent activity sheets published by Winston's Wish (Appendix A) recognises this and suggests that adults help a child create a 'first aid kit'. The first step is to check that a child understands what a conventional first aid kit is and what would be in it. The child is then encouraged to draw a box and decorate it. This is followed up by encouraging her to imagine situations she is likely to find difficult and therefore to feel strong emotions such as sadness, anger or frustration. Examples might be a family outing, an event such as a birthday, and memories brought back by a piece of music or a particular place. It would be at these times that she would want the assistance of an emotional first aid kit to help her cope. The next stage is to think about things that could make her feel better and could be useful in the difficult situations. This might be texting friends, listening to or making music, kicking a ball around, having a nice meal, eating a cream bun. Finally get the child to list or draw pictures of all the helpful things she has thought of all around the first aid box she has drawn and decorated. This 'first aid' sheet the child has created can be carried in a pocket or bag and called upon when she feels particularly pent-up.

Whatever techniques, methods or resources are used, a child with unresolved grief needs to be enabled to name and really experience the feelings that have been denied. It is then that fantasies and 'magical thinking' are likely to be spoken about and the adult can supply the information that the child needs. The child may, of course, try to avoid hearing certain items of information so the adult may have to be quite firm about what needs to be done, e.g. 'I know you really don't want to hear about this' or 'I know this gives you really sore feelings but *this is what we have to do*'.

There are some particularly difficult experiences in a child's life where he or she may need specialist help to deal with the effects. Examples of such events are the imprisonment or mental illness of one or both parents or of a sibling, incest in the family, murder of a member of the family or of a friend. The needs of this child are, of course, the same as for any other child experiencing a loss, but the disturbance in the child is likely to be much greater. Therefore the child may well need to get help from workers with specialist training and support such as child psychotherapists, who can offer consistent and committed care to the child, and preferably to the family as well. Continuity at a time of difficult experience is of enormous benefit.

Whatever the loss the child has suffered, her self-esteem will have been damaged and one of the most important healing processes is the repair to self-esteem. Once children begin to express and share their held-in feelings and the grief work begins, then self-esteem will begin to grow. Children also need to be valued for their efforts in coming to terms with their grief, and they may need to be helped to learn self-control and responsibility more appropriate to their age.

Children also need to be helped to say 'goodbye' to the person and sometimes also to the place that is being grieved. For a planned or anticipated loss or separation, it is likely to be easier to prepare for the change and say 'goodbye'. Where this can be done with the real person and the real place, so much the better. If the loss has been sudden and goodbyes have not been said, then anniversaries or holidays will often raise this need. If it is not possible to say 'goodbye' to the person or place, then a symbolic 'goodbye' using such aids as letters, photographs, drawings and play telephones will help to fill that gap. These techniques can help to round off the emotional work and enable the child to reinvest in her current life, reconnect with emotions and form satisfying relationships again in the present.

Summary

- Recognition of the loss, expression of feeling and acceptance of the new situation are the basic tasks of children's mourning. The counselling attitudes are the same when working with children and adults, but the skills with children are different in various ways, including a more direct, active and playful style.
- Children's grief, like adults', requires the expression of feeling and follows a similar pattern. It can be resolved just like adults' grief if certain conditions are met.
- It is important to respond immediately and openly to children's grief, accepting their feelings whatever they may be.
- If children's feelings become buried and the reactions delayed, then grief may become complicated and it is sometimes necessary to offer extra help. This help includes encouraging the child to express and share her pent-up feelings, exploring fantasies and magical thinking and clarifying facts and realities of the child's life.
- Specific techniques for working with children can be used in such circumstances.
- Children will often need extra help to talk about difficult issues such as incest in the family, imprisonment or mental illness of a parent or other member of the close family.
- A child's self-esteem will begin to improve as grieving progresses, but help may be needed to affirm her growing self-esteem until she is confident enough to manage with her own resources.
- Children need to be encouraged to find ways to maintain the continuing bonds with the lost or dead loved ones. These bonds will be represented for children both through the memories in their minds and through tangible mementoes.
- Some form of 'goodbye' usually needs to be made before a child can be said to have internalised the grieving for her particular stage, and be in a position to move on to her current life tasks.

Part IV

Anger and guilt

Chapter 14

Understanding anger and guilt

We indicated in Chapter 4 that feelings of both anger and guilt are an essential part of any grieving process. We have set aside this chapter for discussing them, not because these feelings are more important than other feelings, nor because they are necessarily the most difficult for the griever or the loss counsellor, but because these feelings are generally experienced as the most powerful. As we mentioned earlier, these are the two feelings that people are most likely to fear and repress, and that our society is prone to deny. Thus a collusive secrecy develops between the frightened individual and the denying community which gives particular power to platitudes such as 'Don't speak ill of the dead'. When feelings of guilt and anger are consistently repressed and denied they find expression in very indirect ways, and can lead to complications or blocks in the grieving process.

Before looking at ways of working with guilt and anger, it is important to understand the origins of these feelings.

Origins of anger and guilt

In Chapter 1 we looked at how our responses to loss are there right from our earliest days. Our first lessons in managing loss happen as we begin to separate from our caring figure, usually our mother. We suggested that by about the age of six months, a baby with a secure attachment has begun to have a marked preference for one person who is recognised as different from itself. As this human connection forms, a baby seems to fall in love with that person. This capacity to love is related to the love the baby is receiving. At this stage the loved person is seen as all good and, in some sense, an extension of the self.

Over the next 18 months more and more physical and psychological separation generally takes place. The way a child reacts to and handles these separations is very dependent on the quality of attachment to the mother. This in turn is dependent on the mother's inner world: her loss history and her capacity to form attachments. Her capacity to psychobiologically attune to and intuit her baby's emotional feelings, to make vital emotional communications and to give care and support, will also be decisive, as will the succour that she in turn receives from her family and surrounding network (Chapters 1, 5 and 9).

If this goes well, then as the intense attachment of the early months begins to wane, the baby begins to explore on its own. The mother is beginning to re-engage with her own life and take steps to live more separately from her baby, but at her baby's pace. This means that she is not always available to meet every need and, naturally enough, the baby hates her and is angry with her. It must seem to the infant, with an infant's understanding, that the all-good mother who loves her, is there when needed, cuddles her and holds her tenderly simply cannot also be the all-bad mother who leaves her, and even chooses to be without her, when she goes out! How could she be? Thus as infants we seem to split up these different feelings, keeping loving feelings in one compartment of the mind and hating and angry feelings in another. In a sense, we do not let hateful and angry feelings 'contaminate' good feelings. Perhaps we even fear that hateful feelings could 'eliminate' the loving feelings or, worse still, 'exterminate' the person we also love so much.

Winnicott (1964) suggested that if the mother's failure to be everything the child wants is attuned well enough to the emotional maturity of the child, then this gradual disillusionment will enable personal growth to occur. The mother not only cannot be everything the child wants, she also will not either do or give the child everything it wants: another form of disillusionment. The child begins to learn that 'life is not fair' and one cannot have everything one wants, which also brings anger when this cannot be accepted. We reach the inevitability of disillusionment when we accept that life will not always be fair.

Disillusionment in a loving environment, where the adults are able to accept and recognise both the toddler's love and hate, stops these feelings being so frightening and unacceptable. This enables the child to learn to tolerate some measure of her hate towards those she loves. Thus, by the time the child is about three years old she has learned to tolerate both love and hate; in other words, ambivalence. In this way the good mother and bad mother will be understood as one 'good enough mother' rather than two separate mothers.

As well as having an inner mental picture of a 'good enough' mother, who is not perfect and will fail us, but will also love us, we seem to develop a similar mental picture of ourselves so that we can allow ourselves to be angry and hating as well as loving. This capacity to love ourselves, including accepting our angry and hate feelings, grows out of our parents' love and acceptance and is the beginning of self-esteem.

Self-esteem is, of course, not the only facet of our internal world to be influenced by our parents. Around the age of five we can observe the beginnings of a conscience, which is initially like an internal message system drawn from the external voices of people around us. The external voices are then 'taken inside' this developing conscience, which gives us an internal sense of what is right and wrong, and helps us maintain a good enough picture of ourselves. By about the age of five we begin to control our behaviour because of messages from our conscience, rather than because of parental commands and the consequent fear of the loss of their love. Initially these messages are, of course, replicas of the do's and don'ts of our parents. Inevitably, therefore, where our parents are too strict or unreasonable our conscience will also be too strict. Conversely, where parents set no limits on standards of behaviour, a child gets little help in developing her own conscience and is then reliant on learning this from other people, such as teachers, employers or even high court judges, later in her life.

Our conscience communicates with us through a sensation of guilt which we frequently experience physically as a churning in the stomach or as a clutching at the heart. It is sometimes difficult to distinguish guilt from fear. The level of guilt is matched to the demands of the conscience, and both grow gradually. When these demands are reasonable then the feeling of guilt is appropriate to the 'naughty' act and we try not to repeat the act.

In our society children are frequently forbidden expression of their angry reactions, and are often left with guilt not just about unreasonable behaviour, but also about their own feelings and thoughts. Then, rather than being helped to manage their angry behaviour in a context of an understanding of their natural feelings, they are left with unreasonably high levels of guilt. Reasonable levels of guilt about behaviour are difficult to develop when the very thoughts or feelings related to the behaviour are not allowed. Feelings of hate in particular are often taboo and consequently denied. Winnicott (1949) pointed out that there are many reasons why a mother might hate her children, yet his list of 18 reasons for hate caused a furore at the time, as the mothers who read Winnicott's words energetically denied their hating feelings! This highlights the difficulty for the child: for if her mother cannot admit to such feelings, how can the child possibly learn to express her own frightening feelings and manage her difficult behaviour? If, however, a mother can express at least some of her hate, but not act on it, then her child learns to do so as well. The child will also be able to tolerate some feelings of hate towards those she loves without having to behave so hatefully that she comes to hate herself. Her self-esteem, which might have been damaged by her hateful behaviour, can be maintained and she can then begin to manage her behaviour.

If feelings of anger and hate are suppressed in early childhood, they often emerge as uncontrollable rage in adults when they are frustrated. A common example nowadays is road-rage, which seems to arise when one driver feels blocked by another and tries to deal with this through a violent, vengeful attack. Possibly the driver was never enabled to understand and manage rage and frustration as a child, so a current frustration turns into revenge against an innocent 'blocker' rather than against the original frustrating relationship.

Revenge is a way of 'making' the attacked person experience a hurt in much the same way as the attacker felt hurt as a child. There seems to be a primitive part of all of us that rushes from the experienced hurt into a rush of blame and then a revenge attack. We can see this played out on the political stage again and again, although there is some evidence of stronger voices calling out for stopping, thinking and understanding rather than rushing into active revenge.

Harold Kushner's book *When Bad Things Happen to Good People* (1982), written after his baby son was diagnosed with and died from an incurable congenital disease, tells how he, like Job, was able to be angry with God for such gross 'unfairness'. He gives a moving account of his guilt, anger, despair and helplessness in the face of such a tragedy. Anger arises when we are frustrated and cannot have what we want, and part of growing up is becoming disillusioned as we gradually realise we cannot have everything we want, nor are we able to control our world. Kushner was able to work his way through intense feelings of hurt and pain and to avoid taking out his revenge on others.

There have also been some extraordinary parents in Northern Ireland who, when their children have been murdered in the sectarian violence, have managed not to act out their revenge but to seek peace and reconciliation.

The deeper the hurt, the more aggressive the revenge is likely to be and the greater the likelihood of a continuous cycle of deprivation, attack and revenge. Sometimes when children are attacked verbally or physically and deprived of love and support by adults, they become deeply hurt and misunderstood and may then take out their revenge on other children. Mary Bell in the 1960s and Robert Thompson and Jon Venables in the 1990s were children whose revenge attacks have damaged their own lives for ever. Perhaps these children were overwhelmed with envy of the apparently more loved children who become their victims. Powerful feelings of envy and the desire for revenge frequently occur when people are coping with loss, particularly when the deaths of children are sudden and violent. The parents of the victims of Bell, Venables and Thompson have been outraged and sought revenge, not least after the court's decision to free these damaged 'children' from prison and to give them new names to protect them from such revenge.

Society's denial of the hurt underlying the revengeful acts is depressingly typical of the general denial of the importance of children's feelings and of the impact of children's experiences on their subsequent behaviour, whether as children or as resposible adults. Any one of us may struggle to manage the disillusionment of not being able to have everything we want when we are filled with intensely painful feelings of envy. Yet if the pain of envy can be faced, then we can begin to recognise positive aspects of envy and make efforts to acquire that which was envied in others for ourselves.

As age creeps inexorably onward, we have to face the pain of losing youth and moving towards death. There are some aspects of modern medicine that make it much harder for us to face the inevitable envy of youth and the subsequent loss and disillusionment that accompany ageing. For instance, various methods of assisted reproduction, such as IVF (in vitro fertilisation) and GIFT (gamete intrafallopian transfer) are used when people are already trying to face the loss of infertility. This can result in people regenerating hope about fertility as they go through several cycles of treatment. Each failed conception is another loss, but it is balanced against having another try. At some point, if unsuccessful, the couple have to face their infertility as well as their envy, for it is likely to seem even more unfair when other people do indeed conceive through assisted reproduction (Syme, 1997). There are also many examples in medicine where 'heroic' treatments can sometimes literally postpone death. These modern methods may tempt us into believing that we can somehow 'control' death. Thus it is quite common to hear people saying 'if' I die rather than 'when' I die. When these methods do not work, we can feel even more cheated and envious of others. Yet gradually we have to face that we cannot have everything we want and that we need to accept the inevitability of death.

Uncomplicated anger and guilt in grieving

In both Anne's and Geoff's stories in Chapter 4 anger and guilt were present; some appropriate, some less appropriate. It is of course reasonable to be angry when we are bereaved or abandoned, yet there is considerable difficulty in acknowledging anger in our society. When asked about their anger, a lot of bereaved will say, 'Of course I'm not angry', yet in the next breath they will express considerable irritation with, for instance, the dead person's employer, or the priest, or the hospital or doctors. This may well be appropriate anger, for mistakes do happen, but frequently such anger, experienced towards someone living, is covering anger that cannot yet be directed towards the dead or lost person, by whom they have been abandoned. This anger is sometimes difficult for those, such as nurses, doctors, counsellors or priests, on the receiving end to manage, but it is quite natural and, fortunately, tends to be short-lived.

Guilt is the other very strong emotion that the grieving feel. Some guilt will be quite reasonable, for most of us will be aware of times when we hurt someone we loved and are aware that we can no longer repair or heal the hurt. However, much of the guilt in grief will arise from our difficulty in tolerating our ambivalent feelings of both love and hate towards the lost person. Yes, we did love them, but there were times when we hated them, even wished them dead or at least gone. These thoughts will be the source of some irrational guilt. For even if we have been allowed to express such negative thoughts and feelings as children, we will still feel some guilt when we have similar thoughts as adults. This guilt is natural and brief.

The combination of realistic and unrealistic guilt frequently leads to some idealisation of the dead. When grievers themselves begin to develop a more rounded remembrance of the dead person, then the idealisation passes quickly and active intervention is not needed. This was illustrated very vividly for a bereavement counsellor leading a group of recently bereaved widows. The following is his account of the session.

> This was my third session with the Smith Street Group. They were all still telling me and each other what wonderful husbands they had lost. What angelic and model husbands they had all been married to! I was just wondering how to confront the group with my disbelief of this idealisation when . . . 'Eeeh . . . but my Jimmy, 'e were a reight bugga 'e were!' [God bless you Mrs Roberts! I thought] . . . and then they all started . . . and the real husbands began to emerge, human beings every one of them. I was not the only one to feel relief, it surged through the whole group. Mrs Roberts, in expressing the other side of her feelings towards her husband, had helped us all. Each woman in that group was enabled to confront her angry feelings and remember the times she had hated her husband as well as those when she loved him. She could thus take responsibility for her ambivalent feelings. The idealisation, and with it her guilt, began to slip away and she could move towards a more realistic, affectionate and human 'Jimmy' in her own memory and in her heart.

In the case of idealisation, the hating feelings towards the lost person are being denied. The reverse can also happen, most commonly in divorce when the absent person may be vilified and any loving feelings denied. Usually both parties have felt very attacked and hurt by the other person. Frequently this hurt has gone unsaid throughout the relationship. The abandoned one may look for evidence to make sense of their hurt feelings and indeed ask other people to confirm that the lost or dead person was insensitive, difficult, selfish or hateful. In this case the counsellor needs to build a safe enough relationship for the griever or divorcee's hurt to be recognised. As the hurtful aspects of the relationship are recognised and the pain acknowledged and accepted, the griever can normally begin to remember the good parts of the relationship and tolerate his or her ambivalent feelings. Where the griever seems to be stuck within the hating aspects of the relationship, the counsellor, in reflecting disbelief in the one-sided portrait being presented, can usually help the griever towards a more realistic picture of the lost person and recognition of the ambivalent feelings. This work is part of the second task of mourning (Table 11.1, p. 117) and enables inappropriate guilt to lift and the grief work to continue.

Thus the anger and guilt are linked to coming to terms with a real relationship with the lost person and also with the ambivalent feelings towards the person who has gone. A major part of work with the grieving is, therefore, to help them explore the relationship through working with the feelings that are hidden or that are at the very edge of awareness. An exploration of these feelings and of the positive and negative aspects of the lost person can create a more realistic picture. With this more balanced, realistic and sometimes affectionate memory, it is actually more possible to internalise the lost relationship. This is as true for separation, divorce and other losses as it is for bereavement.

We have outlined above some of the ways of working with the natural anger and guilt experienced in the typical grief process. Such difficulties with anger and guilt are usually short-lived and, once recognised, the feelings begin to wane and grief moves on. However, when nothing seems to move and a particular feeling seems to be well and truly stuck, then it is likely we are working with more complicated anger and guilt.

Complicated anger and guilt in grieving

In Chapter 5 we looked at how the outcome of grief was markedly affected by external and internal determinants. With this knowledge we are alert to the circumstances where grieving is more likely to be prolonged and complicated. Certain external circumstances, such as coincidental deaths or losses and successive deaths and losses, result in a more prolonged grief, but not necessarily a complicated grief. If the person has developed the capacity to grieve they will eventually manage even the most extreme external circumstances. However, if this capacity has not developed or barely developed, then, whatever the external determinants, the grieving can become complicated with the griever stuck with one particular set of feelings. Without fail, the two emotions that are particularly difficult to manage in complicated grief are anger and guilt. In other words, it is the inability to deal with ambivalent feelings, or to tolerate hate within a loving relationship, that is critical, both during the relationship and after the end of the relationship.

We suggested earlier in this chapter that the ability to tolerate ambivalent feelings develops during the first three years of life. However, some children are not given much help in learning to tolerate ambivalence. When a child is not allowed or enabled to have hating feelings towards those she loves, she 'cannot' be angry with them or hate them. In the child's logic: if she cannot hate her mother at all, then the mother must be 'nothing-but-good'; and if mother is 'nothing-but-good', she, the child, must be 'nothing-but-bad' to have these 'bad' feelings; if she is 'all-bad' then she must deserve to be hated and punished and must therefore be guilty: a very tortuous but common train of thought! It will then be difficult for her to love herself and her self-esteem will not be able to grow. When the capacity to express anger is blocked and guilt is overwhelming, the ability to think is lost. The capacity to repair and forgive is limited and self-esteem will be further damaged. Guilt will be the predominant experience and losses in adult life will be difficult to grieve. Patterns of behaviour then develop that may 'protect' the griever from unwanted or intolerable feeling in the short term, but prevent the grief work from continuing. Some of the patterns that protect a person from difficulties with guilt and anger will be outlined below. When these patterns of denial (idealisation, bitterness, depression, or suicidal ideation) develop and persist, it is important to recognise how they function to protect from deeper feelings.

Idealisation is one way of protecting the self from difficulties with hate and anger in a relationship. The Smith Street Group offered an example of brief idealisation, which quickly disappeared when Mrs Roberts admitted to feelings of hate and enabled the others to do likewise, in many instances remembering them with some affection as well. In complicated grief, however, the idealisation pattern seems to get more stuck. The relationship is regarded as 'perfect' with a denial of natural anger, hurts or disagreements. This can happen between couples in a relationship but also between parents and their children. When one member of the relationship is lost, then a persistent inability to tolerate hateful and angry feelings results in a prolonged idealisation. A sign of this in Western culture might be the creation of a permanent 'shrine'. The shrine is sometimes the dead person's room or it may be the corner of a room set out with pictures and flowers, or may include the urn containing the ashes. In Japan, however, a shrine to the deceased is a sign of respect.

Prolonged idealisation can also occur when difficult losses happen to people who already have severe difficulty in expressing feelings. Imagine, for instance, the situation of parents who have difficulty in expressing anger constructively having an unresolved row with their teenage son. He then rushes out of the house, takes the family car and is killed in an accident. The parents' feelings of guilt and responsibility may be so immense and inexpressible that they lead to idealisation and then the creation of a permanent shrine.

Another fraught situation for people who have difficulty in expressing feelings, and who deny anger and hate, is the long-term nursing of a relative. The survivor may well have hated the relative at times in the past, particularly if they had nursed the relative out of a sense of duty and if they had been hurt when the relative had become spiteful as they aged. If the nursing person was unable to speak of this hurt or to recognise and express their hate, then when the death actually occurs, naturally enough the hurt and hate predominate. This can become entrenched and the griever gets stuck with a bitterness that almost matches the spitefulness of the departed person, thus leading to more hate. Any feelings of sadness and love have become lost. The bitterness seems to prevent any feelings of love, and the griever seems wrapped in the pain of resentment and bitterness rather than the pain of sadness and grief.

This in turn can get covered by a layer of 'guilt', which serves to mask the bitterness or envy. Love can then get blocked out and a position of distant withdrawal seems justified. These defensive layers can make work long and arduous for the counsellor. In the next chapter we shall consider how working with the denied feelings might look in practice.

Summary

- Anger and guilt are the feelings that most people are likely to fear and repress and that our society is most likely to deny.
- From well before six months most babies begin a process of separation from, and have the capacity to develop feelings about, their mothers.
- There seems to be a tendency at an early stage in this separation process to split the all-good-and-all-loving feelings from all-bad-and-all-hating feelings.
- When a mother can manage very gradually to fail to meet the infant's needs at a pace that is attuned to that infant, then the infant will be able to 'understand' that the 'good mother' she loves and the 'bad mother' she hates are one and the same person.
- This 'good enough' mother enables the child, by about the age of three, to tolerate love and hate towards the same person.
- By the age of five the child has begun to develop a conscience of her own and a consequent capacity to feel guilt about her actions.
- When guilt is reasonable in relation to behaviour then it can be listened to, responded to and the wrongs put right. Appropriate guilt can lead to reparation and forgiveness and the child can feel good about herself again.
- When angry and hateful feelings have been denied in childhood, then those adults will fail in a crisis to distinguish between thoughts and feelings on the one hand and action or behaviour on the other hand. In a crisis such as loss, they may build up an inappropriate burden of guilt about both thoughts and feelings. This actually hinders them from moving through the grief process towards a letting go of that which is lost.
- In more complicated grief, when ambivalence cannot be tolerated and guilt is excessive, protective patterns develop and grief fails to progress. Feelings are further denied.
- Those who have severe difficulty in tolerating feelings of anger, envy or hate towards those they have lost develop protective patterns, such as idealisation, which will protect them from unbearable guilt.
- When they have severe difficulty in recognising feelings of love and compassion towards those they have come to hate, they may protect themselves from unbearable pain through vilification.

Chapter 15

Working with anger and guilt in more complicated grief

In the previous chapter we described how complicated grief arises. Complicated grief may be difficult to work with and the counsellor needs to have developed self-knowledge and have integrated the basic counselling attitudes outlined in Chapter 3, so that when sudden difficulties with acceptance, empathy and congruence occur they are recognised as uncharacteristic. If a counsellor realises that she is unexpectedly angry, puzzled, disbelieving or judgemental, then this will lead her to reflect on the process. Is she picking up the client's difficulties with anger and guilt? Or has the client's material sparked off feelings associated with unresolved losses of her own? In Chapters 16 and 18 respectively we consider how a supervisor can help a counsellor recognise and work with more complicated feelings arising in her when with some clients, and to handle situations where her own grief is interfering with her work as a counsellor.

This awareness of the counsellor that the anger or guilt which she is sensing 'does not belong to her' is a very important advanced counselling skill. It enables the counsellor to recognise that she is sensing the frightening feelings behind the protective patterns that develop in more complicated grief. When feelings of anger and guilt are too frightening (Chapter 14) they are avoided or denied and a protective pattern develops. This may avoid feelings of guilt and anger but it prevents the grief work from progressing. The capacity of the counsellor to pick up an underlying feeling is, of course, one aspect of sensitive awareness which requires continued commitment to developing self-awareness. A decision to use such awareness in counselling often grows over a period and arises out of a series of interactions. As responses in an interaction are usually very specific to those two people at that point, it is difficult to give brief and natural vignettes. The examples given here need to be understood as greatly simplified parts of a much more complex whole relationship. The counsellor has to decide at what point in the relationship to use this sensing of the underlying feelings to help the client. The client may be desperately trying not to experience a feeling which, however, needs to be addressed if the grief process is to proceed. The counsellor's skill is to notice and understand the protective mechanism and its function, while still recognising the sense of the avoided feeling. In this way the client can begin to feel safe enough to recognise and accept the dreaded feeling, trusting that the counsellor will not be overwhelmed by it. This can enable the client to face their own feelings.

There are many patterns of behaviour that people use in everyday life to protect themselves from other more frightening feelings. We wisely protect ourselves by being very upset only when we are with safe people, at least as far as we can. Normally the strong feelings in response to loss tend to break through any loosely held protective patterns. Where, however, the capacity to grieve is limited, the protective patterns will be held much more rigidly and the counsellor will find this kind of grief reaction more challenging to work with. In considering the following examples of such 'stuck' patterns, we shall:

1 outline the protective mechanism with an illustrative example;
2 consider the function of the protective pattern;
3 consider the counsellor's likely feelings and possible dilemmas;
4 suggest some possible strategies and verbal responses;
5 consider common counsellor difficulties associated with this pattern.

The 'stuck' patterns

1 Idealisation as a protection against anger or guilt

Mrs Roberts from Chapter 14 helped the other widows to remember their more real husbands through her acceptance of her own angry feelings with her husband Jimmy. Their idealisations of their husbands were short-lived. When, however, 'unacceptable' angry feelings get 'stuck', as they did for Mrs Brown, the idealisation pattern becomes more engrained.

> Mrs Brown, an elderly and highly dependent widow, has talked non-stop about her dead husband Michael, who had gone off fishing against her will on a very stormy day and been drowned.
>
> *Mrs Brown:* He was so wonderful, he was the most perfect husband anyone could ever wish for. There was never an angry word between us . . . He looked after me, cared for me, did the garden, even helped old Mrs Jones next door. We loved each other so much, there was nothing ever came between us . . .

How the pattern functions

Mrs Brown seems here to be protecting herself from any feelings of anger in response to loss. Her anger may be greatly intensified by her additional angry feelings about his going off fishing that day against her will and leaving her alone. His leaving her alone turned out to be not just that Wednesday but for ever, and her anger in response to this fate must have seemed unmanageable to Mrs Brown. To cope, she has denied her anger and covered it over with idealisation. Her grief was stuck.

Counsellor's feelings and dilemmas

The counsellor listening to Mrs Brown might feel some surprise at this paragon of all human virtue, and is then likely to feel some irritation as the eulogy continues and the more complete picture is not recognised. He might be wistfully remembering Mrs Roberts from the Smith Street Group, who, to everyone's relief, had been able to let go of her idealised Jimmy quite quickly! How might the counsellor use this irritation constructively?

Unfortunately, tackling Mrs Brown's idealisation 'head on' might only serve to convince her that her angry feelings really were unacceptable or even dangerous and she would be even less likely to face them. On the other hand, going along with the idealisation of Michael will almost certainly convince Mrs Brown that even her counsellor is frightened by her angry feelings; they must indeed be dangerous!

Counsellor's responses

Somehow the counsellor needs to find a way of highlighting the pattern, recognising its protective function and what is being guarded against: in this case, feelings of anger. If the counsellor can actually name, make sense of, and show an accepting understanding of these 'dangerous' angry feelings, then they are already less dangerous and becoming more recognised. The following counsellor response is just one attempt to combine these elements.

> I get a sense from you, Mrs Brown, that Michael was . . . well . . . a bit of a saint really . . . almost not quite human. I'm thinking that it might be a bit awkward to be cross with a saint? . . . Yet I guess you could have felt quite cross when he left without you that morning.

Perhaps you can think of other responses using your own words that combine these elements and still help to make sense of the protective pattern?

Counsellor's difficulties

Counsellor difficulties associated with this pattern can be the pressure to collude with the idealisation of her husband, Michael, or the temptation to be irritable with this 'ridiculous' picture. A further source of potential irritation might be Mrs Brown's ability to ignore the counsellor's intervention, which might make it necessary to repeat this response on several occasions. It may then be necessary to recognise with her how she refuses to hear certain things. A possible intervention might be:

> Mrs Brown, I notice that every time I raise the possibility of having angry feelings about Michael or Michael's death you seem not to hear me. I guess there's been something really scary about that . . . Yet I wonder if we might be able to look at that now . . .?

It may take some time before there is enough trust for the client to begin to face the cut-off feelings. Discussion with a supervisor should help the counsellor to steer the path between collusion and too rapid confrontation.

2 Vilification as a protection against pain and underlying love

Some vilification is also natural as a part of the response to loss and may indeed be indistinguishable from the initial expression of anger at having been abandoned. When, however, the vilification gets stuck with repeated condemnations it may be to protect the griever from extreme feelings of pain related to the lost love.

> Frank (Table 9.1, p. 87) is talking about his wife Lizzie six months after they separated. His tone is clipped and spiteful.

Frank:	Lizzie was so useless. I was forced to marry her because she threatened to kill herself and the baby if I didn't. She was depressed all the time and never did anything in the house, the place was a tip. Now she won't talk to me and everything goes through my sister Mary. She's trying to get Mary on her side . . . she's spiteful, cunning and stupid and can't even manage the children.

How the pattern functions

At this point Frank seems very bitter. He has not got a good word to say about Lizzie or the children, and seems to be protecting himself against any feelings of the pain and sadness he would have to feel if he could recognise his love for them. Understandably, the more bitter and accusatory he becomes with them, the more Lizzie and the children withdraw from him, thus reinforcing his sense of bitterness and loneliness. His grief seems stuck.

Counsellor's feelings and dilemmas

The counsellor listening to Frank might initially feel fed up with his bitter haranguing and find herself wanting to punish him for being so arrogant and so beastly about Lizzie. Or she might find herself drawn into the anti-Lizzie vilification campaign and find herself thinking that Lizzie ought to 'pull up her socks' or improve in some way. Either way, she is getting drawn into the accusatory pattern and, like Frank himself, is losing touch with Frank's internal world. How might she recognise or confront Frank's protective strategy without being drawn into the accusatory pattern and being punitive in her responses?

Counsellor's responses

The challenge to the counsellor is to recognise the existence and value of Frank's internal world of hidden feelings and fears, while also making sense of the protective pattern and not punishing him. The following two responses attempt, in slightly different ways, to combine these elements.

> I wonder whether hating Lizzie so intensely seems, in some ways, safer than letting yourself feel hurt . . .?
> OR
> I wonder whether hating Lizzie so intensely seems safer than letting yourself feel the longing and pain underneath . . .?

You will be able to find your own words to express this idea of identifying the lost feelings. Obviously, using a non-punitive tone of voice is essential.

Counsellor's difficulties

There are, of course, times when any words we use may be heard as punitive by certain clients. These situations are always worth discussing with a supervisor to help check whether the 'being-punished' feelings in the client are actually coming from the client's internal emotional world, or are indeed an appropriate response to inappropriately punitive or clumsy remarks made by the counsellor.

It is easy for the counsellor to forget that these unpleasant vilification patterns in the client often cover up deep-seated fear and pain. Rather like a hedgehog or cactus, the prickly bits are there to protect the more vulnerable parts underneath. It was a bit like that with Christopher in the next example.

3 Anger as a protection against intimacy and underlying despair

When a trust has been betrayed and an intense intimacy lost, the world may seem to contain only helplessness and despair. To begin to trust anyone else might seem to be courting further rejection. Ferocious anger may be a way of protecting a person from beginning to build a new trust or from feelings of helplessness or despair. They can therefore find themselves avoiding the very closeness or trust they need to help with the grief. Sometimes they can swing between the two positions of a cautious and terrified approach and then vehement avoidance, tinged with longing.

> Christopher (Exercise 10.4, p. 109) talks of his lover Jake, who recently died of Aids. He is angry and isolated and is very frightened of trusting the counsellor. He walks into the first session shouting.
>
> *Christopher:*   Just how do you think you can help me? Do you know what it feels like to have your lover die? You can't give him back to me, can you?

How the pattern functions

Christopher has been deeply hurt and also frightened by Jake's death. The reactions of blame he has met with, in society, and to a lesser extent in his own family, have not helped him with the unreasonable guilt he has experienced in relation to Jake's illness. Some of their gay friends helped enormously while Jake was ill and dying, but they now seem to have drifted away. Christopher is alone in his grief and is very frightened of trusting anyone, especially anyone outside his immediate circle, whom he fears might reject him. Yet he desperately needs someone with whom to share his grief. Anger is often an expression of some kind of hope of renewed contact (remember Tom in Chapter 1); it can also serve to keep someone at arm's length. This is potentially confusing to the unwary counsellor!

Counsellor's feelings and dilemmas

The counsellor faced with Christopher's angry outburst might first be tempted to ignore the anger and work to reassure or calm him down and then to feel very sorry for him, the victim. Or she might be tempted to retaliate and fiercely insist that he stop being angry or even suggest that he 'pull himself together'. She might even find herself drawn into the pattern of dread and blame surrounding Aids.

Counsellor's responses

The counsellor's challenge is not to flinch or to be controlled by Christopher's anger, but to try to recognise its various messages without retaliation, punishment or dread. It is important to be direct and not to 'beat about the bush', nor to use euphemisms. Society's various unrealistic attitudes to Aids make all of this difficult. However, the basic counselling approach of recognising feelings and trying to understand the meaning of behaviours still applies.

The following responses attempt to initiate this process of recognition and unravelling, which could lead to the sort of trust and intimacy which Christopher both longs for and fears.

> That's right, Christopher, I can't give Jake back to you and, you're right, I don't know what it feels like for you. I guess you feel pretty furious about everything and are not at all sure you can trust a stranger like me at this point?
> OR
> Christopher, you are really angry right now and that certainly makes sense to me when I know that you feel . . . possibly . . . so let down. I imagine you might be pretty wary about trusting me in case I let you down too?

Can you now think up other words that could help Christopher to explore his angry feelings and understand more about his dilemma of longing for intimacy and yet fearing rejection? This struggle with trust can cause great loneliness.

Christopher's pattern has many similarities to the previous pattern of vilification illustrated by Frank. There are some differences: Frank was protecting himself from feelings of pain and underlying love, and was grieving a relationship that had been broken, but Lizzie was still alive and his anger was directed towards her. Christopher was trying to protect himself from his dilemma of a longing for intimacy and a fear of rejection, as well as from his underlying feelings of loneliness and despair now that Jake was dead. The counsellor was the one who 'received' the anger, and her challenge is to hear and understand before she moves towards challenging him about both his longing for contact and his lonely withdrawal. It is important that the counsellor finds a way to put his dilemma into words. If she can present the idea in a non-threatening way, then he can begin to articulate it for himself.

Counsellor's difficulties

Again it is important for the counsellor to respond neither defensively nor in a punishing way to Christopher's attack. Recognising the shared responsibility for the relationship can help to take any pity, condescension or retaliation out of the response. Tone of voice, pacing and body language will also influence the sense of caring in the relationship. One of the reasons why Christopher was attacking the counsellor so vehemently may have been to do with his unconscious envy. In his fantasy, the counsellor will seem to him to be someone who is not alone, and who does not have a deep dilemma about whether to approach someone, or to avoid them out of terror of intimacy. He may feel deeply envious of this and unconsciously want to attack and destroy the good things in the counsellor so that he is not so troubled by what she has and he has not. Delicately helping a client to recognise the experience of envy can be very useful in getting to the root of some envious attacks.

The following protective patterns are more complicated and may demand more of the counsellor.

4 Depression as a protection against intense feelings

Depression can protect some people from feelings of unbearable anger and hate by cutting off feeling altogether. Two examples of this follow. In the first one the depression manifests itself as a vague sense of hopelessness (Martha) and in the second one it is experienced as a blankness with no apparent feeling (Peter). Neither of these 'protections' can actually protect anyone from feeling the hopeless blank sensation of depression, but it may dampen the intensity of hate and rage. Prolonged or extended depression in response to loss may be a long tunnel of darkness, hopelessness and sometimes utter despair. It was like this for Martha.

Martha

Martha shuffled in looking grey, drooping and without any sparkle of life. Her boyfriend, Tim, had committed suicide in September last year. He had hanged himself. It is now February and she has so far shown no signs of grieving, but is stuck in a deep feelingless depression. She does not mention Tim.

> *Martha:* Well, it's all right really. I'm just depressed, that's all. I left my job in November, because I wasn't much use at it any-way . . . I don't feel like bothering to go for anything else . . . What's the point? . . . It's all hopeless.

How the pattern functions

Martha learnt long ago that anger and hate were unacceptable feelings to the adults who cared for her. Therefore after Tim's death she could not feel anger towards him, nor hate him for what he had done. Had she done so, she would have been overwhelmed by guilt, so she cut feelings off instead and adopted the protective pattern of despair expressed through hopelessness.

Counsellor's feelings and dilemmas

The very 'feeling-less-ness' of depression can be hard for the counsellor to bear, and he may find himself feeling helpless. A common counsellor response to feelings of helplessness is to set off on a wild goose chase to 'find-the-feeling'. The client is by now, of course, adept at hiding feelings and will reject any help that is likely to evoke feelings, so she can draw the counsellor into just such a chase. This can often be a very intellectual exploration. The overall result is to distance both of them even further from the actual experiencing of the feelings of helplessness. The counsellor needs to be very careful not to be drawn into doing 'all the work'. A simple rule-of-thumb for a counsellor is that when he finds himself doing more than half the work, he should ask himself what is going on. It may be that the counsellor needs to face feelings of hopelessness and helplessness in himself in order to stay with, and truly empathise with, Martha's state rather than 'running away' into being clever.

What can also happen when depression protects a client from anger and guilt is that the counsellor can find himself actually experiencing helplessness, anger or guilt, and sometimes all three together. Having checked with himself that these feelings are in no way his own, the counsellor has to decide how to bring these lost feelings into the open. Again, a way has to be found that is not punitive.

Counsellor's responses

As with other protective patterns, the main strategy is to recognise the pattern and the underlying feelings. This gradual (and it is often very gradual) recognition, expression and acceptance of anger and resentment usually result in the guilt beginning to lift, and with it the depression lightens. The counsellor's response below includes mention of Tim even though Martha avoids any mention of his name or his suicide. The counsellor also uses his own sense of anger as the basis for the suggestion that Martha may be feeling this about Tim.

> Martha, I notice you don't mention Tim or how he died. Perhaps you're not sure it's OK to mention him? Perhaps you're also not sure that you are allowed to be angry about him and what he did?

It is common for depressed clients to be particularly resistant to recognising and accepting the underlying feelings, so it may be necessary to comment on this. The following are examples of such responses.

> I notice, Martha, that when I raise the possibility of your having any feelings you seem not to hear what I'm saying.
> OR
> Martha, I find it interesting that when I mention Tim there seems to be no reaction from you. It's almost as if you didn't know or didn't dare to know whom or what I was talking about.

Counsellor's difficulties

Working with depression is challenging, and often requires enormous patience. Counsellors should keep taking such work to supervision. The supervisor can then help to decide when a depression is so well and truly stuck that referral to someone more specialised is necessary. Consulting with a supervisor is discussed in Chapters 16 and 18, and referral procedures in Chapter 17.

Peter

We mentioned earlier that depression can also manifest itself as blank feelinglessness. This is how Peter in the following example reacted to loss. Again the difficult, hidden feelings are usually anger and hate, but the lack of affect was probably hiding extreme feelings of pain and loss.

> Peter limped in bravely, trying to look cheerful, and yet looking curiously bland and unreal. He had been a sports teacher and an outstanding allround sportsman. When he was 24 he was involved in a climbing accident with his brother in Glencoe and had had to have one of his legs amputated. His physical recovery from the amputation had been continually dogged by pain from his missing leg. He was referred for counselling by his doctor, who noticed that Peter was having unexpected difficulties in managing his prosthesis.
>
> Peter: [Blank voice with little expression] I really am much better now, the doctor's been awfully helpful. I'm most grateful ... They've given me a special car now, you know, as well ... and I can more or less get about ... not as far as Glencoe of course ... [looks slightly surprised] ...

How the pattern functions

Peter seems to be protecting himself from extreme feelings of anger about the accident and his helplessness about his current condition and situation. His previous identity and sense of himself had been that of an extremely ablebodied person. The challenge of managing a prosthesis and adapting to his new identity was proving more than he could bear. However, like Martha he had learned that anger and hate were unacceptable feelings, so he responded by cutting off all feelings about himself or his situation, except that the word 'Glencoe' slipped out.

Counsellor's feelings and dilemmas

The counsellor might feel intense sympathy with Peter's difficult situation and would realise that he would have to draw on every bit of his maturity to manage his new life. Yet she might find herself curiously absent and uninvolved as she heard his string of words, perhaps only coming alive when Peter mentions 'Glencoe'. How might she use this oblique mention of Glencoe to help Peter get in touch with his painful feelings?

Counsellor's responses

As with Martha, the counsellor would have to make choices about which aspect of the protective pattern to highlight and which of the underlying feelings to mention. She might also find her responses unheard.

> Peter, you seemed almost surprised just now when you found yourself mentioning Glencoe. I'm guessing that there is still an enormous number of painful memories associated with Glencoe and what happened there.
> OR
> I can't get much of a sense of what you actually experienced . . . and yet [rising intonation] there must be real feelings underneath. I heard the word 'Glencoe' . . .

Counsellor's difficulties

The counsellor's difficulties would be similar to those of Martha's counsellor. The counsellor might find herself drawn into discussions about climbing or prostheses. She might need to reflect on how well Peter was managing to avoid his painful feelings.

5 Suicidal thoughts as a fantasy of release from pain and despair

Suicidal thoughts in response to loss, whatever the situation, usually grow out of a sense in that person that their feeling-world cannot be understood by anybody else. Often low self-esteem and feelings of hopelessness, helplessness or powerlessness contribute to this position. Sometimes clients mention the word 'suicide' as a way of expressing feelings of despair which, when expressed and recognised, may lift. Others may or may not mention suicide, but their intense feelings of despair may be leading them to think about ways of ending their life as the only apparent way of ending their despair. This was Vilna's position.

> Vilna had been abused both physically and sexually as a child by her own father. Her younger brother Stefan had, as he grew older, become her protector and her best friend. Eventually the abuse had stopped. Stefan had recently married, however, and his young wife, who was very jealous of the relationship between him and Vilna, was encouraging him to

emigrate to America to join her family. Vilna felt sure that they would go and that she would be left alone in Britain to look after her widowed father, who was becoming increasingly infirm and dependent. The rest of her family still lived in the Czech Republic.

Vilna: If Stefan goes, I can see no hope for me. Father will have to come and live with me and I will think only of the past and there will be no one to protect me. Why should I go on living?

Some weeks later:

Vilna: They have gone. I'm all alone, he has moved in and although he can't hurt me any more I can remember only the past. There is no one to protect me now and I can't see why I should go on . . .

How the pattern functions

Vilna seems to see suicide as a way out of her despair, and of escaping from her apparently impossible situation and not feeling her painful and 'unacceptable' feelings. In a sense, her ideas about suicide are a 'comfort' to Vilna in her despair. She will need enormous courage to face these feelings and deal with the situation. She will need to trust her counsellor to stay with her through all these difficulties, so that her feelings of abandonment can be expressed and trust begin to grow again. It is not clear whether she can manage that. Her counsellor is a woman, and the other woman in Vilna's life, her mother, was unable to protect her. Her mother had abandoned her to her father during her life, and now seemed to have done so again through her death. Could Vilna muster the courage to trust another woman? She certainly did not feel she could trust a man, and for this reason had sought a woman counsellor.

Counsellor's feelings and dilemmas

The feelings that the client cannot or dare not express may be felt quite intensely by the counsellor. As with other patterns, the counsellor will need great sensitivity to know when to introduce the client to these 'unfelt' feelings. Without this sensitivity, trust cannot be built. Such trust takes time to build, but it needs to exist before the client can begin to express despair and the underlying anger in words rather than in acts.

The counsellor may experience the 'instinct to save life' when working with someone considering suicide. Human instinct is to save life. Just think of the foolhardy things people do in an emergency to save life! The counsellor may need help from her supervisor to contain this instinct and recognise her fear of the suicidal act itself. Containment of her own fear should enable her to recognise more fully the client's probable feelings of intense pain or despair and hopelessness, along with low self-esteem. These feelings may be masking more deep-seated feelings of anger or hate.

Another strong feeling the counsellor may experience is her own loss of hope, especially if the client seems to give up hope altogether. It is important for the counsellor to hold on to her own sense of hope, while recognising the client's hopeless feelings. If the counsellor found herself struggling with 'hope' in such a situation, it would be essential to take these feelings to supervision. It may also be useful for the counsellor to reflect to the client the possibility that she is holding some unconscious hope for the client, until the client is ready to take it back.

Counsellor's responses

Again in her response the counsellor needs to recognise the different feelings from which the client is protecting herself. These various feelings seem to come in layers. The counsellor's experience as well as the client's has been compared to lasagne, with layer upon layer of different ingredients. Sometimes the 'crust' of despair can seem as impenetrable as over-baked lasagne, and sometimes the underlying anger can spurt up and hit us in the face; just like the tomato sauce if we push through the top layer too vehemently!

It is important for the counsellor to go firmly but gently, gradually letting the layer of despair melt and the underlying feelings emerge in their own time. This firmly-but-gently approach can be expressed through a firm and regular commitment of time with a clear ending, as outlined in Chapter 12, and with a consistent refocusing on the top feeling layer. The following is a counsellor's possible response to Vilna's second statement.

> You don't seem to see any other way out of your situation at the moment than to consider suicide. Your despair must be enormous for you to come to this conclusion. I wonder if it feels as if there is no one who could even begin to understand your despair?

Perhaps you could formulate your own response to Vilna's first statement?

Counsellor's difficulties

It is important for the counsellor to remember that although attitudes towards suicide in the West have become less punitive in the course of the past century, some religious groups do have strongly disapproving views. Counsellors need to be aware of these differences and look out for punitive attitudes in the clients and/or in their close friends and family. Other groups, especially those who believe in reincarnation, are less likely to see suicide as a way out of despair.

Some of the major counsellor difficulties that arise when working with clients experiencing suicidal thoughts and wishes have already been mentioned. In hearing clients talk of suicide, there are two main sources of difficulty. First, the counsellor has to live with the fear that the client may indeed commit suicide. Second, if the counsellor has had experience of suicide in her life, either through her own experiences of persistent suicidal thoughts or through the suicide of someone close, then she will find the threat of suicide difficult to bear.

If a suicide does actually occur, whether threatened or not, then the counsellor will need care from colleagues and consultation with a supervisor. She too has suffered a loss and may experience severe feelings of guilt, failure and possibly loss of self-esteem. It is wise to have extra supervision at such a time to receive the understanding and reflective support that this relationship should give.

Table 15.1 Summary of protective patterns in complicated grief

Griever	Protective behaviour	Denied feelings	Counsellor's responses
1 Mrs Brown	Idealisation of husband	Hate and anger	Recognises incomplete picture and hints at possibility of anger
2 Frank	Vilification of ex-wife	Pain, sadness and underlying love	Recognises incomplete picture, hints at sadness and recognises possibility of loving feelings
3 Christopher	Angry outburst	Pain, loneliness, also longing for trust and intimacy	Affirms reality of loss, recognises angry feelings and hints at hurt, notices possible difficulties with trust in the counselling relationship
4 Martha	Depression as hopelessness	Anger, hate and guilt, and all other feelings	Recognises protective nature of depression and fear of feelings; hints at grief about Tim and anger with him
5 Peter	Depression as blankness	Anger, hate and guilt	Recognises possibility of feelings behind endless words
6 Vilna	Suicidal thoughts and wishes	Despair, underlying anger and guilt	Recognises protective function of suicidal thoughts, despair and hopelessness; hints at underlying anger or unconscious hope

Drawing together the threads

In Table 15.1 we have summarised the protective patterns found in the grievers featured in this chapter. We have also summarised the hidden feelings and the way the counsellor has picked up and used these elements. It may take a long time in more complicated grief for the client to be able to use the counselling relationship to unblock his grief. The counsellor may require great patience.

The use of clarification and confrontation without punishment, which we have described in this chapter, is by far the most complex skill we have considered so far. It not only relies on picking up the griever's underlying feelings but also uses the counsellor's awareness of the protective nature of certain kinds of behaviour. The counsellor will, of course, reflect on how much of this particular feeling belongs to her and how much to the griever, and on how and when to respond to the behaviour or the underlying feelings, or both. Consulting a supervisor to assess how complicated a grief might be, and whether or when it might be appropriate to refer a client, is considered in the next chapter.

Summary

- Difficulties with empathy, genuineness and acceptance may relate to the counsellor's own experiences of loss or may be a sign of complicated grief in the client, or both.
- Sensitivity and self-awareness are enormously important when working with complicated grief as a way of understanding and of working with certain feelings that are avoided.
- The counsellor's task is to recognise the protection and its function without colluding in the denial of the avoided feeling.
- Various patterns of protection arising out of the need to deny certain feelings need to be approached with slightly different counsellor strategies. These are summarised in Table 15.1.

Part V

Professional implications

Chapter 16

Necessary consultation for complicated grief

Some protective behaviour, such as lateness, silence, vilification and idealisation, when understood by the *skilled* counsellor and responded to appropriately, can begin to shift quite rapidly, as outlined in the previous chapter. At other times similar phenomena may evoke a more complex response in the counsellor and need to be thought about in a different way. When counsellors find it difficult to think about and reflect upon a particular experience, this is a sure sign that they need to consult with someone else, probably their supervisor. In this chapter we describe two cases where the counsellor's experiences needed to be taken to supervision. We go on to describe other areas of a counsellor's work where consultation may well be required.

There are many ways in which blocking of the expression of grief can result in challenging behaviours in the counselling relationship. Two kinds of client in particular can evoke intense and sometimes puzzling feelings in the counsellor. These experiences in the counsellor give a really important clue about the client's predicament and their subsequent needs. The first experience the counsellor may struggle with is that of being intensely caught up in, and swamped by, the client's feelings; the second is where the counsellor feels cut out by the client.

'Swamped by feelings'

We saw in the early chapters how important the early attachment relationships were in an individual's capacity to form subsequent attachments. If failure in the first relationship goes unrecognised and therefore unchanged, then subsequent relationships are likely to repeat the pattern of the first one. Those who remain insecurely attached from infancy will not have felt free to explore and will have been using a lot of their energy in making sure that their attachment figures are still around and still attached to them. They are in some sense 'bound' and cannot become separate. They have not been securely enough held to be able to 'move away' from the first attachment relationship and use their creativity for other things. They are stuck with this 'problem of separation'. Like Narcissus, who gazed into the pool and fell in love with the reflection of himself, they see others only as a reflection or extension of them-selves. They seem joined, and cannot get enough distance to get the other person into focus. Thus they never see others as they really are. It is not hard to imagine that people with this sort of 'problem of separation' find enor-mous difficulty in working through the process of grieving, and letting go of the person who had seemed like an extension or reflection of themselves.

When this 'other' person is the parent, then the 'child' will be so consumed by the need to hold on to the 'identical other' that the necessary recognition of separateness in death may be more than that person can tolerate and they may become ill or act in other ways to convert the impossible pain into something else. An interesting twenty-first-century exploration of the dangers of mother–daughter merging is given in Eva Hoffman's novel *The Secret* (2002).

When a person has been able to separate enough from the first attachment figure, but only just enough, they may fall in love with someone who has a similar system of attachments. They have been unconsciously attracted by the identical need in the other, namely to find someone who also longs to fall in love with their own reflection. In this case they have been able to make just enough adjustment to fall in love with the other, who is similar. This way they achieve some degree of separation as well as some fusion, metaphorically like Siamese twins, joined in part and separate in part.

When one of the 'pair' dies, the perceived abandonment makes it impos-sible to imagine surviving when an extension of the self is dead. The con-sequent rage may be enormous. The griever, in not being able to perceive others as different, also cannot conceive that anyone else had a relationship with the deceased and therefore cannot recognise the grief of others related to the lost person. Then even the tenuous relationships that do still exist are threatened by what can look like a competition to be seen as the most hurt and in most pain, the loss and need of the others being totally ignored.

We could think of a person like this as having a very fragile 'psychic skin'. When a counsellor brings an empathic response to this person's pain, the 'skin' seems to break and the psychic pain flows into the counsellor as if they were an extension of the griever. Any sign from the counsellor that they are different or separate (e.g. ending a session) may be met with extreme rage. Counsellors may feel themselves overwhelmed by, and unable to disentangle from, the intense feelings of such clients. More dangerously, they can get caught up in fantasies of a 'special relationship', believing that they under-stand this client in a very special and unique way.

In trying to assess what someone coming for bereavement or loss counsel-ling needs, it is important to think carefully about the impact of that person on oneself. This is illustrated in the following example where Julie, the coun-sellor connected to a hospice, struggled to work with Amanda.

Amanda (38) had just lost her husband Paul (48) to cancer. They had loved one another so much that they had not wanted children, who they thought might have come between them. Anyway, they were both so busy with their careers – she as an opera singer and he as a marketing executive – that they would have had no time for children or for anyone else for that matter; they were sufficient unto themselves. They did, however, have two prize-winning cocker spaniels.

When Paul's cancer of the pancreas was diagnosed, he was given excellent medical care and the staff at the hospice where he died paid much attention to offering them maximum support and helping them to talk to one another about Paul's impending death. However, Amanda's rage about Paul's dying was so intense that staff found it hard to engage with her. They were shocked by her persistent outbursts of temper towards Paul even as he was dying. She also troubled the staff because she seemed to care more for her spaniels than for Paul.

The staff had encouraged her to see the bereavement counsellor and one day, several weeks after Paul's death, she finally went to the first appointment. The counsellor, Julie, was struck by the intensity and bitterness of Amanda's rage with Paul for abandoning her, as she saw it. She was also struck by her sense that, try as she might, she could not seem to get a sense of Amanda's feelings as belonging to Amanda. It was almost as if they were both experiencing the same feelings, and Julie realised that she felt quite swamped by the intensity of Amanda's feelings and struggled to function as her separate self in the counselling relationship.

She decided to take all this to supervision, and in preparing for the supervisory session she went through all the external determinants of grief as well as what she knew of Amanda's loss history. Nothing seemed particularly relevant here. Paul had died in the nearby hospice with an excellent standard of care and with considerable medical support. There had been no other recent losses and, although Paul had been 'young' to die nowadays, it had not been unexpected or sudden. Amanda's family lived in another town, but Paul's family lived close by. Amanda's account of her rage with them made Julie imagine that Paul's family would be finding Amanda's rejecting behaviour difficult and might be keeping some distance. From the way Amanda talked, the counsellor perceived that Amanda saw herself not only as the 'chief mourner' but also the only person affected by his death. Julie began to realise that Paul's family had been pretty much left out of Amanda's account of his death, and wondered if there was anyone at all in relationship with Amanda.

In supervision it became clear that Julie's experience of feeling overwhelmed indicated that Amanda needed to merge with her to feel safe again. In reflecting on this merging experience, Julie and her supervisor wondered whether Amanda had been insecurely attached in infancy. She was therefore insecurely attached to Paul and had merged with him as a way of unconsciously holding onto him. His 'leaving' her had then felt like an infantile abandonment, with the imagined drastic consequences of annihilation. This new merging with her counsellor could be understood to function as a protection against facing the reality of his death.

It was clear that Amanda needed to work long term with a psychotherapist who could very slowly allow her to attach into a secure and dependent attachment relationship and then very gradually begin to differentiate from her therapist as a person in her own right. She would then, in time, be in a position to face all the other losses in her life.

'Feeling cut out'

Some experience of depression is a necessary part of all grieving. At times the depression can get a bit stuck, and then the recognition and exploration of a range of feelings can enable deeper, hidden feelings to emerge and the depression to begin to lift. However, sometimes depression can become prolonged and may become engrained as a rigid protective pattern with potentially dangerous consequences. Natural feelings of anger associated with grief in some people with insecure attachments and damaged self-esteem are often turned against the self and experienced as guilt. Such inappropriate guilt feelings will exacerbate the 'reasonable' guilt feelings associated with loss. This double guilt is intolerable for some people, and can lead to a cutting-off not just of all angry and hateful feelings, but of all feelings. Such lack of feeling in the client may be experienced as confusion or blankness by the counsellor, yet the counsellor knows that the client is depressed. It may be tempting to discount the blankness, but this very experience is also an important diagnostic indicator to be discussed in supervision. An example follows.

> Hamish was Peter's brother mentioned in Chapter 15; it had been in saving Hamish's life that Peter lost his leg in Glencoe. Hamish was overwhelmed with guilt about his own unscathed survival and the damage to Peter's body and self-esteem.
>
> Watching Peter hobbling around had become unbearable for him, so he had given up his job and moved to London, where he knew no one and had become completely isolated and depressed. When collecting his Job Seeker's Allowance one day he had come across a perceptive adviser who spotted his depression and encouraged him to seek counselling. It was this counsellor who, aware of experiencing the cut-off sensation with Hamish, had then been able to take this to her supervisor for consultation about referral. Hamish's depression reached much further back than the Glencoe incident, and was really quite entrenched. After a further assessment consultation he was referred for long-term psychotherapy.

Other areas in which consultation may be required

Sexual abuse in childhood

When one is working with young adult survivors of childhood sexual abuse, the naturally occurring loss of the adolescent stage of development may evoke strong feelings in the survivors of inexpressible anger and helplessness about earlier losses as children. These losses, such as loss of innocence, loss of self-esteem, loss of normal peer relationships, loss of the ability to play, loss of safety and protection and loss of trust, remain unnoticed and the survivor may be overwhelmed by feelings of guilt or anger. Prolonged depression may follow unless these feelings can be recognised. In such cases it is always worth consulting to see whether specialist help is required or whether the counsellor is the appropriate person to work with this client at this time.

Suicidal intent or serious suicidal thoughts

You will remember Vilna from Chapter 15, whose depression, although protecting her from even less tolerable feelings of guilt and helplessness, had in itself become an intolerable experience. Because it is uncomfortable for others too, the depressed person may find themselves very isolated and alone. This can sometimes lead a person to think that suicide might be the only possible response to loss or bereavement. Although suicide may have a number of different psychological roots, it too can often be understood as anger not expressed and turned against the self, or as despair about ever being free of the burden of guilt relating to the loss.

Those who do commit suicide after a loss will have done so for a variety of reasons, and different meanings can be attributed to it. An elderly person who found it impossible to grieve the death of his wife might see suicide as the only way of holding on to her and rejoining her. Someone else overwhelmed by feelings of numbness and despair, or by intense feelings of survivor guilt from long ago, might eventually find it impossible to go on living with these feelings. Another person might consider that the intensely angry and revengeful feelings felt in response to a current loss could only be expressed through the revenge of suicide. And yet another might decide that the only expression for overwhelming guilt feelings would be the most severe punishment imaginable against themselves, namely their own killing.

Whatever the reason or meanings of the act, suicide as a response to loss usually grows out of a sense in that person that their feeling-world cannot be adequately understood by anyone else, so they shut everyone out, including the counsellor. Counsellors sensing this 'shutting out' in the context of suicidal thoughts or ideas should always consult with a supervisor to reflect on possible dangers. The conflict between the principles of autonomy and care usually inherent in this situation needs to be thought through with great care, recognising the low self-esteem and feelings of hopelessness or helplessness that often contribute to this position.

Somatisation: 'weeping through the body'

Some people are unable to tolerate the strength of their feelings and need to block out both the grief and the related tears. Then 'the grief which has no expression in tears makes other organs weep' (Maudsley, quoted by Danbury, cited in McDougall, 1994). In other words, their hidden inner turmoil finds expression through other organs of the body, often resulting in persistent psychosomatic pain. These people may be hard to reach and require specialist help, and any in-depth counselling work should be done with medical consultation (somatic specialist) as well as with supervisory consultation.

Behavioural messages

Another protective pattern that can be difficult to work with is that of self-inflicted hurt such as wrist-slashing, biting or scratching oneself, and head-banging. These acts seem to function as a way of giving some expression to despair, hopelessness and rage as well as giving some protection from really experiencing the feelings. The physical pain and accompanying excitement for some people seem to function as a way of dulling or diverting from the psychic pain of despair. Unfortunately, those around them may find difficulty in 'hearing' this message and may respond with anger and punishment. This probably causes the client to withdraw further and to feel even more hopeless about ever being heard or understood, thus perpetuating what is often a vicious circle of pain and withdrawal.

A similar pattern may appear with eating difficulties, where the protective behaviour may result in antagonising the very people with whom the person is longing, albeit in a rather trying manner, to communicate. The meanings of these behaviours, their persistence and their effect on the counsellor need to be discussed in supervision.

Client behaviour within the counselling relationship

We shall consider here some counsellor difficulties associated with how to respond to silence and how to respond to clients arriving late for sessions.

Silence

Silence can be a comfortable, and often intimate, sharing of time together, or it may be a primitive and frightened withdrawal. Generally that difference is clear to the counsellor and the nature of the silence can usually be explored with the client. It is the frightened silence that can be difficult for the counsellor.

When clients are experiencing deep depression as a protection against painful feelings, even the gentlest of explorations of the silence itself can sometimes seem like an invasion into the very world being protected. The counsellor needs extraordinary patience, as well as firmness of boundaries, to offer the quality of safety the client needs in order to begin to experience a feeling. Prolonged silences should be thought about in supervision.

Persistent lateness

Missing sessions, persistently arriving late or forgetting to pay (if this is relevant) are common behaviours when clients are working through complicated grief. They can all be seen as communications to the counsellor, and may be coming at a stage when anger begins to break through the protection of depression. Because the anger is still largely out of awareness, it is hard for the client to bring it more directly into the session as a conscious feeling or an experience to be thought about. The anger therefore may find its way into behaviour-as-communication (sometimes called 'acting out') and manifests itself as missing sessions, coming late or forgetting to pay. While it is enormously important that the counsellor notice this behaviour, it is also important that the client be encouraged to see the behaviour symbolically, as with the children in Chapter 15. Sometimes the counsellor's attention to such behaviour is experienced as if it were critical. The client needs to be encouraged to recognise that what is seen as critical is in reality an invitation to reflect and think about the process of counselling. A counsellor response incorporating these features might sound a bit like:

> Yes, sure you're 10 minutes late. *I'm* not particularly worried by or interested in the lateness itself. After all, it's your time . . . but I am interested in what you feel about the lateness or in what the lateness might be saying.

When it can be heard, as such, a non-punitive response to this behaviour-as-communication can often enable the client to feel safe enough to recognise the possibility of emerging anger behind the lateness. If the lateness persists and cannot be thought about, supervision should be sought.

Medication

If you are medically qualified, and in a position to recommend prescribed drugs to counteract depression, a dilemma often arises. Is the prescription of anxiolytic drugs a useful way of reducing the fear of feelings and offering temporary relief from the unbearable 'stuckness' of complicated grief? Or is it a message to the client about the unacceptability either of the protective depression or of the avoided feelings? This latter message would simply reinforce the 'dampening' effects of the drugs. Inappropriate prescribing to subdue the effects of ordinary grief is, unfortunately, still common and may reflect the lack of provision of suitable therapeutic help or the prescriber's personal difficulties with grief, or both.

With clients stuck in depression, feelings of guilt or anger may be quick to appear in the prescriber. Thus some prescribing may be more of a response to the doctor's own guilt that the patient is not getting better (as if the doctor could actually do the grief work for the patient!) rather than to the patient's real needs. Alternatively it may be a response to anger with the patient for evoking depressing experiences in the doctor–counsellor (as if the patient actually wanted to be depressed!).

Not prescribing, on the other hand, may also evoke guilty responses in the doctor for not 'taking away' the uncomfortable experiences (as if the drugs actually took away the grief rather than postponing it!). The prescriber may need to take these 'uncomfortable experiences' to supervision. At other times the 'not prescribing' may itself be an angry punitive response to someone who has become dependent on drugs and is now in a position of need and guilty despair.

These are difficult dilemmas that arise for any prescriber. Anxiolytic drugs may help some patients who seem inexorably 'stuck' to accept the 'stuckness', making day-to-day life more bearable. For others, the drugs may take the edge off the feelings that might otherwise be too overwhelming to work with. This can be useful to enable counselling to get started. Or it may enable other life experiences to contribute to change, although perhaps not at a very deep level. However, with many patients in grief, prescribing more often sets up cycles of dependency, which confirm the client's inability to tolerate the very feelings being avoided, thus reinforcing the depression itself. As attitudes towards drug-prescribing and drug-taking change, both prescriber and drug-user may have feelings of guilt about the drugs, which can often outweigh the useful effects the drugs may have. None the less, careful prescribing for certain patients, in consultation with a psychotherapist or counsellor, is often extremely effective.

A psychotherapist will have more training and experience in this area and should be able to make a more accurate assessment about whether someone would be able to benefit from some form of psychological intervention, whether or not drugs are used as an adjunct. Psychotherapists may also be able to decide whether a short or longer-term intervention would be more appropriate. Sharing these decisions with a sensitive colleague or in supervision is strongly recommended.

At the more challenging end of the spectrum of bereavement counselling, it is always wise to consult. This enables counsellors to recognise the importance of their personal responses to the experience of being with the client. In the next chapter we shall consider the range of factors to be considered in making an assessment and in thinking about the referral of a client to another person, agency or setting.

Summary

- An intense feeling experience in a counsellor, such as merging or being cut out, has important informational value that needs to be explored in supervision.
- Other areas where counsellors may have intense feelings and should seek consultation include memories of childhood sexual abuse, suicidal intent or ideation, and self-destructive behaviour.
- Suicide may be a result of the anger or guilt turned against the self, together with a conviction that no one can understand or tolerate their unbearable feelings.
- Other experiences within the counselling relationship where consultation might be sought include persistent lateness or silence.
- Those accorded responsibility for prescribing anxiolytic medication would be wise to seek consultation with an experienced counsellor or psychotherapist about the interface between the psychological and the biochemical aspects of the patient's healing.
- All those working at the more complicated end of the spectrum of bereavement should consult on a regular basis about the efficacy of their work.

Chapter 17

Assessment and referral

Assessment skills

We have placed this skill near the end of the book as it is one of the most complex skills a counsellor uses. Paradoxically, of course, these assessment skills are used in the very first meeting or meetings, yet involve at least all the knowledge and skills we have outlined so far.

At the same time as extending empathy and opening ourselves to a client's story of their loss, counsellors are also trying to assess each client's vulnerability and capacity to grieve. They will have to try to decide what the client needs and whether this can be offered. The client is, of course, also assessing whether the counsellor is right for them. As counsellors listen, an assessment has to be made of which external factors might be influencing the client's needs at that moment as well as beginning to pick up clues about the internal factors likely to affect the grieving process. Above all, counsellors will be getting a sense of how the client is experiencing the relationship, whether the client wants and is able to form a counselling relationship, and what impact the client is having on them.

Counsellors use knowledge about such elements as the relevance of early loss history, for instance, to try to assess the risk of breakdown or unmanageable distress for this client during mourning. In listening to clients' stories, counsellors also need to assess the network of available support and whether the grief work is already under way. In the light of this information a decision must be made about whether the skills and experience of the counsellor are appropriate to continue working with this client at this time. There are indeed so many factors affecting the assessment of a client's suitability for loss counselling or psychotherapy that it may be useful to have a checklist such as the one in Table 17.1 (pp. 198–199).

These factors are not a list of separate items as described in Chapters 2 and 5, but rather a set of linked factors that will affect one another. We shall start at one end with the external circumstances affecting the impact of the loss, and move towards the more internal factors that also affect the grieving process. These internal factors linking with a client's early development will also affect the client–counsellor relationship itself. The effect of the various factors also needs to be understood cumulatively. One or two 'more complex' factors may well be manageable by the less experienced counsellor. However, as the number and degree of more complex factors affecting the client and his loss increases, so the counsellor will need to draw on greater training and experience and, as outlined in Chapter 16, consider referral to someone more experienced.

The components of the checklist in Table 17.1 are based on extensive research and experience, but there are few discrete categories in this complex area and the descriptions are considerably simplified. However, such a checklist can serve as a useful working tool, both to assess someone's suitability for counselling or psychotherapy and in trying to assess the complexity of the loss and grief in any particular individual. The description of a counsellor's competency in terms of 'increasing experience and training' refers to the length and depth of training and to the hours of supervised counselling practice over a given period.

We know that some inexperienced and minimally trained counsellors can sometimes provide just what is needed for a particular individual, even with a number of 'complex factors'. We also know, sometimes only too well, how experienced psychotherapists may struggle with just one or two 'complex factors' when these touch their own areas of vulnerability. The factors down the left-hand side of Table 17.1 are not to be seen as discrete in themselves but rather as a general guide to what tends to complicate grief. It is, of course, the way in which previous losses or other complicating factors have been understood and worked through, rather than just the factors themselves, that affects the course of grief and also the counselling relationship.

In general, where the client is well supported, the grief work is under way and the counsellor senses a developing relationship, the counsellor will probably decide to continue counselling, supported by the necessary supervision. In this case, other factors will be less likely to block the counselling process. Counselling will recognise the grief work that has already been achieved and will enable the work to continue.

Sometimes, however, the counsellor may sense the client's difficulty in relating and may pick up hints of early and damaging loss history. There may also be recognition that the grief process seems to be blocked, possibly by some engrained protective pattern. Usually the counsellor, in regular supervision, will be able to use the skills outlined in Chapter 15 to help work through the protective pattern and the underlying feelings. However, when, as outlined in Chapter 16, the 'blocks' are too rigid and the relationship feels too disconnected or cut off, or when the counsellor has the experience of merging at an early stage, then referral to an experienced psychotherapist may be necessary. If a counsellor is particularly concerned about a client's capacity to grieve without provoking a serious breakdown or mental illness, then a psychiatric assessment from a psychotherapeutically oriented psychiatrist is most helpful

Table 17.1 Factors to be considered in assessing client's suitability for loss counselling and preferable level of competence in the counsellor

Factors \ Levels	*Increasing experience and training of counsellor* → *Increasing complexity of relevant factors*		
Place of death	at home	in hospital	abroad/isolated
Coincidental losses	one person	two people	more than two
Successive losses	one loss in given period	two losses in quick succession	two or more losses in quicker succession
Nature of loss	expected, non-traumatic	sudden, non-traumatic	sudden, traumatic or horrendous
Networks	supportive community	less supportive community	person detached from community
Cultural background	loss-accepting culture	culture ambivalent towards loss	loss-denying culture
Intimacy level of lost relationship	elderly parent or other relative adult sibling	young sibling	spouse or lover child
Life-stage of griever	not in transition some transition (e.g. menopause)	considerable transition (e.g. adolescence)	transition of childhood
Grief history of griever	previous losses largely grieved	most losses grieved	previous losses stirred by current losses
Emotional complexity of relationship lost	straightforward relationship, conflicts largely tolerated	more complex relationship, less tolerance of conflict	complex relationship, guilt and ambivalence largely denied

Table 17.1 continued

Levels / Factors	Increasing experience and training of counsellor → / Increasing complexity of relevant factors		
Degree of isolation and capacity to trust others	relates (either well or badly) to more than one person; capacity to trust	relates to at least one other person with some trust	few, if any, relationships; little capacity to trust
Ability to express feelings	able to express feelings and put thoughts into words	intellectualises many feelings, thoughts get stuck	little feeling expression, muddled thoughts
Ability to tolerate feelings	able to tolerate disturbing thoughts and feelings	some disturbing thoughts and feelings but manages these, largely through use of protective patterns	many disturbing thoughts and feelings, some debilitating use of protective patterns
Desire for change	willing to face the loss and the changes it brings	reluctant to face the loss and subsequent changes	fear or even terror of facing the loss
Preparedness to trust in counselling relationship	open and essentially trusting of the counselling process	apprehensive about trusting either the person or the process of counselling	extreme difficulty in trusting, or, alternatively, inappropriate over-ready trust

in ascertaining whether counselling or psychotherapy is at all appropriate for this person at this time.

Of course these factors affect individuals differently, but when more than a few of the factors listed on the right-hand side of Table 17.1 are present, this particular client may not be able to use counselling or psychotherapy at this time. Further, certain other behaviour and circumstances in a client's life are generally considered to be contraindications for suitability for counselling or psychotherapy. These include: chronic alcoholism or drug addiction; long-term hospitalisation; more than one course of ECT; gross destructive or self-destructive behaviour; and extremely resistant or severe symptoms of fear or obsessive behaviour, where it may be wiser to leave such 'protections' intact. Some people who express their psychic pain through bodily (somatic) pain may be unsuitable for short-term grief counselling, particularly where the somatic pain is resistant. When clients are unreceptive to psychological ways of understanding, longer term psychotherapy may enable change. For others, however, grief may indeed remain stuck and the best help to be given may be to offer 'support' counselling to help shore up their protective patterns.

Referral skills

There are three important initial considerations in relation to referral, whether instituted by the counsellor or the client: first 'Why refer?', second 'When to refer?' and third 'How to refer?'. The counsellor may find reasons during the initial assessment for wanting an immediate referral, or other reasons may arise much later in the relationship. The client may also have good reasons after the first session, or much later in the relationship, to seek referral. Sometimes we refer too early; sometimes too late. Sometimes we are insensitive to the need to refer and sometimes we concur too quickly with a request, or an imagined one, for referral. We must constantly monitor our work, both on our own and with our supervisor, to understand the complexity of the situation and the true basis of our decision. A referral is always a loss for the client and sometimes also for the counsellor.

Reasons for immediate referral

Some of the reasons for immediate referral of a client were outlined in the assessment section above, and concern the degree of fit between the experience and training of the counsellor and the factors suggesting complicated grieving in the client. In general the greater the complexity for the client, the greater the need for sensitivity, good training and sufficient experience in the counsellor. If the counsellor is able to assess straight away that she is not suitably trained or experienced enough to work with this client, then this is good practice and a good reason for immediate referral.

Another reason for immediate referral would be when a client's presenting loss touches a particularly sensitive aspect of the counsellor's own life. If, for example, a client presented with grief for a lost child and the counsellor had had a similar experience that was unresolved, perhaps because it was a recent event, the counsellor would be wise to refer at that point.

A counsellor might also refer immediately if there were clear practical difficulties such as transport, locality, finances or mutual availability of time.

With such incompatibilities it might be more suitable for the client to see someone else.

On such occasions it may be quite clear in the first session that immediate referral is appropriate. However, in other instances this decision cannot be reached in the first or even second session. There are times when the level of make-believe and denial is such that the counsellor may need to consult with her supervisor to consider the possibilities within the relationship and to be able to assess more clearly what is happening for the client. Thus, referral to an experienced counsellor or a psychotherapist may also be appropriate after a number of sessions or at even later stages in the counselling relationship.

Reasons for later referral

If a counsellor absolutely has to leave a job before a counselling relationship has ended, it is clearly important to give the client as much notice as possible about the need for referral. Sometimes the counsellor faces the dilemma of whether to bring information about her own departure into the counselling relationship at a time when the client may be grappling with her grief from long ago. Generally speaking, the longer the client knows, the more time is available to talk about this new loss with the very person who is going to be lost. Helping the client to face up to and grieve the impending loss is an extremely important part of the work.

There are times when the relationship between the counsellor and client meets with great difficulty, and it is sometimes tempting for the counsellor to react by referring rather than thinking about the difficulty. A discussion of the situation with the supervisor will usually enable the difficulty to be resolved within the counselling relationship itself, thus allowing the work to continue.

There are other situations, which may arise later in the counselling relationship, when a counsellor certainly should consider referral. For instance, a sudden bereavement for the counsellor, particularly if the loss is similar to that being experienced by the client, might make it necessary to refer. Another example might be when the counsellor realises, through something that suddenly emerges in the counselling relationship, that the client's loss has evoked a large area of unresolved feeling from the counsellor's past. In consultation with a supervisor, the counsellor may decide that counselling of clients should stop for a period, probably with the counsellor seeking counselling for herself. Or the supervisor may suggest that the counsellor have extra counselling help with her own grief for the very purpose of enabling the established counselling relationship to continue. Wherever possible it is, of course, preferable to continue the counselling relationship once it is under way, and not create yet another loss. There are many reasons for this, but with loss counselling in particular the potential for feelings of rejection and the propensity to feel anger and guilt are very frequent and powerful. In such circumstances referral can exacerbate these feelings of rejection, anger and guilt in the client. The supervisor has an important role in helping the counsellor to make a decision about referral. This includes the arrangements for the referral of the client, as well as ensuring that the counsellor gets the help she needs.

When referral has to happen, it is essential that the 'referring counsellor' remember that the client may well feel 'as if it were her fault'. Therefore the reasons for referral should be as clear as possible. The 'receiving' counsellor or psychotherapist will need to work through the referral with any referred clients who may well have guilt feelings and, almost certainly, feelings of anger towards the initial counsellor for the sense of rejection that the referral may have evoked.

Timing of referrals

We have recognised above that it is often very difficult to assess, in the first or even the second session, whether or not referral is appropriate. This is a difficult skill. It may also be difficult to get the timing right, and some of the difficulties in referral timing can be understood and worked through in supervision.

Trainee counsellors are sometimes inclined to refer earlier than appropriate, particularly when they fear the strong feelings that often emerge quite quickly in loss counselling sessions. This can result in the counsellor feeling unsure that they can maintain the 'secure base' for the griever. Supervision often helps to clarify the counsellor's feelings in such a case and will enable the relationship to continue.

Sometimes counsellors in training, and indeed other more experienced counsellors at any stage in their career, have the enthusiastic but omnipotent idea that they can do anything and everything. They cannot then distinguish between recognition of their own limitations and 'failure' in the work. They may then fail to refer appropriately early. Supervision can help trainees to see when being able to recognise their own limitations is an important part of professional development and is not necessarily a failure in the relationship.

At other times counsellors become so over-involved with the bereaved person that they do not make an appropriate referral soon enough. This may arise through a fear of separation, which the counsellor picks up from the griever but does not recognise or respond to appropriately. Supervision can enable the counsellor to recognise the client's fear of separation and can help the counsellor to work with this. If a referral is indeed appropriate at this stage, the supervisor may need to help the counsellor with her 'fear of failure' in the relationship. This fear may have contributed to the counsellor's failure to understand the client's needs in the first place.

There are times when an early referral or a late referral is appropriate. Good referrals require considerable counselling skill. Using supervision to explore the counsellor's own thoughts and feelings is important in attempting to clarify the reasons, timing and responsibility for referral.

Method of referral

It is important to be as clear and unambiguous as possible about the need to refer. Stating your feelings and responsibility as straightforwardly as you can sometimes helps prevent the client feeling 'as if it were her fault'. It is important to clarify your role and responsibility in the referral process and to recognise the client's feeling in response to your referral suggestion. Here are two attempts to be open and clear with Joe as it becomes obvious early in the relationship that it is appropriate to refer him to someone more experienced.

Early stage referral

You will remember Joe from Exercises 10.1, 10.3 and 10.4. It is now his third session and you feel distinctly puzzled at his odd behaviour. He seems lifeless and listless. You feel increasingly uncomfortable about his capacity to relate to you and his difficulty with expressing feelings. You decide to try to be open with him. You might say something like this:

> Joe, I'm feeling a bit uncomfortable about what's happening in here right now. I'm not sure *I'm* going to be able to help you much at this stage. I think I might like to get another opinion on this . . . How does this idea strike you?
> OR
> Joe, I think I'm sensing some feelings in you that may be difficult for you, and I think they are difficult for me too at this point. I'm wondering if perhaps you and I might get some help with that?

Of course you would find your own words for this, but the gist of the responses expresses a carefully honest and non-critical approach. If Joe is then able to hear that the counsellor is neither accusing him nor punishing him, he might recognise that she was not the right person to work with him on those difficulties at that time. The counsellor needs to recognise and understand any feelings of rejection evoked in Joe. This would help Joe to recognise and work with such feelings with both the referring and the 'receiving' counsellor to whom the referral is made.

Referral at an early stage may be relatively straightforward if there has been very little time for a relationship to develop and there are thus likely to be less strong feelings of rejection in the client. When, however, there are reasons to refer later in the relationship, the feelings aroused in the client by the referral are likely to be much stronger, and to need more time to be worked through. Let us think about the feelings that might be evoked in Alice, whom you will also remember from Exercises 10.1 (p. 103) and 10.4 (p. 109), when her counsellor decides to refer her for more specialised help. You will remember the complex difficulties she faced in grieving Brendan's death. This was exacerbated by her husband's refusal to accept Brendan's addiction and also by the general persecution of Aids sufferers in the community. First let us consider the referral itself.

Later stage referral

Let us imagine you have been working with Alice now for some months. She has gradually begun to trust you and has survived the painful anniversary of Brendan's death, but somehow things don't seem to be moving. Alice has suddenly become icy cold and seems to be withdrawing from you and the counselling relationship. This withdrawal is puzzling and disturbing. You discuss this with your supervisor and together you reach the painful conclusion that Alice may need help from someone with more skills and experience than you. You might say something like either of the following:

> Alice, I'd like to take a look at where we are. I recognise that we've done a lot of work together but I'm thinking that perhaps there may be some work you need to do with someone who's more experienced than me. I wonder what you think about this?
> OR
> Alice, we've worked together for some months now and I've seen your courage in facing and grieving Brendan's death. Now I'm beginning to wonder whether perhaps facing Brendan's death has brought you into contact with even deeper losses in your life. Perhaps you and I could talk about whether I'm the right person to continue working with you from now on in considering these deeper losses?

It is always difficult to predict how grievers will respond to a counsellor's thoughts and recommendations about referral. Some people feel relief at the counsellor's recognition of their difficulties without judging or blaming them, and relief that they themselves do not need to ask for more trained help. They may, of course, also feel sadness at the thought of losing the current counselling relationship. This in its turn may touch off other sadnesses from past separations, which will need to be recognised and 'contained' in some way so that they can be 'carried over' to the next relationship. You might then say something like the following in response to someone's sadness.

Counsellor: I'm feeling sad too about our separation . . . and I wonder if the sadness in here is touching the pain of the great sadness out there about your mother who you lost long ago?

Client: Mm – yes, I suppose so.

Counsellor: I guess one of our tasks is to somehow parcel up that sadness about your mother for now, so that you can then carry it on to your work with your new therapist. The sadness we share in here now about our separation is different from the sadness about earlier times.

Returning now to Alice, she seemed to accept the need for referral to someone more experienced, yet her response was full of anger. You were as clear as you could be about your responsibility in referring, yet for Alice the very notion of 'passing her on', however rational she knew it to be, had awakened raw experiences of rejection from earlier times. Her natural response to rejection was one of anger.

Alice: [Angrily] Right! You may as well ring 'the loony bin' straight away!

Counsellor: Alice, I hear your anger towards me and I guess that in some way it must *feel* as if I'm rejecting you just like you were rejected in the past.

Alice: [Resentfully] Well, you are rejecting me aren't you – you're sending me away aren't you?

Counsellor: [Firmly and gently] No, Alice. I'm not *sending* you away; I'm suggesting you seek someone better able to work with you on the losses from long ago. A part of you knows that's right and that this now is different from being sent away. Another part of you is, I guess, remembering very painful feelings associated with being sent away so that it feels *as if* I were sending you away. The very painful feelings of rejection you are experiencing in here are probably making you feel angry with me now [rising intonation].

Alice: Yes, I am feeling angry. I know I shouldn't be.

Counsellor: Your angry feelings in here certainly make sense to *me* as a response to the rejection which you remember so acutely from back then.

As Alice was gradually able to recognise and express her angry feelings and have them accepted, she was able to understand that the real rejection happened in the past. Sadly, she now needed to change her therapist to continue with the work. As so often happens, when her anger was understood it began to subside and she was able to think and to see that the counsellor was not actively rejecting her. She could then begin to experience her sadness at the separation from this counsellor. Recognition, expression and acceptance of the feelings evoked by the referral are necessary for a successful handing-over to take place. This very referral process may enable the griever to begin to separate the real rejection, which happened in the past but is remembered in the present, from the necessary but, of course, painful separation from the current counsellor. The way the 'receiving' therapist works with the feelings of grief associated with the separation from the original counsellor will be an important factor in creating trust in the new relationship.

A client may occasionally seek referral as a way of avoiding painful issues, but generally a client who is avoiding difficult feelings with a counsellor will simply miss sessions or prevent issues being discussed in the session. If the relationship is well established the client is likely to hope, however secretly, that the counsellor will notice and help with the difficulties. The request for referral in this case can be seen as a metaphor for the need to avoid pain or to avoid relationships (see particularly Chapters 12 and 15).

As mentioned earlier, clients also seek referral for appropriate reasons. When referral is suggested by a client, the counsellor needs to remember that it is a measure of the trust in the relationship that the client has been able to come and discuss the referral. It would be all too easy just to stay away or try to approach someone else without the counsellor's knowledge, or perhaps do both. In this case it is the counsellor who needs to remember that this referral request from the client is different from the counsellor's experiences of hurtful rejections from the past. The counsellor may also need to hold on to the recognition of the trust that has brought the client with this request. The counsellor may use supervision to help work out which kind of 'referral' is being sought.

Assessment and referral are complex skills. They rely on the fundamental attitudes and basic skills mentioned earlier, on practical training, on a realistic assessment of one's own strengths and weaknesses, and on continuous supervision of the counselling relationship.

The next chapter deals with the function and processes of supervision.

Summary

- Assessing the suitability of a client for counselling requires a very complex set of skills.
- The sense of relationship, the internal factors and, to a lesser extent, the external factors all need to be taken into consideration in assessing a client's need.
- Reasons for immediate referral include a mismatch between the client and the counsellor, recent counsellor losses or specific practical difficulties.
- Reasons for later referrals include the counsellor having a sudden similar loss herself or having insufficient training and experience to work with the 'difficult' client material emerging later in the counselling relationship. Supervision will usually enable these difficulties to be worked through and the referral to be avoided.
- Reasons for inappropriate timing of referrals include fear of strong feelings, over-involvement with a client, 'omnipotence' or poor assessment skills.
- In making referrals it is important for the counsellor to be clear and openly accepting of responsibility for the referral. Client feelings of guilt, anger or rejection need to be recognised, accepted and worked through.

Chapter 18

Supervision

Functions of supervision

Supervision has been referred to in several chapters. We now come to discuss what we really mean, and why we consider it to be so important. The word 'supervision' in counselling refers to a relationship between a counsellor and another, usually more experienced counsellor, who ideally has had some further training in counselling supervision. It is sometimes called 'consultative support' in order to avoid confusion with other meanings of 'supervision', which entail ideas of 'inspection' or 'overseeing', with the corresponding suggestions of incompetence or formal assessment. Practising counsellors meet regularly, either individually or in small groups (three to four people), with their supervisor or with peer groups to talk through and reflect upon their counselling sessions. The choice of individual, small groups or peer group supervision might be simply pragmatic, and based on availability and financial constraints. However, it is important to recognise that peer group supervision is only suitable for experienced counsellors, and even then it should not be the sole supervision. A fairly typical duration and frequency for individual supervision would be one hour every fortnight, and for peer and small group supervision 1½ hours every fortnight. Obviously trainees need considerably more supervision.

In this book we give ideas of how counselling attitudes, sensitivity and knowledge might look when translated into 'skills'. We also likened the integration of counselling skills into the counselling relationship to the integration of skills required in the co-ordination necessary to ride a bicycle. But of course the counselling relationship is more than that; it is a living interchange between two human beings, who are both experiencing and learning within that relationship. One of the ways in which the counsellor learns from, and about, the counselling relationship and about how to develop it more effectively is through the confidential supervision relationship. In supervision a counsellor is able to focus on the interaction with the client in a collaborative and supportive environment. The supervisor recognises and works with the feelings experienced in the counselling session, as well as those experienced in the supervisory session.

Such a 'place for feelings' is very necessary, for in choosing to enter the world of other people's losses counsellors are entering something different from the normal and the everyday. There are times when it may seem barely worthwhile to the counsellor to enter the painful world of a bereaved person. Clients can be consistently ungrateful, can get stuck in suicidal feelings and do occasionally succeed in committing suicide. Counsellors can think they have lost their way and feel useless, helpless and drained. It is hardly surprising, then, that counsellors can come to believe they have nothing more to give, or have been a failure. At times like this it is tempting to 'soldier on', to 'keep one's head down', to 'get on with it' and not make time to reflect on what is going on in the counselling relationship. Individuals, teams and organisations can all collude in this process of 'head down', 'soldier on' and denial of the necessity for supervision. This denial may occur out of the mistaken but common belief that remembering and reflecting on pain 'only makes it worse'. Yet it is this very reflecting and sharing, in the context of a secure and professional supervisory relationship, that can offer comfort and care for the counsellor's struggle with the client. Supervision can also offer a place to reflect upon the skills and interventions that are being used, as well as those that are being avoided. It can then enable the counsellor to ponder the reasons for avoidance of certain skills or feelings, or to wonder why certain rules of counselling practice are suddenly particularly difficult to follow.

A loss counsellor can expect supervision to function in three ways.

- As a safe and secure base in which to feel, and to reflect upon feelings, images and associations that arise; the restorative function.
- As a place to develop appropriate skills and abilities through reflecting upon and learning from the nitty-gritty of the relationship; the formative function.
- As a place to reflect as honestly and openly as possible about the quality of the counselling work and its relationship to professional standards and codes of practice; the normative function.

Although these 'restorative, formative and normative functions of supervision' (Inskipp and Proctor, 2001) are described as if they were discrete entities, they are in practice seldom totally separate. We start by describing each function in turn, then give a brief illustration of how they interweave.

The restorative function

For an inexperienced counsellor, a sense of security will be enhanced through training. This fosters self-awareness and self-acceptance, and confirms and develops skills. None the less, even for the most experienced counsellor, the very strong feelings associated with the void, emptiness, suicidal despair and essential loneliness of human existence, and which emerge in the process of grieving, can evoke fear and insecurity. The counsellor who wishes to remain receptive to this experience in others (i.e. to enable the work of Task 2) needs to be allowed to feel such emotional disturbance within the safer setting of the supervisory relationship. To create a safe environment for this type of exploration, the supervisor needs to demonstrate the attitudes of empathy, warmth and genuineness, and hence create an accepting environment. In such a climate the counsellor can feel secure enough to explore, ponder and reflect upon the counsellor–client relationship in a way that ensures and develops the effectiveness of that relationship. We can draw a parallel here between supervision and John Bowlby's work on attachment.

In Chapter 1 we mentioned Bowlby's work, in which he showed that parents who are secure within themselves, and who are not over-anxious about themselves or their world, offer their children a secure base from which to explore. This, in turn, leads to the children feeling secure enough to be able to explore, enjoy and understand the world. Of course, children will get hurt and frightened in the course of their explorations, but they will return to the secure base for comfort and healing before setting out again. In a similar way the supervisor who is personally secure offers a 'secure base' where the counsellor can return for comfort and healing. The counsellor is then in a better position to 'set out' and offer a secure and predictable relationship to a client. This will be very necessary for a client who is hurt, frightened and in need of security in a world that has become chaotic and unpredictable through loss.

To offer such a secure base, the supervisors need their own supervision. A further way in which the security of supervision is enhanced is through a clear contract. Guidance on contracting is given in the *Ethical Framework for Good Practice in Counselling and Psychotherapy* published by the British Association for Counselling and Psychotherapy (BACP) (2002).

Obviously the restorative function of supervision has similarities to personal counselling, but only in so far as the environment of acceptance is essential to create trust. Beyond that, the focus is different. In supervision the primary focus is the counsellor's client; in personal counselling the focus is on the counsellor.

The formative function

For an inexperienced counsellor, supervision often focuses on the task of relating theoretical ideas, such as those outlined in Chapters 1 to 9, to the actual practice of counselling. There is likely, therefore, to be a substantial training aspect to supervision in the early stages. The counsellor will also be helped to look very closely at which skills were used in the session and which were not. Further areas of exploration would be to look at the consequences of these interventions and to help the counsellor become more aware of responses, and sometimes reactions, to the client and, in return, to consider the client's reactions. As the counsellor gains experience, supervision focuses more and more on understanding what is going on in the relationship. We sometimes use the word 'process' to mean 'what is going on in the relationship'. Reflecting upon this process of the counselling relationship and trying to understand the particular pattern of grief constitute the 'meat', as it were, of supervision. Other less conscious processes relating to supervision will be considered later in this chapter.

The normative function

Supervisors within almost any context will have some responsibility to ensure that the counsellor's work is appropriate and falls within defined ethical standards. Given that the primary purpose of supervision is to ensure that the counsellor is addressing the needs of the client, the supervisor will be concerned with ethical issues of counselling. This includes concern about confidentiality, respect for the client's beliefs and values, and maintenance of the boundaries between counselling and friendship. The supervisor also needs to recognise whether the counsellor is too depleted by the work to continue counselling, or too affected by the losses brought to the work to continue without having a break from counselling, further training, personal counselling, or even all three. The supervisor's task within this function is to monitor the overall quality of the work. The UK Council for Standards in Bereavement Care has developed and published *Standards for Bereavement Care in the UK* (2001). This is complementary to the *Ethical Framework for Good Practice in Counselling and Psychotherapy* published by BACP (2002). The latter outlines the ethical standards expected of any member of BACP regardless of where they are working, and whether they are acting as a counsellor, supervisor or trainer or using counselling skills. The combination of these two documents sets the standards that any counsellor working with the bereaved should also expect of themselves.

The interweaving of supervisory functions

To show how these various supervisory functions interweave in the supervision of loss counselling, we shall return to Angie's story in Chapter 12.

Angie's story

You will remember that Angie was able to pick up the threads of her life after Oliver's death: not without great pain and sorrow, but with increased sensitivity and a new maturity. After that there followed a period of enormous personal and professional development for Angie. Gradually she was able to invest her renewed energy into her work and grow in confidence and personal strength. About 3½ years after Oliver's death Angie met Paul, who himself was suffering loss. His ex-wife Sally, from whom he had separated four years previously, but who had continued to live down the road, had decided to move to northern Scotland, taking his four-year-old daughter Katie. Angie not only 'knew' about loss in the historical sense of having experienced loss herself, she also 'knew' about loss in the sense of knowing that the feelings of grief need to be heard and understood. She knew that it would take time for ambivalent feelings to be disentangled and resolved and that the process cannot be rushed. Having a clear and continuing bond with her late husband, Oliver, she was therefore not only able to wait for Paul to grieve the profound loss of Sally and Katie, but also able to help him in his grief. Knowing that Paul's loving feelings towards Sally and Katie did not prevent loving feelings growing in their own relationship, Angie was able to share with Paul the sense of her continuing bond with Oliver as she told Paul about him. This helped Angie to treasure even more the precious memories of the man who had died so young. In turn, this helped Angie to manage feelings of retrospective jealousy about Sally, and Angie and Paul's relationship developed through the sharing of their separate griefs; they were married two years later and went on to have two children of their own.

Over the years, as the children became more independent, Angie realised that she was interested in going forward for selection as a bereavement counsellor. In thinking about the selection process, she wondered whether the wound of Oliver's death 10 years earlier had healed enough for her to be in a position to offer herself for counselling training. She thought that it had.

Angie was indeed selected as a counsellor, took part in initial training and began working with her first clients. She had group supervision at the training centre and saw her individual supervisor once a fortnight.

One day a new client, Debbie, came in to see Angie and quickly burst into tears. The following is the story she had to tell.

Debbie's story

Debbie was a student and had recently gone to university. The day before she had left home for university she had received a letter out of the blue from her boyfriend, John, her first love, saying quite coldly that the relationship was finished. He was going to college, she to university, and their ways ought to part. Debbie had been distraught at this news and had sought comfort from her mother, but her mother seemed to reject her feelings and kept insisting that 'there were other fish in the sea'. This made Debbie feel even worse, and it was at that point that she had sought counselling at the agency where Angie worked.

Two days after this initial session Angie took the work to her supervisor, David. In Exercise 18.1 we give an account of this supervision session.

Exercise 18.1 A typical supervision session

The first memory Angie had was that Debbie had been very distressed, and that she was grieving the loss of her young man, John, at much the same age she had been when Oliver died. She then remembered that she had wondered momentarily whether she should refer Debbie to someone else. However, she had felt secure enough in herself to leave the idea of referral and get on with the work with Debbie in the session. In supervision she wanted to review this decision, and to consider further whether the empathic skills she had used had been appropriate and effective. As Angie talked with her supervisor, David, about her initial assessment she realised that she had noticed three crucial factors that had suggested to her the appropriateness of a counselling relationship for Debbie. First, Debbie had talked of student friends in a way that made Angie think she was well supported. Second, Angie noticed Debbie's open distress and anger, which seemed to indicate that the grief work was under way. Finally, Angie had sensed a growing trust and developing relationship as the counselling session progressed. Angie herself felt well supported in the supervisory relationship so she decided, encouraged by her supervisor, that she should continue with Debbie rather than refer.

As the supervision session proceeded, Angie remembered Debbie's anger, and also began to remember, with poignant intensity, how angry she herself had felt when she had experienced feelings of abandonment by Oliver. Gradually as she talked about those feelings of loss, abandonment and anger, she became aware that Debbie's anger was different from her own. However, she realised that she had the capacity to understand and empathise with Debbie. She also realised, with David's help, that she had worked through the tasks of mourning about Oliver enough to be able to work with Debbie on her grief. This enabled Angie to focus on the feelings in relation to Debbie that she was still aware of from the session. She could remember the interventions she had used, and reflect on what their effect might have been on the counselling relationship. She could then consider alternative interventions and think with her supervisor about how she might have ended the session more effectively. This led on to a brief discussion about the particular importance of firm boundaries in loss counselling.

Identify examples of the restorative, formative and normative functions of supervision and make notes of your own.

In the supervision session outlined in Exercise 18.1 (p. 212), we have shown how the three main functions of supervision interweave. At the beginning of the session, supervision is mainly formative, as Angie reflects on the relationship with Debbie. In reflecting on her feelings of anger, the function of the supervision moves into the restorative mode; and then back into the formative mode, as Angie returns the focus to understanding Debbie and working with Debbie's anger. There are further examples of the movement from formative to reflective and back again before the final part of the supervision, which is normative.

Uses of feelings

The counsellor's feelings

In the description of a supervisory session in Exercise 18.1 (p. 212) we focus on the various feelings that are evoked in the counsellor and are a particularly important part of supervision. First of all this focusing helps the counsellor to discover whether these feelings belong more to the client or more to the counsellor. If they belong to the counsellor it is important to establish whether they can be contained within the supervisory session, and then used to understand more about the client; or whether they signal the need for personal counselling for the counsellor. This focus on the counsellor's feelings is both restorative, in that it helps contain the feelings naturally evoked by working with loss, and formative, in that the discovery may be made that certain feelings, experienced by the sensitive counsellor, may well be the very feelings denied by the client (Chapter 15). Awareness of the existence and nature of all these feelings is an important part of the counsellor's development and is part of what enables clients to work through Task 2.

We shall now return to Angie to look in more detail at how the supervisor helps the counsellor use her feelings remembered from the counselling session. In her supervision session with David we see how Angie's feelings were contained and then used to give a clue to Debbie's difficulties.

Use of counsellor's feelings to locate denied feelings in the client

In the session described in Exercise 18.1 Angie found that her feelings about Oliver, reawakened by the counselling work, could be heard and contained within the supervision session. She was then able to focus back on to her session with Debbie. As she did this she became aware of an intensely sad and aching feeling in herself, which she had first felt as she listened to Debbie raging about this 'awful' John. Debbie seemed still to be protecting herself from feelings of pain and sadness by raging at and vilifying John. (This is similar to Frank's behaviour in Chapter 15.) Angie seemed to sense the feelings that Debbie dared not. David, Angie's supervisor, in pondering about these feelings with her, helped her to see that not only the anger but also the feelings of sadness and pain belonged to Debbie. They then discussed ways in which Angie might reflect back the anger and rage that Debbie was expressing, and hint at the sadness and longing of which Debbie seemed unaware. This would give Debbie an opportunity, within the context of the counselling relationship, to experience the feelings of which she was afraid.

Use of counsellor's feelings to recognise the counsellor's need

When the feelings stirred up in a counsellor by a particular client keep distracting the counsellor from the counselling relationship, they may be signalling to the counsellor that certain ungrieved losses in her own life need attention. The following account is given by a counsellor who experienced powerful feelings in the counselling session, which later in supervision she recognised as her own.

> About 10 years ago now I remember how, towards the end of a counselling session with Jenny, I felt my throat tighten and tears coming to my eyes. Jenny was grieving the loss, through abortion, of the only child she might have had with the man who had just left her.
>
> Of course I might well have shed tears for Jenny in her hitherto unrecognised grief, but my tears here were strangely distracting and I felt uncomfortable and angry in the session. A few days later in my supervision session I was able, in a safe place, to ponder these feelings and discovered great pain and sadness about a miscarriage I had had some 16 years previously. The relationship with my baby's father had also been lost and therefore we could never grieve the miscarriage together. It became clear that my personal material related, not just to the miscarriage but to the relationship itself, had been re-stimulated in me by Jenny's experiences. The exploration of Jenny's experiences had uncovered more grief in me than could be appropriately dealt with in supervision. I felt considerable relief when my supervisor suggested that I should have some further counselling in order to explore and work through the feelings from my own grief.
>
> On realising that these distractions came from a past experience of mine, I understood what had interfered with my listening to Jenny. After the supervision session I was able to get help with my own grief. When I met Jenny again the following week I was able 'to be' with her more fully, undistracted by feelings which belonged to my past.

This example illustrates how the supervisor had helped this counsellor to express and understand some of her feelings about her own miscarriage, and lost relationship. The counsellor quickly recognised her own need to get help with her grief. This then enabled the counsellor to empathise with Jenny's conscious feelings, as well as focusing on her feelings at the edge of awareness. She was now responding to Jenny the person and to her feelings, rather than simply reacting to material that Jenny had brought. A clear advantage had been gained for both parties as a result of good supervision.

Not all feelings experienced in a session are necessarily distracting from the client. In supervision a counsellor will recall many feelings as she remembers a session. A counsellor, for instance, might talk about a feeling of being deskilled. Supervision could help her understand whether the deskilled feeling related quite straightforwardly to poor use of skills; or whether the feelings of deep insecurity or hopelessness in the client were being experienced by the counsellor, as if they were her own. Obviously many other feelings felt by the counsellor when recalling a counselling session in supervision can be used to understand what may be happening in the relationship. In the example with Jenny, a source of learning for the counsellor occurred when feelings, expressed by the griever during the session, immediately re-evoked forgotten and unresolved feelings that had gone underground in the counsellor long ago. In supervision she was quickly aware of the feelings and their source and acknowledged what needed to be done. It sometimes happens, however, that feelings or processes from the client do not reach the counsellor's conscious awareness and so she brings them or 'reflects' them unconsciously into the supervision relationship.

Reflected feelings in the parallel process

This phenomenon of unconscious material from the counselling relationship finding its way into the supervisory relationship was first pointed out by Harold Searles (1955). He described how the processes in the one relationship are repeated or reflected in the processes in the other relationship. This is the basis for what is called the 'parallel process' that happens in supervision and can be picked up by the supervisor noticing uncharacteristic behaviour in the counsellor.

When the counsellor unconsciously parallels the client's behaviour in supervision it can throw light on the counselling relationship. Something like this happened to a counsellor in supervision when recalling counselling Christopher, whom you met in Exercise 10.4 (p. 109) and in Chapter 15.

> Christopher talked of his lover Jake who had recently died of Aids. He was angry, isolated and very frightened of trusting me. He came into the first session more or less shouting, 'Just how do you think you can help me? Do you know what it feels like to have your lover die? You can't give him back to me can you?' I had responded with something like,

'Christopher, you are really angry. Your anger certainly makes sense when you have been so let down. I guess you might be really wary about trusting me in case I let you down too?' I felt reasonably sure that this response was appropriate yet Christopher replied with a 'Yes, but why should I trust you anyway?' And so the session continued with Christopher apparently unable to hear, to take in or to use anything I said. By the end of the session I felt pretty useless.

I took this case to supervision hoping, or so I thought, to get some help with this 'difficult' client, but found myself exceedingly resistant to what I usually regarded as excellent supervision. My responses of 'Yes, but . . .' soon reached my supervisor's awareness and she was able to point out how the process of 'yes-but resistance' from the counselling session was being reflected in supervision. Once I had become aware of how I was resisting in supervision I realised that this process of resistance was mirroring Christopher's. I could then reflect with my supervisor on how I might constructively use Christopher's process of resistance, rather than just be dragged down and made impotent by it. Once I was able to understand the function of Christopher's resistance I became more confident in exploring the pain and intimacy he was avoiding.

Use of the supervisor's feelings

There is another way in which unconscious material from the counselling session finds its way into the supervisory session. A supervisor may pick up an unconscious feeling, which can arise quite suddenly. In paying attention to this 'stray' feeling the supervisor can often provide reflective illumination for the counsellor. Angie's supervisor, David, picked up just such a strong feeling during the first supervision session soon after Angie had seen her new client, Debbie.

You will remember how Debbie had sought comfort from her mother who had ignored Debbie's feelings, insisting that 'There were other fish in the sea'. It was at this point that Debbie had sought counselling. Angie subsequently told David about her session with Debbie. In the following passage David describes part of this supervisory session with Angie.

I was listening to Angie talking about Debbie's sudden loss and something to do with Debbie's mother, when I noticed Angie's curious blankness. Then I found that I wasn't really listening to Angie any more and was feeling inexplicably angry. I quickly reflected on whether I might be feeling angry about anything in my own life outside the session. I thought not. I returned to Angie, pretty certain that this feeling in me was something to do with Angie and possibly also with her relationship with Debbie. I stopped Angie's talk with some difficulty and invited her to reflect on whether this inexplicable angry feeling which I was experiencing could have anything to do with the counselling relationship between her and Debbie. Angie reflected on this. She gradually became aware that she too had been unable to concentrate fully on Debbie, when Debbie was talking about her mother.

As Angie reflected on her own blankness about Debbie and her mother she found herself beginning to feel angry. At this point I had wondered if this was Debbie's anger, which Angie was beginning to feel (see Table 15.1, p. 183), but she seemed to draw away from Debbie and towards her own past. She then suddenly remembered telling her own mother of Oliver's diagnosis. Her mother, no doubt trying to be helpful at the time, and perhaps not realising the depth of the relationship between Angie and Oliver, had said something like 'Never mind dear, there are other pebbles on the beach'. Angie also remembered that she had been so shocked and numbed by the news of Oliver at that point, that she had felt relatively little about her mother's response, and certainly had not been angry.

She had subsequently been enabled through counselling (Chapter 12) to express her feelings of grief about Oliver's death and now, in supervision, reflected briefly upon that experience. Her sense was that the 'wound' had largely healed. It was then that she began to experience and to express anger about her own mother's response. This was anger which she had not been able to feel at the time of Oliver's death and which had gone underground. Having been unable to experience or express her own anger with her own mother then, Angie had been unable later to recognise that Debbie was angry with *her* mother now.

I then understood why Angie had been unable to experience the angry feelings in the session with Debbie. I also understood why she had needed to bring them unconsciously, masked by her blankness, into the supervision session. Once Angie had expressed anger about her own mother's similar remarks, she found that she was still angry. This at last was Debbie's anger, which had been denied in the counselling session. We were then able to focus on the related counselling tasks. She could see that Debbie might be needing to recognise, understand and accept her anger with her mother, rather than just her anger with John for leaving her.

These examples show two ways in which unconscious material appears in the supervision session. Others occur whenever processes that happen in the counselling session are, often without the counsellor's awareness, reflected or 'paralleled' in supervision. The supervisor's awareness of these processes is an enormously useful contribution to the understanding of the counselling relationship. It can often unravel complicated feelings that block the counselling process.

Supervision for the unexpected

Another important aspect of supervision is its capacity to 'hold' the counsellor when there are sudden or unplanned endings such as when a client becomes seriously ill and subsequently dies, or suddenly dies.

If a client in counselling or psychotherapy discovers that they have a terminal illness, the counsellor has many issues to think about and decisions to make. Frequently one's supervisor would be the best person to consult. If one decides to continue therapy throughout the illness, then there are many questions to consider. Hospitals, for instance, often do not offer much privacy and it may be equally difficult to get both privacy and quiet in a private house. Both Joy Schaverien (2002) and Sue Wheeler (1996) give moving accounts of what it is like to be in a counselling relationship with someone when they are seriously ill. In both of these cases the client was terminally ill, so they worked together right up to the client's death.

If a client dies through illness or suicide, counsellors will have to face their own feelings about their client dying as well as drawing on much of what has been said in this book. A supervisor would normally be the first person to consult, to share one's feelings with and think about practical issues. Decisions need to be made about such things as what contact, if any, should be made with the family and the appropriateness of attending the funeral. Counsellors will also need to pay attention to their own needs for support and care (Syme, 2003), possibly spending some time with a therapist if personal losses are evoked and become unmanageable.

Supervisors may also have an important role in 'holding' a counsellor's clients if the counsellor should suddenly become seriously ill or die. Counsellors themselves need to make arrangements for such eventualities by making a 'professional will' (Syme, 1994). In such an event clients need to be informed quickly and need to have the opportunity to explore and express their feelings and thoughts about this sudden loss. A supervisor or an experienced colleague would be the usual choice of 'professional executor'. This person, or two people if there are many clients, would know who the clients were, how to inform them, and what was to be done about them, their records and financial arrangements. Clearly the counsellor needs to discuss these arrangements with the relevant person before the event. Given the temptation to deny our mortality, we may delay making these arrangements and leave a difficult mess behind. The next of kin are likely to be bereft under such circumstances, so it is important that counsellors make these arrangements in advance and inform their next of kin who their 'professional executor' is to be and where to find the relevant information. Counsellors working in agencies should check that similar arrangements are in place.

The value of supervision

In this chapter we have considered the three main functions of supervision and tried to show how these interrelate in practice. We have shown how both the counsellor's and the supervisor's feelings constitute a rich and necessary resource for understanding the counselling process. We have also drawn attention to the supportive role of supervisors when the unexpected happens, such as the death of either a counsellor or a client. What has been implied throughout this chapter, but perhaps needs stating more explicitly, is that the quality of the relationship between the counsellor and the supervisor is paramount. It is when both counsellor and supervisor can drop their judgemental attitudes, face the anxieties inherent for both in the supervisory relationship and manage to be genuine with each other that the supervision is likely to be most effective.

We have talked here of the necessity of supervision for all counsellors, and of the special quality of supervision for all those working with loss and grief. The importance of supervision is highlighted by BACP. This counselling organisation insists that accredited counsellors, regardless of their experience, receive a minimum of 1½ hours of supervision per month. This commitment to ongoing supervision and continued personal development is essential during training and throughout the working life of all counsellors.

Supervision itself has training-like qualities in its formative function, but cannot replace a training course in counselling skills or counselling. A loss-counselling training course, like all counselling training, needs to be largely experiential in nature. It would include training in specific skills, study of at least one model for understanding human development and knowledge about loss itself. Various opportunities for self-exploration, both individually and in groups, would be given. Any more advanced course in counselling will include supervision in groups and individually, or preferably both, as an integral part of the course. Supervision on a loss-counselling training course enables the integration of skills, knowledge and the various levels of loss experience into counselling practice.

Many counselling courses integrate the theory and practice of loss into the whole course, while others simply offer a 'loss' component within a more general counselling course. When selecting a course it is important to consider your own learning needs; the length, general aim and target group for the course; the specific objectives and assessment procedures of that course; the balance between self-exploration, knowledge and skills; the availability of supervised counselling practice; and the experience and qualifications of the trainers. A professional counselling course will have firm structures for making a clear ending to the course, which will enable participants to experience an ending where self-exploration and understanding can take place. They will also recognise that finishing a counselling course is just the beginning of setting off on one's own, and will try to ensure that good supervisory structures are in place for those completing the course.

Counselling trainers themselves need to address all these issues, and to assess their own training skills and levels of supervision. They are also responsible for clear publicity about the courses offered and for 'safe enough structures' for personal development work within the course. BACP produces relevant helpful publications on ethical issues in training and information on accredited courses.

Summary

- Supervision is a necessary professional relationship between one or more loss counsellors and a more experienced counsellor trained as a supervisor. It focuses on the well-being of the clients and the care and development of the counsellors.
- Care for the counsellor is particularly important in the lonely business of loss counselling, where the pain of grief is a consistent element of the work.
- The tendency in our culture to deny pain can lead to a similar tendency to deny the need for supervision.
- Supervision functions in three main ways:

    (a) As a restorative base where the feelings stirred up by grief work may be expressed, contained and reflected upon.
    (b) As a formative or developmental forum for studying the theoretical implications, the interventions and the processes of the counselling relationship.
    (c) As a place for monitoring the quality of counselling through such normative elements as maintaining appropriate boundaries and practising ethically.

- Supervisory activities sometimes fulfil more than one function simultaneously, and at other times supervision moves almost imperceptibly from one function to another.
- Some feelings and processes that are not conscious in the counselling relationship may be brought unconsciously into the supervisory relationship. The supervisor's awareness and use of this material is an integral part of supervision.
- Supervisors should ensure that arrangements are in place for the management of the death of a counsellor or a client.
- A competent training course in loss counselling will include a large experiential element to ensure that loss counsellors are aware of the role that loss plays in their lives.

Chapter 19

Epilogue

We hope that as you approach the end of this book you will have learned or discovered things relevant to you. For us, drawing on our knowledge and experience and having to formulate our ideas in order to write this down has certainly been a learning process! And yet, in the end these ideas are not new, only recombined and reformulated for our times.

Human life is characterised on the one hand by love and connectedness, and on the other by separation and loss. We ignore and avoid this truth at our peril. Kalish (1985) warns that 'Anything that you have, you can lose; anything you are attached to, you can be separated from; anything you love can be taken away from you. Yet if you really have nothing to lose, you have nothing.'

In the 12 years since we wrote the first edition of this book there have been some eight million deaths in Great Britain alone. There have also been many hundreds of thousands of divorces and other loss experiences for children and adults. They have all had the opportunity to discover how central love and loss are to their lives. They can only avoid grieving if their capacity to love has been 'killed'.

Art can enable us to get inside the skin of others and thus put us in touch with our own feelings. Music, poetry and other media have helped humans express love, fear, wonder and awe through all recorded time, but perhaps the most passionate expression of all has been that of loss and sorrow. It is through their expression that feelings can be thought about and the urge towards death turned again towards life.

As bereavement counsellors we are also part of humanity, reaching out to connect with those who are feeling at their loneliest and most vulnerable. For us there are three cardinal rules. They have all been said before, but are worth saying again.

1. If in doubt; say nowt!

That is, when someone is trying, however hesitantly and confusedly, to put their sorrow into words, for heaven's sake, don't get in the way! Learn how to use silence to let someone else find their words.

2. Know thyself

The Delphic oracle was well aware, before Freud, that whoever does not know their own history is destined to repeat it. If we are really going to understand the experience of grief in another (and to help them, we must), then we have to know and experience the story of our own griefs.

3. Grief is the price we pay for love

We leave the last words to Tennyson.

> 'Tis better to have loved and lost
> Than never to have loved at all.
> *In Memoriam A.H.H.*, canto XXVII

Appendix A

Useful resources

Age Concern England, Astral House, 126–128 London Road, London SW16 4ER. Tel.: 020 8765 7200. Email: ace@ace.org.uk. Provides services to elderly people in the UK.

Aids: The Terrence Higgins Trust, 52–54 Gray's Inn Road, London WC1X 8JU. Tel.: 020 7831 0330 and THT direct helpline: 0845 1221200. Email: info@tht.org.uk.

Alzheimer's Society, Gordon House, 10 Greencoat Place, London SW1P 1PH. Tel.: 020 7306 0606. Fax: 020 7306 0808.
Email: info@alzheimers.org.uk. Website: www.alzheimers.org.uk.

ARC (Antenatal Results & Choices), 73 Charlotte Street, London W1P 1LB. Tel./Fax: 020 7631 0280. Helpline: 020 7631 0285.
Email: arcsatfa@aol.com. Website: www.arc-uk.org.

Association for Post-Natal Illness, 145 Dawes Road, Fulham, London SW6 7EB. Tel.: 020 7386 0868. Fax: 020 7386 8885.
Email: info@apni.org. Website: www.apni.org.

Barnardo's, Tanners Lane, Barkingside, Ilford, Essex IG6 1QG. Tel.: 020 8550 8822. Fax: 020 8551 6870.
Email: dorothy.howes@barnardos.org.uk. Website: www.barnardos.org.uk.

British Association for Counselling and Psychotherapy (BACP), 1 Regent Place, Rugby, Warwickshire CV21 2PJ. Tel.: 0870 443 5252. Fax: 0870 4435160. Minicom: 0870 443 5162.
Email: bacp@bacp.co.uk. Website: www.bacp.co.uk.

British Humanist Association, 47 Theobalds Road, London WC1X 8SP. Tel.: 020 7430 0908. Fax: 020 7430 1271. Email: info@humanism.org.uk. Website: www.humanism.org.uk. Helps with ideas for a non-religious funeral or cremation.

Broken Rites, Secretary Johann Martin, 93 York Road, Teddington, Middlesex TW11 8SL. Tel.: 020 8943 4688.
Email: secretary@brokenrites.org. Website: www.brokenrites.org. Inter-denominational self-help and support group for separated and divorced wives of clergy and ministers.

CancerBACUP, 3 Bath Place, Rivington Street, London EC2A 3JR. Tel.: 020

7696 9003. Fax: 020 7696 9002. Freephone helpline: 0808 8000 1234. Website: www.cancerbacup.org.uk. Cancer information service.

CARE Confidential, PO Box 6906, Chelmsford, CM1 3YQ. Helpline: 0800 028 2228. Email: careconfidential@aol.com.
Website: www.pregnancy.org. uk. For pregnancy and post-abortion concerns.

Carers UK, 20/25 Glasshouse Yard, London EC1A 4JT. Tel.: 020 7490 8818. Fax: 020 7490 8824.
Email: info@ukcarers.org. Website: www. carersonline.org.uk.

Child Bereavement Trust, Aston House, High Street, West Wycombe, Buckinghamshire HP14 3AG. Tel.: 01494 446648. Fax: 01494 440057. Info and support line: 0845 357 1000.
Email: enquiries@childbereavement.org.uk.
Website: www.childbereavement.org.uk. A charity that cares for grieving families by training and supporting the professional carers.

Childline (UK HQ), Studd Street, London N1 0QW. Tel.: 020 7239 1000. Fax: 020 7239 1001. Helpline: 0800 1111. Website: www.childline.org.uk. Confidential telephone service for abused children.

Compassionate Friends, 53 North Street, Bristol BS3 1EN. Tel.: 0117 966 5202. Fax: 0117 914 4368. Helpline: 0117 953 9639.
Email: info@tcf.org.uk. Website: www.tcf.org.uk. A nationwide organisation of bereaved parents and their families.

Contact a Family, 209–211 City Road, London EC1V 1JN. Tel.: 020 7608 8700. Helpline: 0808 808 3555. Website: www.cafamily.org.uk. For families with disabled children.

COSCA, Counselling and Psychotherapy in Scotland, 18 Viewfield Street, Stirling, FK8 1UA. Tel.: 01786 475 140. Fax: 01786 446 207.
Email: cosca@compuserve.com. Website: www.cosca.org.uk.

Cruse Bereavement Care, Cruse House, 126 Sheen Road, Richmond, Surrey TW9 1UR. Tel.: 020 8939 9530. Fax: 020 8940 7638. Helpline: 0870 1671677. Email: info@crusebereavementcare.org.uk.
Website: www.crusebereavementcare.org.uk.

Divorce Recovery Workshop, 69 Elmdon Lane, Marston Green, Birmingham B37 7DN. Tel.: 07000 781889. Email: drw@drw.org.uk.
Website: www.drw.org.uk. National organisation that helps people cope with the trauma of the breakdown of a major relationship.

Families Need Fathers, 134 Curtain Road, London EC2A 3AR. Tel.: 020 7613 5060. Fax: 020 7739 3410. Email: fnf@fnf.org.uk. Organisation committed to continued shared parenting after separation and divorce.

Fostering Network, 87 Blackfriars Road, London SE1 8HA. Tel.: 020 7620 6400. Fax: 020 7620 6401.
Email: info@fostering.net. Website: www.fostering.net.

FSID (The Foundation for the Study of Infant Deaths), Artillery House,

11–19 Artillery Row, London SW1P 1RT. Tel.: 0870 787 0885. Fax: 020 7222 8002. Helpline: 0207 233 2090.

Email: fsid@sids.org.uk. Website: www.sids.org.uk/fsid.

Gay Bereavement Project, Helpline: 020 7403 5969.

Gingerbread, First Floor, 7 Sovereign Close, Sovereign Court, London E1W 3HW. Tel.: 020 7488 9300. Fax: 020 7488 9333. Advice line and membership: 0800 018 4318. Email: office@gingerbread.org.uk. Website: www.gingerbread.org.uk. The organisation supports lone-parent families.

Hospice Information, Help the Hospices, Hospice House, 34–44 Britannia Street, London WC1X 9JG. Tel.: 0870 903 3903. Fax: 020 7278 1021. Email: info@hospiceinformation.info.

Website: www.hospiceinformation. info.

Incest Crisis Centre, Helpline: 01246 559889.

Jewish Bereavement Counselling Service (JBCS), PO Box 6748, London N3 3BX. Tel.: and fax: 020 8349 0839. Email: jbcs@jvisit.org.uk. Help in bereavement.

MATCH (Mothers Apart From Their Children), c/o BM Problems, London WC1N 3XX. A non-profit voluntary organisation – no office/phone, post is forwarded by an agent to committee members in their own homes. Website: www.matchmothers.org.

MENCAP (Royal Society for Mentally Handicapped Children and Adults), 123 Golden Lane, London EC1Y 0RT. Tel.: 020 7454 0454. Fax: 020 7696 5540. Email: information@mencap.org.uk. Website: www.mencap. org.uk.

Miscarriage Association, c/o Clayton Hospital, Northgate, Wakefield WF1 3JS. Tel.: 01924 200799. Website: www.the-ma.org.uk.

NAPAC (The National Association for People Abused in Childhood), 42 Curtain Road, London EC2A 3NH. Freephone helpline: 0800 085 3330. Email: mail@napac.fsnet.co.uk. Website: www.napac.org.uk.

National Association of Widows, 3rd Floor, 48 Queens Road, Coventry CV1 3EH. Tel./Fax: 024 7663 4848.

Email: info@nawidows.org.uk. Website: www.nawidows.org.uk.

National Council for Hospice and Specialist Palliative Care Services, First Floor, 34–44 Britannia Street, London WC1X 9JG. Tel.: 020 7520 8299. Fax: 020 7520 8298. Email: enquiries@hospice-spc-council.org.uk. Website: www.hospice-spc-council.org.uk.

National Council for One Parent Families, 255 Kentish Town Road, London NW5 2LX. Tel.: 020 7428 5400. Fax: 020 7482 4851. Freephone lone parent helpline: 0800 018 5026. Email: info@oneparentfamilies.org.uk. Website: www.oneparentfamilies.org.uk. For UK lone parents/single parents.

Natural Death Centre, 6 Blackstock Mews, Blackstock Road, London N4 2BT. Tel.: 020 7359 8391. Fax: 020 7354 3831.

Email: ndc@alberyfoundation.org. Website: www.naturaldeath.org.uk.

NORCAP (National Organisation for Counselling Adoptees and Parents), 112 Church Road, Wheatley, Oxfordshire OX33 1LU. Tel.: 01865 875000. Fax: 01865 875686.
Email: enquiries@norcap.org. Website: www.norcap.org.uk.

Parentline Plus, 520 Highgate Studios, 53–79 Highgate Road, Kentish Town, London NW5 1TL. Tel.: 020 7284 5500. Free confidential helpline: 0808 800 2222. Website: www.parentlineplus.org.uk. National charity offering help and information for parents and families.

Post Adoption Centre, 5 Torriano Mews, Torriano Avenue, London NW5 2RZ. Tel.: 020 7284 0555. Fax: 020 7482 2367. Advice: 020 7485 2931. Email: advice@postadoptioncentre.org.uk.
Website: www. postadoptioncentre.org.uk. Offers a specialised, innovative and creative approach to working with adoption issues.

Postnatal Depression Project, Wallace House, 3 Boswell Road, Edinburgh EH5 3RJ. Tel.: 0131 538 7288. Fax: 0131 552 2319.
Email: pnd.cos@uk.uumail.com. Offers group and individual counselling as well as infant massage and support in Edinburgh area with links in other Scottish cities.

Relate (Marriage Guidance Association), Herbert Gray College, Little Church Street, Rugby CV21 3AP. Tel.: 01788 573241. Counsellors also work with separating couples and individuals. Website: www.relate.org.uk. For Scotland, website: www.couplecounselling.org.

Samaritans, The Upper Mill, Kingston Road, Ewell, Surrey KT17 2AF (Head Office). Email: jo@samaritans.org. Website: www.samaritans.org.uk. Has branches in all major cities and towns. For local telephone number look in your local telephone directory under 'S' or emergency. Offers emotional support to anyone in need.

SANDS Stillbirth and Neonatal Death Society, 28 Portland Place, London W1B 1LY. Tel.: 020 7436 7940. Helpline: 020 7436 5881. Fax: 020 7436 3715. Email: support@uk-sands.org. Website: www.uk-sands.org.

Scottish Institute of Human Relations, 18 Young Street, Edinburgh EH2 4JB. Tel.: 0131 226 9610. Fax: 0131 226 9611. Glasgow Office: 13 Park Terrace, Glasgow G3 6BY. Tel.: 0141 332 0011. Fax: 0141 332 3999. Email: info@sihr.org.uk. Website: www.sihr.org.uk. Offers psycho-analytically informed psychotherapy and counselling for individuals, groups, children and families in the two major cities, with links throughout Scotland and North-East England.

Spinal Injuries Association. Freephone: 0800 980 0501.
Email: sia@spinal.co.uk. Website: www.spinal.co.uk.

Way Foundation, PO Box 6767, Brackley NN13 6YW. Tel.: 0870 0113450. Email: info@wayfoundation.org.uk.
Website: www.wayfoundation.org.uk. An organisation that acknowledges the needs of men and women widowed young.

Winston's Wish, The Clare Burgess Centre, Gloucestershire Royal Hospital,

Great Western Road, Gloucester GL1 3NN. Tel.: 01452 394377. Fax: 01472 395656. Family Line: 0845 2030405. Guidance and information for families of bereaved children.

Email: info@winstonswish.org.uk. Website: www.winstonswish.org.uk.

wpf Counselling and Psychotherapy, 23 Kensington Square, London W8 5HN. Tel.: 020 7361 4800. Fax: 020 7361 8808.

Email: counselling@wpf.org.uk. Website: www.wpf.org.uk.

Useful websites

www.allaboutsikhs.com – Contains articles on Sikh funeral ceremonies.

www.bacp.co.uk – Contains information about counselling and counselling-related agencies.

www.buddhanet.net – Information on all aspects of bereavement in a Buddhist culture.

www.intellectualdisability.info – Learning resource for students and professionals.

www.mabf.org.uk – The Grief Centre (MABF). Bereavement support and training organisation.

www.merrywidow.me.uk – Survival guide to widowhood.

www.rd4u.org.uk – For young people coping with bereavement. Email: info@rd4u.org.uk.

www.samm.org.uk – Support after Murder and Manslaughter.

www.shaareyzedek.org – Guidance on rules and practices of traditional Judaism.

www.skylight.org.nz – New Zealand-based, it carries useful information for children and young people dealing with change, loss and grief.

www.thearc.org – Resource for information about learning disability.

www.uh.edu – Go onto site and search for Muslim Students' Association: extensive information about beliefs and mourning customs.

www.uk-sobs.org.uk – Survivors of Bereavement by Suicide.

Further reading

We list here books, or parts of books, that we think are useful background reading to each chapter. We have also included novels and biographical material that are a 'good read' and that we have found both moving and illuminating. This list is not exhaustive; a recent search on a bookseller's website produced 3,349 books on bereavement and 22,377 on death!

We have reprinted the list from the first edition, amending dates and publishers where they have changed and deleting books that we know to be out of print. We have added some of the books we have come across in the past 12 years. We are, of course, aware that the growth of interest in loss and grief has resulted in many publications in and around this subject, some of which we have discovered and many we have not.

Chapter I

Bowlby, J. (1979) Lecture 7 in *The Making and Breaking of Affectional Bonds*, London: Tavistock Publications.
Holmes, J. (1993) *John Bowlby & Attachment Theory*, London: Routledge.
Parkes, C.M. and Stevenson-Hinde, J. (1982) Part 1 in *The Place of Attachment in Human Behaviour*, London: Tavistock Publications.
Skynner, R. and Cleese, J. (1993) *Families and How to Survive Them*, London: Vermillion.
Viorst, J. (1989) Part 1 in *Necessary Losses*, Englewood Cliffs, NJ: Prentice Hall.

Chapter 2

Hindle, D. and Vaciago Smith, M. (1999) Chapter 3 in *Personality Development; a Psychoanalytic Perspective*, London: Routledge.
Holmes, J. (1993) *John Bowlby & Attachment Theory*, London: Routledge.
Holmes, J. (2001) *The Search for the Secure Base*, Hove: Brunner-Routledge.

Chapter 3

Rogers, C.R. (1967) Especially Parts I and II in *On Becoming a Person*, London: Constable and Robinson.

Tolan, J. (2003) *Skills for Person Centred Counselling and Psychotherapy*, London: Sage.

Chapter 4

Books about death and bereavement

Archer, J. (1999) *The Nature of Grief: the Evolution and Psychology of Reactions to Loss*, London: Routledge.

Dickenson, D., Johnson, M. and Katz, S. (eds) (2000) *Death, Dying and Bereavement*, 2nd edn, London: Sage.

Ironside, V. (1997) *You'll Get Over It*, London: Penguin Books.

Kübler-Ross, E. (1997) *On Death and Dying*, New York: Simon & Schuster.

Littlewood, J. (1992) *Aspects of Grief*, London: Routledge.

Morrall, C. (2003) *Astonishing Splashes of Colour*, Birmingham: Tindal Street Press.

Orbach, A. (2003) *Counselling Older Clients*, London: Sage.

Parkes, C.M. (1996) *Bereavement: Studies of Grief in Adult Life*, 3rd edn, London: Routledge.

Terry, P. (1997) *Counselling the Elderly and their Carer*, London: Macmillan.

Thompson, N. (ed.) (2002) *Loss and Grief: a Guide for Human Services Practitioners*, London: Palgrave.

Walter, T. (1999) *On Bereavement: the Culture of Grief*, Buckingham: Open University Press.

Novels, biographies and self-help books that have helped us and other grievers understand more about our experiences of death, dying and various other losses

Abrams, R. (1999) *When Parents Die*, 2nd edn, London: Routledge. Aimed at 15–25-year-olds.

Ashworth, A. (1999) *Once in a House on Fire*, London: Picador.

Carr, S. (2000) *The Boys are Back in Town*, London: Hutchinson.

Chang, J. (1993) *Wild Swans. Three Daughters of China*, London: Flamingo.

Collick, E.M. (1986) *Through Grief*, London: Darton, Longman & Todd.

Craven, M. (1980) *I Heard the Owl Call My Name*, London: Picador.

Faulks, S. (1994) *Birdsong*, London: Vintage.

Forster, M. (2000) *The Memory Box*, London: Penguin.

Golden, T.R. (2000) *Swallowed by a Snake: the Gift of the Masculine Side of Healing*, 2nd edn, Gaithersburg, MD: Golden Healing Publishing.

Golden, T.R. and Miller, J.E. (1998) *When a Man Faces Grief/A Man You Know Is Grieving*, Fort Wayne, IN: Willowgreen Publishing.

Hale, S. (2003) *The Man Who Lost His Language*, London: Penguin.

Hill, S. (1977) *In the Springtime of the Year*, London: Penguin.

Hollins, S., Dowling, S. and Blackman, N. (2003) *When Somebody Dies*, London: Royal College of Psychiatrists. Story told in pictures for people with learning disabilities.

Hollins, S. and Sireling, L. (2003) *When Dad Died*, London: Royal College of Psychiatrists. Story (including a cremation) told in pictures for people with learning disabilities.

Hollins, S. and Sireling, L. (2003) *When Mum Died*, London: Royal College of Psychiatrists. Story (including a burial) told in pictures for people with learning disabilities.

Humphry, D. with Wickett, A. (1978) *Jean's Way*, New York: Dell Publishing.

Jones, M. (1988) *Secret Flowers*, London: The Women's Press.

Johnston, J. (1989) *The Christmas Tree*, London: Review.

Kohner, N. and Henley, A. (2001) *When a Baby Dies*, 2nd edn, London: Routledge.

Kohner, N. and Thomas, J. (1993) *Grieving after the Death of Your Baby*, Bourne End, Bucks: Child Bereavement Trust.

Kushner, H. (1981) *When Bad Things Happen to Good People*, London: Pan.

Lambert, A. (1997) *Kiss and Kin*, London: Black Swan.

Lewis, C.S. (1961) *A Grief Observed*, San Francisco: Harpur.

Lively, P. (1985) *Perfect Happiness*, London: Penguin.

—— (1990) *Passing On*, London: Penguin.

Martin, T. and Doka, K. (1999) *Men Don't Cry . . . Women Do*, Philadelphia: Brunner/Mazel.

McCourt, F. (1997) *Angela's Ashes*, London: Flamingo.

McCrum, R. (1998) *My Year Off: Rediscovering Life After a Stroke*, London: Macmillan.

McEwan, I. (2002) *Atonement*, London: Vintage.

Morrison, B. (1993) *And When Did You Last See your Father?* London: Granta Books.

Picardie, R. (1998) *Before I Say Goodbye*, London: Penguin.

Rinpoche, S. (1992) *The Tibetan Book of Living and Dying*, London: Rider.

Rollin, B. (1998) *Last Wish*, Oxford: Public Affairs.

Rose, X. (1995) *Widow's Journey. A Return to Living*, London: Souvenir Press.

Rosen, M. (2002) *Carrying the Elephant: a Memoir of Love and Loss*, London: Penguin.

Sanders, C.M. (1992) *Surviving Grief . . . and Learning to Live Again*, New York: John Wiley and Sons.

Sanderson, M. (2003) *Wrong Rooms*, London: Scribner.

Sebold, A. (2003) *The Lovely Bones*, London: Picador.

Sheepshanks, M. (1998) *The Bird of My Loving*, London: Penguin.

Tatelbaum, J. (1993) *The Courage to Grieve*, London: Hutchinson.

Taylor, L.M. (2000) *Living with Loss*, Edinburgh: Constable.

Wallbank, S. (1991) *Facing Grief: Bereavement and the Young Adult*, Cambridge: Lutterworth Press.

Wallbank, S. (1992) *The Empty Bed*, London: Darton, Longman & Todd.

Woods, P. (1998) *Diary of a Grief*, York: William Sessions.

Zorza, R. and Zorza, V. (1980) *A Way to Die*, Westminster, MD: Random House.

Anthologies

Astley, N. (ed.) (2002) *Staying Alive: Real Poems for Unreal Times* (especially Part 10), Tarset, Northumberland: Bloodaxe.

Benson, J. and Falk, A. (eds) (1996) *The Long Pale Corridor*, Tarset, Northumberland: Bloodaxe.

Dobson, D. (ed.) (1998) *Aspirations*, London: Runnymede Publishing.

Dobson, D. (ed.) (1994) *Inspirations*, London: Runnymede Publishing.

Enright, D.J. (ed.) (1987) *Death*, Oxford: Oxford University Press.

Whitacker, A. (ed.) (1984) *All the End Is Harvest*, London: Darton, Longman & Todd.

Chapter 5

Bowlby, J. (1980) *Attachment and Loss: Volume 3: Loss: Sadness and Depression*, London: Penguin.

Parkes, C.M. (1975) *Bereavement: Studies of Grief in Adult Life*, London: Penguin.

Raphael, B. (1985) *The Anatomy of Bereavement*, London: Routledge.

Worden, J.W. (1983) *Grief Counselling and Grief Therapy*, London: Tavistock.

Chapter 6

Aries, P. (1994) *Western Attitudes towards Death: from the Middle Ages to the Present*, London: Marion Boyars Publishers.

Gorer, G. (1977) *Death, Grief and Mourning*, Manchester, NH: Ayer Co. Publishing.

Parkes, C.M., Laungani, P. and Young B. (eds) (1997) *Death and Bereavement across Cultures*, London: Routledge.

Chapter 7

Ainsworth-Smith, I. and Speck, P. (1999) *Letting Go: Caring for the Dying and Bereaved*, 2nd edn, London: SPCK.

Albery, N., Elliot, G. and Elliot, J. (1997) *The New Natural Death Handbook*, London: Rider.

D'Ardenne, P. and Mahtani, A. (1999) *Transcultural Counselling in Action*, 2nd edn, London: Sage.

Feild, R. (2003) *The Invisible Way: a Time to Love and a Time to Die*, Edinburgh: Floris Books.

Gibran, K. (1991) *The Prophet*, London: Pan.

Gill, S. and Fox, J. (1997) *The Dead Good Funerals Book*, Ulverston: Engineers of the Imagination.

Huntingdon, R. and Metcalfe, P. (1992) *Celebrations of Death*, Cambridge: Cambridge University Press.

Kübler-Ross, E. (1986) *Death: the Final Stage of Growth*, Englewood Cliffs, NJ: Prentice Hall.

Lago, C. and Thompson, J. (1989) 'Counselling and race', in W. Dryden, D. Charles-Edwards and R. Woolfe (eds) *Handbook of Counselling in Britain*, London: Routledge.

Neuberger, J. (1999) *Caring for Dying People of Different Faiths*, St Louis: Butterworth-Heinemann.

Chapter 8

Fraiberg, S.H. (1997) *The Magic Years*, New York: Simon & Schuster.

Krementz, J. (1988) *How it Feels when a Parent Dies*, New York: Alfred A. Knopf.

Noonan, E. (1983) *Counselling Young People*, London: Routledge.

Chapter 9

Bowlby, J. (1979) Lecture 5 in *The Making and Breaking of Affectional Bonds*, London: Tavistock Publications.

Hindmarch, C. (2000) *On the Death of a Child*, Oxford: Radcliffe Medical Press.

Skynner, R. and Cleese, J. (1993) *Families and How to Survive Them*, London: Vermillion.

Chapter 10

Jacobs, M. (1999) *Psychodynamic Counselling in Action*, 2nd edn, London: Sage.

Mearns, D. and Thorne, B. (1999) *Person-Centred Counselling in Action*, 2nd edn, London: Sage.

Manthei, R. (1997) *Counselling. The Skills of Finding Solutions to Problems*, London: Routledge.

Nelson-Jones, R. (2000) *Practical Counselling and Helping Skills*, 4th edn, London: Sage.

Chapter 11

Thompson N. (ed.) (2002) *Loss and Grief: a Guide for Human Services Practitioners*, London: Palgrave.

Worden, J.W. (1991) *Grief Counselling and Grief Therapy*, London: Routledge.

Chapter 12

Mander, G. (2002) *A Psychodynamic Approach to Brief Therapy*, London: Sage.

McLoughlin, B. (1995) Sections I and II in *Developing Psychodynamic Counselling*, London: Sage.

Murdin, L. (2000) *How Much Is Enough?* London: Routledge.

Chapter 13

Books about how to work with children and related issues

Christ, G.H. (2000) *Healing Children's Grief*, Oxford: Oxford University Press.

Crossley, D. and Stokes, J. (2001) *Beyond the Rough Rock: Supporting a Child who has been Bereaved through Suicide*, Gloucester: Winston's Wish.

Daniels, D. and Jenkins, P. (2000) *Therapy with Children: Children's Rights, Confidentiality and the Law*, London: Sage.

Dyregrov, A. (1991) *Grief in Children*, London: Jessica Kingsley.

Harris-Hendriks, J., Black, D. and Kaplan, T. (2000) *Guiding Children through Trauma and Grief*, 2nd edn, London: Routledge.

Jewett, C. (1994) *Helping Children Cope with Separation and Loss*, 2nd edn, London: Free Association Books.

Kroll, B. (1996) *Chasing Rainbows: Children, Divorce and Loss*, Lyme Regis: Russell House Publishing.

Silverman, P.R. (1999) *Never too Young to Know*, Oxford: Oxford University Press.

Smith, S.C. (1999) *The Forgotten Mourners*, 2nd edn, London: Jessica Kingsley.

Ward, B. (1995) *Good Grief 1. Teacher's Pack. Exploring Feelings: Loss and Death with under 11*, London: Jessica Kingsley.

Ward, B. (1995) *Good Grief 2. Teacher's Pack. Talking and Learning about Loss and Death*, London: Jessica Kingsley. For secondary schools and FE colleges.

Wells, R. (1988) *Helping Children Cope with Grief*, London: Sheldon Press.

Books that children have found helpful

We have given a rough indication of the appropriate age-group, knowing that children go back and forwards in their reading ages.

3–7 years old

Althea (1982) *When Uncle Bob Died*, London: Happy Cat.

Brown, L.K. and Brown, M. (1996) *When Dinosaurs Die. A Guide to Understanding Death*, London: Little, Brown and Company.

Burningham, J. (2003) *Granpa*, London: Red Fox.

Clark, E.C. (2003) *Up in Heaven*, London: Andersen.

Cole, B. (2000) *Two of Everything*, London: Red Fox.

Cole, H. (1997) *The Best Day of the Week*, London: Walker.

Cooke, T. (2001) *The Grandad Tree*, London: Walker.

Crossley, D. (2000) *Muddles, Puddles and Sunshine*, Stroud: Hawthorn Press.

Gerstein, M. (1989) *The Mountains of Tibet*, London: HarperCollins

Gray, N. (2000) *Little Bear's Grandad*, London: Little Tiger Press.

Heegaard, M.E. (1992) *When Someone Very Special Dies*, Minneapolis: Woodland Press. Can be obtained through Cruse Bereavement Care.

Joslin, M. (1998) *The Goodbye Boat*, Oxford: Lion Publishing.

Kerr, J. (2003) *Goodbye Mog*, London: Collins.

Stickney, D. (1984) *Water Bugs and Dragonflies*, Princeton, NJ: Pilgrim Press.

Varley, S. (1992) *Badger's Parting Gifts*, London: Collins.

Viorst, J. (1975) *The Tenth Good Thing about Barney*, New York: Aladdin Paperbacks.

Warfel, E.S. (2001) *The Blue Pearls*, Bristol: Barefoot Books.

Weiss, L. (1996) *My Book about our Baby who Died*, Bourne End, Bucks: Child Bereavement Trust.

Many traditional fairy tales also explore loss and separation, e.g. *The Babes in the Wood*, *Snow White and the Seven Dwarfs*, *Rumpelstiltskin*.

8–13 years old

Alexander, S. (1995) *Leila*, Edinburgh: Polygon.

Almond, D. (1998) *Skellig*, London: Hodder Children's Books.

Amos, J. (1997) *Separations: Divorce*, Isleworth: Cherrytree Books.

—— (2002) *Separations: Death*, Isleworth: Cherrytree Books.

Hartnett, S. (2002) *Thursday's Child*, London: Walker.

Kaye, J. (2002) *The Straw Girl*, London: Walker.

Magorian, M. (1996) *Good Night Mr Tom*, London: Penguin.

Marshall, J.V. (1980) *Walkabout*, London: Penguin.

Saint-Exupéry, A. (1974) *The Little Prince*, London: Egmont.

Thebo, M. (2003) *Wipe Out*, London: Collins.

Townsend, S. (2002) *The Secret Diary of Adrian Mole, Aged 13¾*, London: Penguin.

White, E.B. (1993) *Charlotte's Web*, London: Penguin.

Wilson, J. (2001) *Vicky Angel*, London: Corgi.

Wilson, J. (2002) *The Cat Mummy*, London: Corgi.

13 years upwards

Blume, J. (1998) *Tiger Eyes*, London: Piccolo.

Bowler, T. (2003) *Starseeker*, Oxford: Oxford University Press.

Chambers, A. (1995) *Dance on my Grave*, London: Red Fox.

Dickens, C. (2003) *Nicholas Nickleby*, London: Penguin.

—— (2003) *Oliver Twist*, London: Penguin.

Howker, J. (2003) *Badger on the Barge and Other Stories*, London: Walker.

—— (1996) *Isaac Campion*, London: Walker.

Hoy, L. (1987) *Your Friend Rebecca*, London: Red Fox.

Serrailer, I. (1960) *The Silver Sword*, London: Puffin.

Wallbank, S. (2000) *My Father Died*, Richmond: Cruse Bereavement Care.

Wallbank, S. (2000) *My Mother Died*, Richmond: Cruse Bereavement Care.

Zindel, P. (1996) *The Pigman's Legacy*, London: Red Fox.

Chapter 14

Bowlby, J. (1980) Lectures 1 and 2 in *The Making and Breaking of Affectional Bonds*, London: Tavistock Publications.

Rowe, D. (1983) *Depression: the Way Out of Your Prison*, London: Routledge.

Skynner, R. and Cleese, J. (1993) *Families and How to Survive Them*, London: Vermillion.

Viorst, J. (1998) Chapters 3, 5, 9 and 16 in *Necessary Losses*, Englewood Cliffs, NJ: Prentice Hall.

Winnicott, D.W. (1984) Part II in *Deprivation and Delinquency*, London: Tavistock Publications.

Chapter 15

Jacobs, M. (1999) *Psychodynamic Counselling in Action*, 2nd edn, London: Sage.

Kennedy, E. and Charles, S.C. (2002) *On Becoming a Counsellor*, Dublin: Gill and Macmillan.

Gil, E. (1995) *Outgrowing the Pain*, New York: Bantam Doubleday. Useful for those who have been sexually abused.

McLoughlin, B. (1995) *Developing Psychodynamic Counselling*, London, Sage.

Shannon, P. *Bereaved by Suicide* (leaflet), London: Cruse Bereavement Care.

Wertheimer, A. (2000) *The Special Scar. The Experiences of People Bereaved by Suicide*, London: Routledge.

Chapter 16

Bass, E. and Davies, L. (2002) *The Courage to Heal*, London: Vermillion. Useful for those who have been sexually abused.

Evans, J. (2003) *An Invisible Child*, Lewes: The Book Guild.

Fraser, S. (1989) *My Father's House*, London: Virago Press.

Harrison, K. (1997) *The Kiss*, London: Fourth Estate.

Martindale, B., Morner, M., Rodriguez, M.E.C. and Vidit, J.P. (eds) (1997) Chapters 2, 4 and 5 in *Supervision and Its Vicissitudes*, London: Karnac.

Shipton, G. (ed.) (1997) *Supervision of Psychotherapy and Counselling; Making a Place to Think*, Buckingham: Open University Press.

Chapter 17

Jacobs, M. (1999) *Psychodynamic Counselling in Action*, 2nd edn, London: Sage.

Kennedy, E. and Charles, S.C. (2002) *On Becoming a Counsellor*, Dublin: Gill and Macmillan.

Palmer, S. and McMahon, G. (eds) (1997) *Client Assessment*, London, Sage.

Chapter 18

Clarkson, P. (ed.) (1998) *Supervision; Psychoanalytic and Jungian Perspectives*, London: Whurr.

Dryden, W. and Thorne, B. (1991) *Training and Supervision for Counselling in Action*, London: Sage.

Hawkins, P. and Shohet, R. (2000) *Supervision in the Helping Professions*, Milton Keynes: Open University Press.

Inskipp, F. and Proctor, B. (2001) *Making the Most of Supervision*, Twickenham: Cascade Publications.

Jacobs, D., David, P. and Meyer, D.J. (1995) *The Supervisory Encounter*, London and New Haven, CT: Yale University Press.

Martindale, B. (ed.) (1997) *Supervision and Its Vicissitudes*, London: Karnac.

Schaverien, J. (2002) *The Dying Patient in Psychotherapy*, London: Palgrave.

Shipton, G. (ed.) (1997) *Supervision of Psychotherapy and Counselling: Making a Place to Think*, Buckingham: Open University Press.

Multimedia

In thinking about relevant films and videos, it was almost impossible to know where to begin as most of what touches the heart is loss or the fear of it. This list contains films we remember having used or that have moved or helped us over a range of different losses. We have divided them into 'Training Material' and 'Other Multimedia', but this division is somewhat arbitrary.

Training material

Grief in the Family. Leeds Animation Workshop. Tel./Fax: 0113 2484997. This animated video looks at the ways children and young people respond to grief, and what the adults around them can do to help.

Loss Counselling in Practice. An Interactive Training Video. S. Lendrum and G. Syme. Available from Concord Video and Film Council Ltd, 22 Hines Road, Ipswich IP3 9BG. Tel.: 01473 726012. Fax: 01473 274531. Email: concordvideo@btinternet.com. Website: www.concordvideo.co.uk. Concord has a wide range of video training material on death and bereavement, which can be hired or bought.

Other multimedia

Children of a Lesser God (U) (1986) Director: Randa Haines.
Dying Young (15) (1991) Director: Joel Schumacher.
Fly Away Home (U) (1996) Director: Carroll Ballard.
My Life (15) (1993) Director: Bruce Joel Rubin.
Rain Man (U) (1988) Director: Barry Levinson.
Schindler's List (PG) (1993) Director: Steven Spielberg.
Spoonface Steinberg (PG) (1998) video release (Director: Betsan Morris Evans) from the BBC radio play by Lee Hall. (Also released as an audiotape by BBC.)
The Son's Room (PG) (2001) Director: Nanni Moretti.
The Pianist (15) (2002) Director: Roman Polanski.

Truly, Madly, Deeply (PG) (1990) Director: Anthony Minghella.
Wild Strawberries (PG) (1957) Director: Ingmar Bergman.

Useful **BACP** publications

Accreditation of Training Courses
Counselling and Psychotherapy Resources Directory
Ethical Framework for Good Practice in Counselling and Psychotherapy
Training in Counselling and Psychotherapy Directory
Handbook of Counselling in Britain (1989) Edited by W. Dryden, D. Charles-Edwards and R. Woolfe. Published by Routledge in association with the British Association for Counselling and Psychotherapy.

BACP also publish information sheets including:
Time-limited to open-ended counselling – how to handle the transition
Satisfactory Endings
What is Counselling?
What is Supervision?

References

Ainsworth, M.D.S., Blehar, M.C., Waters, E. and Wall, S. (1978) *Patterns of Attachment: a Psychological Study of the Strange Situation*, Hillsdale, NJ: Lawrence Erlbaum Associates.

British Association for Counselling and Psychotherapy (2002) *Ethical Framework for Good Practice in Counselling and Psychotherapy*, Rugby: BACP.

Blake, W. (1992; first published 1794) 'On Anothers Sorrow', in *Songs of Innocence and of Experience*, London: The Folio Society.

Bowlby, J. (1953) *Child Care and the Growth of Love*, Harmondsworth: Pelican.

—— (1969) *Attachment and Loss: Volume 1: Attachment*, London: Penguin Books.

—— (1979) *The Making and Breaking of Affectional Bonds*, London: Tavistock Publications.

—— (1980) *Attachment and Loss: Volume 3: Loss: Sadness and Depression*, London: Penguin Books.

Brown, G.W. and Harris, T. (1978) *Social Origins of Depression*, London: Tavistock Publications.

Crossley, D. (2000) *Muddles, Puddles and Sunshine*, Stroud: Hawthorne Press.

Freud, S. (1917) 'Mourning and Melancholia', in J. Strachey (ed. and trans.) *The Standard Edition of the Complete Psychological Works of Sigmund Freud*, Vol. 14, London: Hogarth Press (1961).

Fromm, E. (1978) *To Have or To Be*, London: Jonathan Cape.

George, C., Kaplan, N. and Main, M. (1985) *The Berkeley Adult Attachment Interview. Unpublished Protocol*, Berkeley: Department of Psychology, University of California.

Gray, J. (1997) *Men Are from Mars, Women Are from Venus*, London: HarperCollins.

Harlow, H.F. (1961) 'The development of affectional patterns in infant monkeys', in B.M. Foss (ed.) *Determinants of Infant Behaviour: Volume 1*, London: Methuen.

Heegaard, M.E. (1992) *When Someone Very Special Dies*, Minneapolis: Woodland Press.

Hesse, E. (1999) 'The adult attachment interview', in J. Cassidy and P.R. Shaver (eds) *Handbook of Attachment*, New York: Guilford Press.

Hobson, P. (2002) *The Cradle of Thought*, London: Macmillan.

Hockey, J. (1990) *Experiences of Death: an Anthropological Account*, Edinburgh: Edinburgh University Press.

Hoffman, E. (2003) *The Secret*, London: Vintage.

Holmes, J. (1993) *John Bowlby & Attachment Theory*, London: Routledge.

Holmes, J. (2001) *The Search for the Secure Base*, Hove: Brunner-Routledge.

Inskipp, F. and Proctor, B. (2001) *Making the Most of Supervision*, Twickenham: Cascade Publications.

Jewett, C. (1984) *Helping Children Cope with Separation and Loss*, London: B.T. Batsford.

Jones, E. (1962) *The Life and Works of Sigmund Freud*, London: Hogarth Press.

Kalish, R.A. (1985) *Death, Grief and Caring Relationships*, 2nd edn, Pacific Grove, CA: Brooks/Cole.

Kroll, B. (1996) *Chasing Rainbows: Children, Divorce and Loss*, Lyme Regis: Russell House Publishing.

Kushner, H.S. (1982) *When Bad Things Happen to Good People*, London: Pan.

Main, M. (1994) 'A move to the level of representation in the study of attachment organisation: implications for psychoanalysis'. Annual Research Lecture to the British Psycho-Analytical Society, London, 6 July.

McDougall, J. (1994) 'Grief and the psychosoma'. First Keynote Lecture, Fourth International Conference on Grief and Bereavement, Stockholm.

Mearns, D. and Thorne, B. (1999) *Person-Centred Counselling in Action*, 2nd edn, London: Sage Publications.

Mørch, D.T. (1982) *The Evening Star*, London: Serpent's Tail.

National Funerals College (1996) *Dead Citizens Charter*, London: National Funerals College.

Parkes, C.M. (1972) *Bereavement: Studies of Grief in Adult Life*, 1st edn, London: Tavistock Publications.

Parkes, C.M. (1996) *Bereavement: Studies of Grief in Adult Life*, 3rd edn, London: Routledge.

Raphael, B. (1984) *The Anatomy of Bereavement*, London: Unwin Hyman.

Rochlin, G. (1967) 'How younger children view death and themselves', in E.A. Grollman (ed.) *Explaining Death to Children*, Boston: Beacon Press.

Rogers, C.R. (1967) *On Becoming a Person*, London: Constable.

Rosenblatt, P.C. (1997) 'Grief in small-scale societies', in C.M. Parkes, P. Laungani and B. Young (eds) *Death and Bereavement across Cultures*, London: Routledge.

Schaverien, J. (2002) *The Dying Patient in Psychotherapy*, London: Palgrave.

Schore, A.N. (2001) 'Minds in the making: attachment, the self-organising brain, and developmentally-oriented psychoanalytic psychotherapy', *British Journal of Psychotherapy*, **17**: 299–328.

Searles, H.F. (1955) *The Informational Value of the Supervisor's Emotional Experience. Collected Papers on Schizophrenia and Related Subjects*, London: Hogarth.

Spitz, R. (1945) *Hospitalism. The Psychoanalytic Study of the Child. Volume 1*, New York: International Universities Press.

Stern, D. (1985) *The Interpersonal World of the Infant*, New York: Basic Books.

Stroebe, M.S. and Schut, H.A.W. (1995) 'The dual process model of coping with loss'. Presented at the International Work Group on Death, Dying and Bereavement, St Catherine's College, Oxford, 26–29 June.

Suttie, I.D. (1935) *The Origins of Love and Hate*, London: Kegan Paul.

Syme, G. (1994) *Counselling in Independent Practice*, Buckingham: Open University Press.

Syme, G. (1997) 'Facing the unacceptable: the emotional response to infertility', *Human Reproduction*, **12**: 183–187.

Syme, G. (2003) *Dual Relationships in Counselling and Psychotherapy: Exploring the Limits*, London: Sage.

Tannen, D. (1992) *You Just Don't Understand*, London: Virago.

Tonkin, L. (2001) *Remembering: a Book to Help Grieving People of All Ages*, Christchurch, New Zealand: Port Hills Press.

Trevarthen, C. (1990) 'Growth and education of the hemispheres', in C. Trevarthen (ed.) *Brain Circuits and Functions of the Mind*, Cambridge: Cambridge University Press.

Trevarthen, C. (1993) 'The self born in intersubjectivity: the psychology of an infant communicating', in U. Neisser (ed.) *The Perceived Self: Ecological and Inter-personal Sources of Self-Knowledge*, New York: Cambridge University Press.

Truax, C.B. and Carkhuff, R.R. (1967) *Towards Effective Counseling and Psycho-therapy: Training and Practice*, Chicago: Aldine Publishing Co.

UK Council for Standards in Bereavement Care (2001) *Standards for Bereavement Care in the UK*, London: London Bereavement Network.

Van Eerdewegh, M.M., Bieri, M.D., Parilla, R.H. and Clayton, P.J. (1982) 'The bereaved child', *British Journal of Psychiatry*, **140**: 23–29.

Viorst, J. (1989) *Necessary Losses*, London: Positive Paperbacks.

Wheeler, S. (1996) 'Facing death with a client: confrontation or collusion, counter-transference or compassion', *Psychodynamic Counselling*, **2**: 167–178.

Winnicott, D.W. (1949) 'Hate in the counter-transference', *International Journal of Psycho-Analysis*, **30**: 69–75.

—— (1964) *The Child, The Family, and the Outside World*, London: Penguin Books.

—— (1971) *Therapeutic Consultations in Psychiatry*, New York: Basic Books.

Worden, J.W. (1983) *Grief Counselling and Grief Therapy*, 1st edn, London: Tavistock Publications.

—— (1991) *Grief Counselling and Grief Therapy*, 2nd edn, London: Tavistock Publications.

Author index

Subject index

Page numbers in bold type indicate a substantial discussion of the topic